THE EUROPEANISATION OF REFUGEE POLICIES

To my family

The Europeanisation of Refugee Policies

Between human rights and internal security

SANDRA LAVENEX
University of Zurich, Switzerland

Routledge
Taylor & Francis Group

LONDON AND NEW YORK

First published 2001 by Ashgate Publishing

Reissued 2018 by Routledge
2 Park Square, Milton Park, Abingdon, Oxon OX14 4RN
711 Third Avenue, New York, NY 10017, USA

Routledge is an imprint of the Taylor & Francis Group, an informa business

Copyright © Sandra Lavenex 2001

Publisher's Note
The publisher has gone to great lengths to ensure the quality of this reprint but points out that some imperfections in the original copies may be apparent.

Disclaimer
The publisher has made every effort to trace copyright holders and welcomes correspondence from those they have been unable to contact.

A Library of Congress record exists under LC control number: 2001089136

ISBN 13: 978-1-138-72887-5 (hbk)
ISBN 13: 978-1-138-72885-1 (pbk)
ISBN 13: 978-1-315-19030-3 (ebk)

Contents

Preface and Acknowledgements

This book, which is the result of a PhD thesis written at the European University Institute in Florence between 1995 and 1999, has two main goals. The first is to provide a long-term and comprehensive analysis of the dynamics and the constraints behind the Europeanisation of refugee policies. The second, and related, goal is to highlight the institutional and normative environment in which these changes take place. European cooperation in refugee policies since the early 1980s is thus investigated from a multilevel perspective. Developments at the level of the EU are analysed against the background of the international refugee regime and in the context of the simultaneous and interlinked transformations of domestic refugee policies in two important member states, France and Germany. Conceptualising these changes both in terms of shifts in the balance between state sovereignty and EU competence and between human rights and internal security considerations, this work has something to say about the role of the nation state in the European Union and, more specifically, about the prospects for political unification.

I am grateful to several institutions and individuals, who have contributed in many ways to the process of writing this book. First of all, I would like to thank the European University Institute in Florence for offering me three years of research support in a highly stimulating and aesthetically splendid working environment. I couldn't think of a better place to write a PhD. I am also grateful to the Swiss National Science Foundation, which generously offered a grant for terminating this study. The final draft of the manuscript benefited from the benevolent support of my new employer, the University of Zurich, and in particular from Prof. Ruloff's team at the Centre for International Studies in Zurich.

Many friends and colleagues have provided help and assistance during the writing of this book, and I'm grateful to them all. Particular thanks are due to the members of my examining jury, Adrienne Héritier, Klaus Eder, Didier Bigo and Thomas Risse, for their critical reading of the thesis and their friendly and encouraging support during my research. I would also like to thank Maureen Lechleitner for her organisational support. In addition, this work benefited from fruitful and enjoyable conversations with several members of the European Forum on International Migration at the European University Institute in 1998, as well as from conversations with various colleagues at academic conferences and elsewhere. In particular, I would like to thank Roland Bank, Michael Bommes, Grete Brochman, Kirsten Dauck, Thomas Diez, Adrian Favell, Elspeth Guild, Virginie Guiraudon, Hans-Martin Jaeger, Christoph Knill, Dirk Lehmkuhl, Andrea Lenschow, Matthias Leo Maier, Sabine Schweitzer, Joanne van Selm, Nina Spaelti, Emek Uçarer, Patrick Weil, Antje Wiener and Catherine Wihtol de Wenden for many fruitful conversations. Of course, I am also indebted to my various interview partners in the EU institutions, the UNHCR, NGOs and national administrations in Germany and France for sharing their insights into the Europeanisation of refugee policies with me.

Finally, I would like to thank my brother, my parents and my grand-parents for their constant interest, their questions, their confidence and support. The book is dedicated to them.

Abbreviations

AT	Amsterdam Treaty
BAFl	Bundesamt für Flüchtlinge
BGBl	Bundesgesetzblatt
BR Drs	Bundesratsdrucksache
BR PlPr	Bundesratsplenarprotokoll
BT Drs	Bundestagsdrucksache
BVerfGE	Bundesverfassungsgerichtsentscheidung
CAHAR	Ad Hoc Committee of Experts on the Legal Aspects of Refugees of the Council of Europe
CDMG	Committee on Migration, Refugees and Demography of the Council of Europe
CDU	Christlich Demokratische Union
CEECs	Central and Eastern European Countries
CFSP	Common Foreign and Security Policy
CIREA	Centre for Information, Discussion, and Exchange on Asylum
CIREFI	Centre for Information, Discussion, and Exchange on the Crossing of Borders and Immigration
COREPER	Committee of Permanent Representatives of the Member States at the European Union
COSAC	Conference of European Affairs Committees of the Parliaments of the European Union
CRR	Commission de Recours des Réfugiés
CSCO	London Conclusions on countries in which there is generally no risk of persecution
CSU	Christlich Soziale Union
DAF	Division Asile aux Frontières
DC	Dublin Convention
DICCILEC	Direction centrale du contrôle de l'immigration et de la lutte contre l'emploi des clandestins
DLPAJ	Direction des libertés publiques et des affaires juridiques du ministère de l'interieur
EC	European Community (Treaty)
ECHR	European Convention on Human Rights and Fundamental Freedoms

ECJ	European Court of Justice
ECOSOC	United Nations Economic and Social Council
EIS	European Information System
EU	European Union (Treaty)
EURODAC	Draft Convention for the comparison of fingerprints of applicants for asylum
FASP	Independent Association of Police Unions
FAZ	Frankfurter Allgemeine Zeitung
FDP	Freie Demokratische Partei
FN	Front National
FR	Frankfurter Rundschau
GC	Geneva Convention on the Status of Refugees
GG	Grundgesetz
ICG	Intergovernmental Conference
JHA	Justice and Home Affairs
JO	Journal Officiel
HLWGAI	High Level Working Group on Asylum and Migration
LM	Le Monde
MNS	Migration News Sheet
NGO	Non-Governmental Organisation
OFPRA	Office Français pour la Protection des Refugiés et Apatrides
PC	Parti Communiste
PS	Parti Socialiste
RMUA	London Resolution on manifestly unfounded asylum applications
RPR	Rassemblement pour la République
RSTC	London Resolution on a harmonised approach to questions concerning host third countries
SA	Schengen Agreement
SCGI	General Secretariat of the Inter-ministries Committee for European Economic Cooperation
SEA	Single European Act
SIS	Schengen Information System
SM	National Federation of Young Lawyers' Union, and the Union of Judges
SNAPC	Independent Union of Plainclothes Policemen
SPD	Sozialdemokratische Partei Deutschlands
SZ	Süddeutsche Zeitung
UDF	Union Démocratique Française
UNHCR	United Nations High Commission for Refugees

Introduction

"Whether one examines the tragic displacement in the former Yugoslavia, the passionate debate on asylum in Germany, the long discussions on harmonizing immigration and asylum policies in the European Community, the concern over illegal immigration and the battles against xenophobia throughout Europe, the drama and complexity of the refugee problem in Europe today is evident." (Sadako Ogata, United Nations High Commissioner for Refugees 1993: 10)

Almost fifteen years after the beginning of intergovernmental cooperation in asylum and immigration matters, the establishment of a common European asylum system has become a priority in the European Union. This priority has its legal base in the Treaty of Amsterdam, which defines common asylum and refugee policies as central elements in the development of an "area of freedom, security and justice". Its political background rests with the enduring politicisation of asylum seekers in the member states and recent experiences with massive refugee flows in the context of the Yugoslav crisis.

Which role can the European Union play in the field of refugee policy, and how does this role relate to traditional asylum regimes in selected member states? These are the central questions addressed in this book. The Europeanisation of refugee policies opens new dimensions in the process of European integration. Unlike the broader phenomenon of migration, which occurs on a voluntary basis, the notion of asylum derives from international human rights and liberal republican understandings about the relationship between the state and the citizen. In this line of thought, the state is both the cause and the solution of the asylum problem. On the one hand, refugees are defined as individuals who have been violated in their basic human rights and have lost the protection of their country of origin. On the other hand, the loss of protection invokes the responsibility of the international community; it is another state which, by granting asylum, warrants the protection of these fundamental rights. This human rights base of the refugee concept means that the Europeanisation of refugee policies has implications that go well beyond the hitherto dominant economic logic of

1

European integration. Can the EU, under its current institutional setting, be a "country" of asylum? The endeavours to implement fundamental rights at the EU level are a recent phenomenon, and they started only after the adoption of significant measures relating to asylum seekers and refugees at the intergovernmental level.

A second feature which distinguishes the field of refugee policy from the main body of the European *acquis* is that it touches a core aspect of state sovereignty, namely the right of the state to admit or reject the entry and stay of non-nationals on its territory. With the free movement of persons in the single market, member states have effectively lost their sovereign discretion over admission, residence and expulsion of Community nationals, empowering these individuals with equal rights enforced by a supranational authority through the European Commission and the European Court of Justice. Indeed, this freedom of movement has been fundamental to the building of an "ever closer union among the peoples", as stated in the preamble to the Treaty on the European Community. In contrast, member states have resolutely safeguarded their discretion towards persons from outside the Community, now usually referred to as "third country nationals". This is clearly reflected in the elaboration of the so-called "compensatory measures" to the abolition of internal border controls in the Schengen framework, resulting in the reinforcement of external borders. The issue of asylum seekers and refugees occupies a peculiar position in this triangle of European integration, state sovereignty and immigration as they form, together with the right to family unity, the only exception to the right of the state to select their admission under international law. This exception is codified in an international regime with the customary norm of non-*refoulement*, which prohibits the return of individuals to a place where they fear inhuman or degrading treatment or punishment or persecution on defined grounds. It is this normative commitment of Western European liberal democracies which constitutes the distinctive quality of Europeanisation in this particular policy field and which distinguishes it from the principles of the market place. This commitment raises the question of normative accountability in the increasingly political Union, and points at the challenge of embedding the re-organisation of powers and responsibilities in a common canon of values and norms in the multilevel polity.

These difficulties facing the development of a common asylum system in the fragmented and incomplete European polity are exacerbated by the contested nature of the asylum concept today and the destabilisation of the post-World War II refugee regime. Coupled with the multiplication of migration flows world-wide and the end of East-West ideological antagonisms, the normative core of the asylum concept has become increasingly blurred. The collapse of the old bipolar system, the persistence of ethnic and political conflicts all over the world, growing economic disparities, as well as increasing numbers of refugee and asylum seekers have led to a growing perception of the refugee problem as a threat to national stability and internal security. With the official halt to foreign labour recruitment in the mid-1970s, the asylum right – together with the right of family reunification – has become the main legal avenue for immigration in Europe, contributing to an overburdening of asylum systems in the principal receiving countries and to the widespread perception of an abuse of asylum procedures. As a result of this, Western countries have increasingly tightened their provisions regarding the admission and processing of asylum claims. Together, the multiplication of the causes of forced migration and the attempt to limit the exposure to refugee flows have contributed to a conceptual confusion regarding the definition of refugees and their protection, expressed most conspicuously in the inconsistent approaches developed towards the admission of Bosnian and Kosovo refugees in the 1990s. As this book shows, these changes have not occurred in an isolated environment: they were directly linked to the emergence of intergovernmental cooperation at the European level and the gradual development of a common set of policy instruments. Against the background of the normative tensions inherent to the refugee concept, this restrictive trend places the Europeanisation of refugee policies between two conflicting paradigms: the commitment to international human rights on the one hand and the preoccupation with the safeguarding of internal security on the other.

Starting from the fragmented structure of the European multilevel polity and the contested nature of the refugee issue today, this book analyses the scope and the limits of an evolving common European refugee policy from the beginnings of intergovernmental cooperation in the mid-1980s until today. Throughout, the emphasis is on the interaction between the development of common measures at the European level with political structures and processes in Germany and France. These two countries have a strong humanitarian tradition in relation to the admission of asylum seekers and refugees, they were the motors of intergovernmental cooperation in this field, and they carried out significant reforms in the 1990s, culminating in the amendment of their national constitutions. The interaction between developments at the European and the domestic levels is conceived of in institutional and ideational terms. Firstly, Europeanisation leads to a re-organisation of the political institutional arenas. It confers new competences to the supranational actors and alters the division of authority and resources in the domestic polity, thereby strengthening the position of particular members of the domestic constituency and weakening the position of others. It is shown that cooperation among justice and home affairs officials has led to a structure of "intensive transgovernmentalism" between bureaucratic networks, which limits the influence of supranational actors at the European level and strengthens the position of national executives, particularly the interior ministries, at the domestic level. This institutional structure has also weakened the role of other international organisations traditionally in charge of safeguarding the international refugee regime, particularly the Council of Europe and the United Nations High Commission for Refugees (UNHCR). Secondly, Europeanisation alters the factual and normative representation of social problems and thereby modifies the terms of political discourse. Addressed in the context of the single market project, the asylum question has been framed as a challenge to the free movement of persons in Europe. By emphasising the priority of control and internal security over the humanitarian value of refugee protection, this frame limits the prospects for the development of a comprehensive refugee policy at the European level and has facilitated the limitation of national humanitarian traditions in France and Germany. In these two countries, reference to the need of implementing intergovernmental agreements (in particular the Schengen and Dublin Conventions) and the alleged aim of harmonising domestic policies provided crucial elements in the legitimation of incisive asylum reforms, culminating in the amendment of the asylum right of the national constitutions in 1993. With the transfer of asylum and immigration matters to the Community's first pillar, the Amsterdam Treaty symbolises the departure from earlier intergovernmental coordination and assigns greater powers to supranational institutions. Still, the provisions on an "area of freedom, security and justice" are marked by the legacies of fifteen years of intensive transgovernmentalism, reflected recently in the failure to agree on a common approach or some form of "burden"-sharing with regard to Kosovo refugees.

The book is divided into four chapters. The first chapter provides an introduction into the field of refugee policy and identifies the theoretical implications of studying the process of its Europeanisation. Starting from the observation that refugees and their protection have always been contested concepts, this policy field is situated at a crossroads between two fundamental principles of the modern nation state system: the particularism of state sovereignty on the one hand, determining the right of the state to control the entry and stay of aliens on its territory, and the universalism of human rights on the other, as these apply to every human being, irrespective of their his/her national origin. Depending on which principle one emphasises, different consequences follow for the conceptualisation of refugee policy. This is illustrated in a more philosophical discussion of refugee protection - from the "realist" and "idealist" perspectives - which helps to abstract it from current public and political debates, and provides the deeper normative context, against which the following chapters analyse the development of a common refugee policy in the European Union. The theoretical approach of the study is presented in the third section. Here, the question of Europeanisation is conceived of as an institutional and ideational process, which impacts on policy-making structures in the member states and alters the terms of policy discourses. This approach combines constructivist understandings on the role of ideas and norms in political processes with an institutionalist focus on the role of power, authority and rule in the emerging European multilevel polity. The choice for this approach is motivated by the political nature of refugee policy, which has its base in the fundamental values underpinning modern liberal democracies and the challenge of redistribution and solidarity implied in the adoption of a common refugee policy. The focus is thus on the mechanisms which drive the development of a common asylum system in the incomplete European polity and in particular the interaction between evolving principles, norms and rules at the European level with domestic asylum regimes in the member states.

In Chapter Two, the empirical study of the Europeanisation of refugee policies starts with an analysis of the post-World War II regimes before the onset of European cooperation in this matter. This chapter begins by introducing the normative framework of the international refugee regime and presents the constitutive pillars of refugee policies in Germany and France from a historical perspective. The country studies are divided into a first section on the principles and norms structuring the German and French asylum systems and a second section recapitulating the main policy developments until the late 1980s.

The emergence and evolution of European cooperation in asylum and immigration matters from the mid-1980s onwards is analysed in Chapter Three. Starting with a short discussion of earlier cooperation processes in the framework of the Council of Europe, this chapter scrutinises the specific institutional configuration of cooperation in this policy field, as it has evolved from purely intergovernmental negotiations in the Schengen and Ad Hoc Group on Immigration, to cooperation under the third pillar of the Maastricht Treaty and, finally, partial Communitarisation in the Treaty of Amsterdam. It argues that what we see is the emergence of a new mode of policy-making in the EU - referred to as intensive transgovernmentalism - which challenges what we have come to know as the Community method. The second focus of this third chapter analysis is on the contents of this cooperation and the factual and normative definition of the refugee problem in the policy instruments adopted at the European level. This includes the two intergovernmental treaties of 1990, the Schengen and the Dublin Conventions, the totality of resolutions, conclusions and joint positions adopted under the European Union Treaty, as well as the new normative elements introduced with the Treaty of Amsterdam. The chapter ends with an assessment of the progress achieved so far in the development of a common European refugee policy and scrutinises the emerging links between the development of an "area of freedom, security and justice" and the affirmation of fundamental rights at the European level.

The impact of this European cooperation in asylum and immigration matters on domestic asylum policies in Germany and France is analysed in Chapter Four. The first section deals with the processes leading to the incisive reforms of asylum laws including the amendment of the national constitutions in 1993 and highlights their entanglement with developments at the European level. The focus is on the impact of Europeanisation on the institutional settings structuring the political realisation of these reforms and on the role of European arguments in their formulation and legitimation in political discourse. The degree, to which the 1993 reforms implemented the European *acquis* in this field, is assessed in the second section. Finally, the third section examines the continuities or discontinuities of specific national traditions in a long-term perspective up to the year 2000. These case-studies highlight the role of specific domestic structures - such as federalism and fragmentation in Germany or the tradition of republicanism in France - in the processes of Europeanisation; at the same time, they also point at the scope and limits of the current system of cooperation in asylum matters.

The Conclusion recapitulates the main findings of the book, with regard to the manner in which evolving European structures interact with domestic political institutions and processes in the construction of Europe. Linking up with the broader debates on the adoption of a European charter of fundamental rights, the Conclusion recalls the civic and normative foundations underpinning the notion of asylum and discusses the opportunities and challenges facing the establishment of a common asylum system in the European Union.

1 Refugees, the State, and European Integration

In contrast to the main body of the European *acquis*, which focuses on economic matters, the development of a common refugee policy addresses a deeply political issue which is directly linked to questions of human rights and state sovereignty. Defined as persons who, having been violated in their basic human rights and having lost the protection of their country of origin, seek refuge in another country, the notion of refugees derives from universal human rights. Conversely, the admission of refugees and the granting of protection are subject to the fundamental norm of state sovereignty which provides the right of states to admit or refuse the admission of aliens into their territory. The right of asylum was formalised in parallel with the codification of international human rights in an international regime and in national laws after World War II. With the multiplication of migration flows world-wide and the end of East-West ideological antagonisms (Loescher 1993; Zolberg et al. 1989), however, the normative core of the asylum concept has become increasingly blurred. The consequence is that today, the emergent European refugee policy faces a fundamental confusion, namely the difficulty to determine who deserves which kind of protection – and who does not.

This first chapter presents the normative questions underlying the integration of refugee policies and discusses the concept of Europeanisation used in this book. It argues that the analysis of European integration in this policy field - which is closely tied to normative political understandings and humanitarian values - requires an extension of dominant approaches to Europeanisation, allowing for the consideration of the ideational dynamics and constraints of the integration process. Starting with a definition of refugee policy as a matter of national sovereignty, international interdependence and human rights, this chapter exemplifies the contested nature of the refugee concept by presenting two opposed philosophical perspectives which are deduced from two classical approaches to the state and international relations. These are on the one hand the "Hobbesian" or realist view and, on the other, the "Kantian" or idealist perspective. These two opposed philosophical views highlight the inherent tension which characterises refugee policy as a matter of national sovereignty and human rights, that is particularist and universalist respectively. Although presented in an abstract manner, these two views are at the basis of contemporary debates on refugees and constitute the two extreme poles, between which a common European refugee policy will situate itself.

The approach developed to analyse the Europeanisation of refugee policies is discussed in the third section. The development of a common refugee policy represents an instance of political integration which consists of the institutionalisation of organisational structures and substantive guidelines of policy-making in this area. Taking a multilevel perspective on the interaction between domestic and European levels of governance in this process of Europeanisation, a combination of new institutionalism with the ideational approach of frame analysis is proposed.

Defining Refugees: Between Human Rights and State Sovereignty

From a political science perspective, refugees are an intriguing phenomenon located at the interface of national sovereignty, human rights, and international interdependence. Theoretically speaking, refugees are a vivid expression of the tension between two constitutive principles of the modern state system: on one side is the principle of territorial sovereignty, which determines the right of states to control entry into their territory, and on the other is the universality of human rights norms, which apply to every human being across national boundaries.

As a phenomenon, the protection of refugees is as old as recorded human history. Its conceptualisation, however, is closely linked to the emergence of the modern state system and the confirmation of the principle of state sovereignty as "the institutionalization of public authority within mutually exclusive jurisdictional domains" (Ruggie 1986: 143) during the course of the 19th century (Hathaway 1991: 1; Goodwin-Gill 1996: 9). The implementation of this general principle dates back to the American and French revolutions and to the idea that sovereignty resides with the people rather than the monarch. This idea implied the demarcation of a "people" within a given territory, which in turn led to the institutionalisation of citizenship. Citizenship was first and foremost a means of defining the criteria of membership in the "people"; secondly, its rules determined the relationship between the rights and duties of the citizen regarding the state and vice-versa. Thus, the birth of the nation state went hand in hand with the demarcation of boundaries between territories and peoples (Brubaker 1992: 21ff).

At the same time, this social closure took place in the context of republican notions of universal human rights, as expressed in the Virginia

Bill of Rights, the American Declaration of Independence of 1776 and the French Declaration of the Rights of Man and Citizen of 1789 (see Habermas 1996a: 231ff). These civil and political human rights (e.g. the right to life, the prohibition of torture, the right to liberty and to the security of persons, freedom of expression et cetera) were to secure the primacy of personhood vis-à-vis the state. They thus limit its freedom of action vis-à-vis the individual. With this function, civil and political human rights became "the modern pillars of legal legitimacy and political power" (Habermas 1994: 1). In accordance with the theories developed in the age of enlightenment (esp. those of Locke and Rousseau), these rights were at the same time the basis for the jurisdiction and legitimisation of a state government. They were defined in direct relation to the state; indeed, their safeguard is one of the latter's major functions. From this results the fact that their observance may be claimed only vis-à-vis the state as the responsible entity.

Whereas the principles of human rights and territorial sovereignty are conceptually complementary within a given national community, they turn out to be contradictory in a transnational perspective. In contrast to the bounded concept of sovereignty, the notion of human rights is universal and applies to all human beings independently of their nationality or membership of a particular state. This universal validity derives from the consideration that these norms are founded exclusively on moral considerations independent from political or historical aspects (Habermas 1996a: 223). While this tension between the universalism of human rights and the particularism of the social order was already present in the idea of the social contract - which establishes the relationship between the rulers and the ruled - it was subsequently amplified with the confirmation of nationalism as integrating factor in the late 18th and 19th centuries. This demarcation of the "sovereign people" along national ideas of common descent and culture had the effect of emphasising the particularistic and exclusionary elements of the modern state system (Habermas 1996a: 128ff).

These intrinsic tensions in the modern nation state system are crucial in understanding the theoretical foundations for international migrations. Since borders represent a condition for popular sovereignty in a state, "movements across the boundaries of the space it administers necessarily engage its vital interests" (Brubaker 1992: 25). The principle of national popular sovereignty presupposes the maintenance of a certain degree of exclusion. It depends on the ability of the state to maintain a coherent sense of belonging, including its ability to control the composition of its population. From this perspective, a loss of control over immigration would threaten the basis of its legitimacy (Jacobson 1996: 4).

While the principle of territorial sovereignty implies the right of states to refuse foreigners entry into their territory, the concept of refugees constitutes an exception to this prerogative of states (Hathaway 1991: 231). In contrast to the general phenomenon of international migration, the central characteristic defining the concept of refugees is its foundation in the idea of universal human rights. Independent from its codification in international and national law after World War II, this exception derives from the definition of a refugee as a person whose basic human rights have been violated. Considering that the safeguard of these rights is incumbent upon the state, refugees can be conceptualised as the very product of the above-mentioned tension between particularism and universalism. Having lost this basic level of protection from their country of origin, these individuals are an anomaly in the nation state system. Seeking the protection of another state, they are a transnational phenomenon which conflicts with the territorial organisation of states and rights. They are a vivid expression of the unsolvable tension between the particularism of a cultural "primordial" community and the universalist "civic sentiments" of an egalitarian legal community in the modern state system (Habermas 1994: 131; 1996a: 139).

It is this transnational quality which defines refugees as a matter for international relations. Given the world's division into territorial states, the production of refugees is automatically a problem of international interdependence: "Jointly, these territorial jurisdictions exhaust the inhabitable surface of the earth. In such a world, a person cannot be expelled from one territory without being expelled into another, cannot be denied entry into one territory without having to remain in another" (Brubaker 1992: 26). As a consequence, their "right-less" situation requires the remedial action of another state in the international community (Goodwin-Gill 1996: 167). Thus, refugees are a classic example of international interdependence; their production by one state automatically impacts upon other states. At the same time, the denial of protection by one potential host country directly shifts the responsibility to provide shelter to another.

This international quality of refugees is discussed in the next subsection from the perspective of two opposed normative approaches in international relations theory.

Two Views on Refugees

As has already been indicated in the previous sections, refugee policy is characterised by an intrinsic tension between the principles of human rights and national sovereignty. As a consequence, the notions of refugees and refugee protection are contested concepts, whose perception and definition follow either more statist or more humanitarian concerns. The socio-philosophical implications of this dichotomy are reflected in the evolution of the discipline of International Relations (IR), in which the tension between particularism and universalism has been a major feature since its establishment at the beginning of the 20th century. Long dominated by a (neo-)realist paradigm which concealed the more philosophical roots of the discipline, normative studies reappeared with a "forty years detour" (Smith 1992) after the end of the Cold War right at the beginning of the 1990s. Today, the resurgence of more "philosophical" issues in IR studies can be observed, such as, for example the concept of sovereignty, the role of human rights norms, or more generally the re-apparition of normative theory (e.g. Brown 1992; Clark/Neumann 1996; Griffiths 1992; Hoffman 1994).

This section presents two fundamentally opposed views on the refugee question which derive from two major classical theoretical traditions in IR theory, namely realism and idealism. While these two paradigms in IR have both led to a large variety of different approaches, their philosophical basis can be identified in a set of core assumptions which essentially contrast with regard to their concept of the relationship between human rights and state sovereignty. An illustration of the different cognitive and normative implications existing between the realist and idealist perspectives on the refugee question highlights the contested nature of refugees and helps to unveil certain - often implicit - normative orientations which underpin most discussions on this topic. The identification of these diverging normative orientations helps to abstract from momentary impressions of the refugee issue and provides useful analytical categories in the empirical study of policy change.

The Realist View: the Primacy of the State

From a realist perspective, refugee protection is a clear prerogative of the state and must be seen on the basis of the three fundamental realist premises of statism, rationalism and self-help.

The concept of *statism* implies that, for realists, the key actors in the international system are the sovereign states. Their sovereignty has both an internal and an external dimension. Internally, it refers to the supreme authority of the state to make and enforce law within a given territory. The basis of this authority is the idea of a social contract existing between the people and the state as the guarantor of security. The internal organisation of power precedes the development of a civil society. Accordingly, the safeguarding of internal security is the first priority of the state. State leaders are seen as fully rational persons who act in order to protect the "national interest". From this derives the fact that, in periods of crisis, human rights and other values are subordinated to the necessity of preserving internal order. The realist concept of human rights is one which only applies between the state and its citizens; they are not universal in the sense of the common basic rights of mankind, but are state-specific (see Krasner 1993b: 140). This leads to the external dimension of sovereignty which consists of the exclusive control of a state over its territory. There is no authority allowed to interfere with the internal affairs of states; the international system is characterised by anarchy. In the absence of a common power, realism sees the international system as free from norms or common principles. Similarly, every state is fully autonomous with regard to its own population and societal values.

From this idea of anarchy results the two other key concepts of realism: that is, rationality and self-help. Firstly, the notion of *rationality* refers to the utilitarian behaviour of states as power-maximisers in the international system. Under anarchy, their relationship is seen as a wholly distributive zero-sum game, gains for one state equal losses for another. Consequently, states act under a competitive logic and seek to maximise their power in terms of the "size of population and territory, resource endowment, economic capability, military strength, political stability, and competence" (Waltz 1979: 131). This competitive logic is contradictory to the agreement on common norms or principles, with the exception of the rule of non-interference in the internal affairs of other states. Thus, as far as realists consider the pursuit of ideas and values in foreign policy, this is necessarily interpreted as part of power politics; notions of "universal" norms are merely the reflection of the norms valid in respective hegemonic states (Carr 1946:87). And, the pursuit of human rights in foreign policy is seen as the imposition of one state's own moral principles upon another (Morgenthau 1973: 4; see also Krasner 1993b: 141).

The second and interrelated consequence of anarchy is the notion of *self-help* and the constant preoccupation of states with their survival. While traditional realists derive this principle from the image of man who, in the Hobbesian tradition, is in a constant state of war with other men, neo-realists such as Kenneth Waltz derive it from the structure of the international system. In contrast to the domestic organisation of power, where the state is responsible for defending the rights and security of its citizens, in international relations states can realise their security only through self-help. This means that every state has the right to pursue its foreign policy as it sees it fits (Krasner 1993b). As a consequence, realist theories are mainly concerned with questions of "high politics", such as questions of war and peace. Economic or other goals are subordinated to the overall national interest in survival. Ideas, norms or values do not impact upon international relations.

From this perspective, the issue of refugees must be seen primarily in the context of state sovereignty, including the control of its territory and population. Given the repudiation of the notion of universal human rights, for a realist, a refugee does not differ from other voluntary migrants. Their common definition consists of their quality as transborder-phenomena; they leave one state to enter the territory of another. The fact that refugees may have been violated in their basic rights does not represent a common international concern since these rights are only subject to the respective country of origin and are not a universal value. Hence, states may have two different approaches to these migrants; either refugees are actively used as an instrument of foreign policy[1] or they constitute a threat to the internal security of the country concerned. If a state cannot rationally control the flow of migrants anymore, then both emigration and immigration represent challenges to its internal stability. Here, therefore, migration becomes a security threat. From a realist perspective, uncontrolled immigration not only undermines a state's sovereign authority over its own territory, but it also threatens its social, economic and political fabric. Accordingly, large-scale refugee flows can seriously affect relations between the sending and receiving countries and ultimately may represent a threat to peace.[2]

The Idealist View: the Primacy of the Individual

Liberal thinking in IR originates in various philosophical and theological writings from the early sixteenth century onwards which, rejecting the idea that war is the natural state in international relations, articulated the conditions necessary for peace in the international system. While the label "liberal" has been used for a whole variety of approaches this discussion focuses the label of "idealism" according to the Kantian tradition in liberal thought.

From a Kantian perspective, the central unit of analysis in the international system is not the state, as in realism, but the *individual* as part of a universal "community of mankind". In this view, the state fulfils only the minimal role of ensuring the rights of its people; the sovereign is not the state but the individual. The purpose of states is not the pursuit of specific national interests, but promoting the realisation of universal values. In "The Idea for a Universal History with a Cosmopolitan Purpose", Kant proposes a major structural reform of the state system by introducing a centralised power in charge of determining and enforcing the law above the states. This would prevent independent sovereignties from manipulating the rights of individuals and would allow the safeguarding of universal norms by a "united power and the law-governed decisions of a united will" (printed in Reiss 1991: 41ff). In this view, states are not the ultimate form of political organisation, but are "necessary staging-posts in a wider process of creating a functioning peaceful world society" (Williams/Booth 1996: 77).[3] The underlying idea of this claim is the assumption of a basic harmony of interests existing among individuals which itself derives from membership of mankind. The latter is defined by a common set of universal rights applying to each individual as autonomous moral agents independent of their membership of particular groups, cultures or ideologies.[4] This assumption of the existence of a universal moral order signifies that states are not legitimated as particular communities of values and thus challenges the notion of national sovereignty and independence.

While this liberal tradition acknowledges the existence of war in the nation-state system, the idea of international relations contrasts sharply with the realist notion of anarchy. Indeed, it sees international relations in a progressive way. The central actors in this process are individuals who, with the growth of interaction and interdependence with each other, automatically develop higher degrees of reason, law and *morality*. Three conditions are seen as promoting this moral progress. Firstly, it derives from the overall moral imperative to find a means of abolishing war. The second condition is the ability to learn from experience and the aspiration to create common laws and institutions. Thus, the strengthening of the international legal order promotes the mutual rights and duties both of and among states and peoples (Hurrell 1990: 200). Finally, focusing on the transnational interaction between individuals, especially through trade, this liberal tradition believes in the growth of interdependence and understanding among different peoples (see Hurrell 1990: 194ff). Thus, for liberals, the international system is not characterised by anarchy - in which rational, power-maximizing sovereign states compete with one another - but by the existence of universal values, growing interdependence, and the increasing institutionalisation of common laws and regimes structuring these interactions. International relations are not fully distributive zero-sum games, but are necessarily positive-sum games which strengthen universal values and the conditions for peace.

Accordingly, the dominant principle in international relations is not self-help and states' constant preoccupation with survival but, rather, *cooperation* and the overcoming of national boundaries and inequalities. With the rise of interdependence "the peoples of the earth have ... entered in varying degrees into a universal community, and it has developed to the point where a violation of rights in *one* part of the world is felt *everywhere*" (Kant, "The Perpetual Peace", in Reiss 1991: 107ff). Not only does mankind form a community of rights, but it also possesses a common responsibility for the protection of those rights. International law is founded on the rights of the individual; it aims at protecting freedom and establishing global justice (Williams/Booth 1996: 81ff). The liberal notion of justice is intrinsically linked to the idea of distributive justice and of the need to overcome political and economic disparities in the world. The conditions for attaining distributive justice are the moral obligations of individuals towards each other and the establishment of social institutions which are able to enhance equal access to resources (Hoffman 1994: 35). This global responsibility also has an internal dimension within the contemporary state organisations. This is most clearly expressed in the third "definitive article" of "The Perpetual Peace" where Kant claims the principle of "universal hospitality" towards strangers in someone else's territory, since "no-one originally has any greater right than anyone else to occupy any portion of the earth" (in Reiss 1991: 106). While Kant acknowledges that strangers do not possess the right to settle down in another country, they have the right to be treated with hospitality and should never be turned away or directed towards places where their lives would be threatened (ibid.: 105f). From this perspective, moral principles precede political considerations: "The rights of man must be held sacred, however great a sacrifice the ruling power may have to make" (Kant: "The Perpetual Peace", Appendix One: "On the Disagreement Between Morals and Peace in Relation to Perpetual Peace", in Reiss 1991: 125).

If one tries to define the notion of refugees within this idealist perspective, it becomes obvious that it differs very much from the realist concept. Refugees are not primarily a question of state sovereignty or territoriality, but individuals as carriers of rights. Refugees are not to be equated with voluntary migrants who want to enter into relations with the members of a foreign country. They are persons who have been violated in their fundamental rights and who are in need of protection. Violations of human rights in this perspective are not a matter of state sovereignty, but a common concern for a cosmopolitan community. Since human rights are common to all human beings, regardless of their membership of a particular country, culture or group, their protection is a common good and a condition for peace. The protection of human rights is thus a common responsibility held by all of the international community.

Two conclusions can be drawn from this notion of humanitarian interdependence. Firstly, the international community has a responsibility to prevent human rights abuses and the production of refugees. For this purpose, states must cooperate in the fight against the root causes of flight, including economic cooperation and, if necessary, humanitarian intervention (Hoffman 1994: 33f). Secondly, the international community has a common responsibility to provide protection for these individuals. This duty poses a limit on states' discretion over the composition of their population and over entry into their territory. From this perspective, fundamental rights are superior to any political considerations regarding the national interest; their protection must be held sacred. A limit to this duty is only conceivable if the intake of refugees is of such proportions that it threatens to violate the fundamental rights of other individuals within the country. From this derives the view that refugees are not a question of power politics or competition, but that they are a common concern for all of humanity which requires both cooperation and solidarity among states and individuals.

European Integration and Refugees

With this contested nature of refugee protection in mind, this study analyses the impact of European integration in asylum and immigration matters on changes in the integrative principles of refugee policy. European integration is thereby understood as the emergence of new political and ideational structures which interact with domestic and international structures in the maintenance or the transformation of a policy field. This topic has a European and a national dimension: it refers to the processes of *Communitarisation*, which concern the development of refugee policies at the European level including their scope and contents; as well as the processes of *Europeanisation*, which refer to the impact of these European structures and policies on the domestic refugee regimes in selected member states (France and Germany).

The Europeanisation of this policy field has several intriguing aspects. In contrast to the main body of economic integration, it refers to the integration of a core issue of state sovereignty, namely the authority of a state to control the entry into its territory and the composition of its population. The right of asylum has always been a very sensitive national matter which became formally implemented in Western European legislation after World War II. In France and Germany, it was enshrined as a subjective right in their national constitutions and became a strong and highly value-loaded symbol of humanitarian commitment. At the same time, the international community established an international regime rooted in the United Nations system with the purpose of promoting international cooperation regarding the protection of refugees.[5] These characteristics of the policy field as a matter of human rights and national sovereignty move the question of Europeanisation closer to what is a growing interest in the role of human rights norms and the conditions for their implementation in international relations studies. From this perspective, the study of European integration in this policy field can be re-phrased as an investigation of the conditions, under which Europeanisation – understood as a specific form of international cooperation – promotes, weakens or transforms the impact of human rights norms in refugee policy.

Against this background, the questions addressed in this book are: how did European cooperation in this policy field evolve, what are its main institutional features and what are its leading ideas? How far are common structures of policy-making emerging, and how far do these structures include shared causal and normative understandings about the nature and the scope of a common European refugee policy? Seeking to identify the interaction of this integration with domestic refugee policies in selected member states, the second emphasis of this study lies in the question: how far does Europeanisation - considering that domestic asylum policies are very much shaped by specific national histories, norms and values - lead to a convergence of refugee policies in Germany and France? Coming back to the definition of the policy field given above, the substantive dimension of this question thus reads: in what way does Europeanisation impact on the relationship between realist and idealist elements in the area of refugee policy?

Europeanisation, Institutions and Ideas

The concept of Europeanisation departs from earlier approaches to European cooperation in that it is less interested in the conditions or constraints for the transfer of sovereignty to independent, supranational structures than in the transformation of traditional modes of governance across policy-making levels and arenas. Breaking with the traditional limitation of international relations and domestic policy analysis to their respective levels of analysis, these studies investigate the linkages between European level institution-building and domestic processes and examine their impact on changes in structures of authority and rule (e.g. Andersen/Eliassen 1993; Cowles/Caporaso/Risse 2000; Héritier et al. 1994; Jachtenfuchs/Kohler-Koch 1996a; Mény/Muller/Quermonne 1996; Olsen 1995a and 1995b).

In this study, the process of Europeanisation is seen as a process of institutionalisation, which not only implies a transfer of tasks, powers and responsibilities between the levels of government but, rather, is a dynamic interaction between institutions and actors at the European and the national levels. This institutionalisation has two main aspects: it firstly refers to the development of new rules of governance, and secondly to the establishment of new "structures of meaning and schemes of interpretation which explain and legitimize practices and rules" (Olsen 1995a: 5). The first aspect of Europeanisation thus concerns changes in the rules of interaction as defined by the vertical and horizontal distribution of tasks, powers and responsibilities across levels of government and within the levels of governments among various political institutions (Olsen 1995a: 10f) and includes the redistribution of resources across political levels and arenas. This more organisational aspect is at the core of the literature on Europeanisation has already been investigated in a variety of studies. In contrast, the second aspect, which refers to changes in the cognitive structures - ideas and norms - in which political action is embedded (Olsen 1995a: 5), remains underexplored and needs further conceptual and empirical investigation. Two points underline the importance of this ideational dimension in the field of refugee policy. The first point is its character as a core element of national sovereignty and its highly normative and moral quality deeply embedded in national histories, traditions, and - in the case of France and Germany - even national constitutions. The second point refers to the problem of coordination implied in the Europeanisation of this policy field. Unlike the main body of the European *acquis*, the rationale for refugee protection cannot follow the principles of the market place and cannot be justified in terms of economic gains. The establishment of a common European refugee regime based on supranational structures poses a challenge of redistribution among the member states and raises the problem of coordination between national interests and collective goals. In contrast to areas such as welfare state policies or democracy, where this problem of coordination refers to a lack of solidarity and homogeneity among the units of the European polity (Scharpf 1999), the question of refugees extends the need of solidarity to third country nationals whose admission cannot be justified in economic terms (in contrast e.g. to labour migration). The act of admission thus presupposes an agreement about the substance of the collective interest in having a common refugee policy, and ultimately about the values ensuring commitment and compliance to this common policy. Considering the contested nature of refugee protection both in normative and empirical terms, this study thus adopts an interpretive approach which underlines that "meaning is not something that can be taken for granted", but that the "creation, communication, and understanding of meaning require attention" (Yanow 1995: 111).

   In analysing the Europeanisation of refugee policies between internal security and human rights, this study links up with critical security studies which focus on the discursive processes, by which new issues - e.g. societal, environmental, economic - are constructed as problems of internal and international security (Lipschutz 1995; Waever 1993; 1995 and 1996a). The central questions are: "*what* is being secured?", "how do *ideas* about security develop?" and "how do they become *institutionalized*?" (Lipschutz 1995: 1-2). Hence, the problem of analysis becomes the process of securitisation, "a process which depends on the social construction of the threat or the risk" (Bigo 1996: 14; see also Huysmans 1995: 66). In order to make these changes empirically and analytically operational, this thesis has for the concept of "frames" as it has been introduced in policy-analysis by Markus Jachtenfuchs (1993; 1996) and Rein/Schon (1991). This concept has strong affinities with Pierre Muller's and Bruno Jobert's notion of "référentiels" and Frank Nullmeier's "politology of knowledge". It is seen as a useful tool for studying the hitherto very abstract and underspecified notions of "ideas" and "knowledge" in processes of policy change. The central dependent variable is the development of shared, inter-subjective understandings over given problems in public or political discourse. These understandings reflect the actor's perception and definition of the problem and provide the basis for the development of interests and the formulation of policies (Muller/Jobert 1987; Nullmeier/Rüb 1993, Nullmeier 1993; Jachtenfuchs 1993, 1996). According to these authors, the identification of these clusters of knowledge is crucial to an understanding of continuity and change in political behaviour since they provide the cognitive and ideational basis upon which policies are formulated.

Against this background, the interesting question which needs to be addressed in this study is: by which mechanisms can European integration lead to an approximation of traditional refugee discourses in the member states and the emergence of convergent policy frames? In the following section, an analytical model that responds to this question is developed by focusing on two explanatory variables: (1) the institutional impact of European integration on traditional policy-making arenas and (2) its ideational impact on policy discourse.

Europeanisation as an Institutional Process
The institutional dimension of Europeanisation refers to changes in the regulatory structures of governance in the multilevel polity and includes the question of power distribution within a given field of political interaction. As regulatory mechanisms, institutions are formal and informal organisational rules which structure political interactions (Thelen/Steinmo 1992: 6). They are the procedural determinants of a system of governance. Classically, they include the rules of electoral competition, the structure of the party systems, the relations among various branches of government, and, in many political-economic studies, the structure and organisation of economic actors at the domestic level (see Ikenberry 1988: 226f).

In this study, institutions refer to the specific characteristics of the multilevel polity as interaction between domestic and European political structures. The underlying idea is that the evolution of (hitherto predominantly) intergovernmental cooperation in asylum matters at the European level goes along with a re-organisation of political structures and processes at the domestic level and that it changes traditional cleavage structures and the distribution of power and competences in the multilevel constituency. In the literature, this more organisational dimension of institutions includes two broad categories. Firstly, as was already mentioned, these are the distribution powers and competences among the actors involved: the rules of access to the policy-making arena and to material and non-material resources (e.g. financial, legal, personal, technical, informational). This aspect refers to the capability to act, to introduce the own perceptions, interests and value judgements into the decision-making process as well as the capability to enforce agreed rules in cases of non-compliance. Secondly, the organisational dimension includes the process of "structuration and routinisation" (Olsen 2000: 5), referring to the behavioural and procedural standards or customary practices which structure the relationship between the various actors in making publicly binding decisions (see Schmitter 1996: 3).

In this study, these factors are translated into the following categories:

- The *Composition* of the decision-making or discourse arena: polity and policy specific characteristics of the actors involved in policy discourses. This includes the characteristics of intergovernmental groups and negotiations, as well as the role of supranational bodies at the European level (Chapter Three), and the characteristics of centralism and unitarism versus federalism and fragmentation, party systems, parliaments, resort-autonomy, and the role of the judiciary at the domestic level (Chapter Four).
- The division of *competences* among the actors involved. This includes the negotiations in Schengen and Ad Hoc Group on Immigration, under the Maastricht Treaty (third pillar) and the Amsterdam Treaty at the European level, and the legislative procedures at the domestic level.
- The *inter-organisational relations* both horizontally and vertically between the actors involved in the various arenas. This refers to the relations between the intergovernmental groups and between these groups and the EU supranational bodies at the European level and at the domestic level the vertical relations between the domestic arena and intergovernmental /supranational bodies and horizontally between domestic actors.
- The *operational mode* applied in policy discourse: at the European level, this includes the secrecy versus publicity of intergovernmental

negotiations and, at both levels, the presence of a more technocratic versus political approach, as well as the concentration versus the fragmentation of the discourse arena.

Europeanisation as an Ideational Process

As constitutive mechanisms, institutions fulfil a more substantial role since they "shape how political actors define their interests" (Thelen/Steinmo 1992: 2). This notion of institutions has recently experienced an important reception in IR studies which deal with the role of international norms as independent variables on states' behaviour. While historical institutionalists include in this notion mainly normative understandings as implemented in formal laws, general principles of a given polity or policy-specific ideas (e.g. Keynesianism in Hall 1989; 1992 and Weir 1992), sociologists move the notion of institutions very closely to that of culture and include everyday life conceptions, such as symbolic systems, cognitive scripts and moral templates that guide human behaviour (Di Maggio/Powell 1991; Scott/Meyer 1994). From this perspective, cognitive frames also represent institutions once they are taken for granted as "social facts" (see Eder 1992: 20). For the purpose of policy analysis, the development of frames has been defined as processes "by which people construct interpretations of problematic situations, making them coherent from our various perspectives and providing ourselves with evaluative frameworks within which we can judge how to act" (Rein/Schon 1991: 264). More specifically, once implemented in the policy-making process, frames represent the ideational core of a particular policy field which not only expresses the dominant interpretations of the political actors but which also includes directions for action. They can develop into legitimating features providing ethical and identity orientations in public or political discourse. Thus, once implemented in a system of political governance, policy frames themselves become independent variables shaping actors' perceptions and interpretations of the world.

In studying the relationship between policy ideas and policy-making, it is important to note that "ideas do not float freely" (Risse-Kappen 1994), and that the emergence and institutionalisation of policy frames is usually characterised by the existence of conflicting views and political struggles over facts, values, interpretations and consequences. This dependency of frames from the advocacy activities of particular groups or organisations implies that their implementation in public policies will usually reflect the position of the most influential actors. Therefore, the distribution of power among the actors involved in framing processes and the institutional procedures guiding their access and interaction in the relevant policy arena are crucial in examining the emergence and the effects of particular policy frames. Nevertheless, once implemented in public policies, these frames become independent from the underlying power relations and can continue to affect the course of policy making, even after the social power relations that facilitated their emergence have changed (Coleman 1998: 634).

The elements of policy frames can be differentiated into distinct cognitive orders that highlight different aspects of a system of reference organising the assessment of external events or specific situations. These cognitive orders are heuristic devices that help to highlight the different dimensions of human knowledge. They are, however, only analytical distinctions that in reality are often interrelated and overlapping. The distinction is between "factual" causality-oriented knowledge, "normative", value-driven knowledge, and the "affective" emotional presentation of a discourse (Habermas 1981: 130ff). The *factual* dimension of a frame comprises the sphere of empirical facts. It refers to the world of observable and measurable data. This data should not, however, be regarded as objective realities, but are is itself a social construction. The evaluation of this information follows the criteria of truth; factual knowledge can be described as true or false. The second dimension of social *norms* refers to the sphere of moral responsibilities. These moral responsibilities derive from the norm and rule regulated context of social interaction. This context provides the values according to which action is assessed. In this sense, it suggests both a desirable and a condemnable state of affairs, since it generates general expectations about the goodness and the badness of action. Finally, the *affective* dimension here refers to the emotional expression of a discursive process, that whether the discourse presents itself in an emotional, polarised manner, or whether is follows a more technocratic, "objective" appearance. Given its interest in the process of Europeanisation, this study focuses on the following aspects of the europeanising asylum frame: the manner, in which it conceives of the dominant issue of concern (protection, borders, freedom of movement, abuse of asylum procedures etc.), the dominant image of refugees (individuals as carriers of rights, bogus asylum seekers, or just neutrally as a cross-border phenomenon), the conception of international interdependence (solidarity and cooperation versus competition and protectionism), and the policy-style invoked (securitarian, technocratic or humanitarian).

The scope of the discourse analysed in policy analysis can be delimited with regard to the range of political actors included in the relevant communication processes as identified by the institutional analysis and the material used in the empirical analysis. This policy specific notion of frames largely corresponds to the policy specific ideas or paradigms examined by historical institutionalists such as Peter Hall and Margaret Weir. The common characteristics of these ideational factors are (1) their social and intersubjective nature in contrast to cognitive beliefs held by individuals; (2) their institutionalised nature, which goes along with a certain degree of stability and resistance to change in contrast to free-floating and volatile ideas; and (3) their identifiability and specificity in a specific policy-area and a specific polity. These ideational factors need not be moral; they are collective expectations which can have functional and non-ethical origins and purposes. The intersubjective and policy-specific nature of policy frames distinguishes them from two other kinds of ideational structures impacting on political action: the general political principles or "public myths" describing a particular polity as a whole and legal norms. Applied to the European multilevel polity, three types of ideational structures are thus identified: (1) *principles* as general and accepted models of order, including historical memories which contain value criteria for distinguishing right from wrong, and just from unjust; (2) *legal norms*, as implemented in international, European and national law, both formal and informal; and (3) once established as "social fact", the European *policy frame*, which structures the interpretation and the orientation of action in a specific policy field. Interpretations of particular principles and legal norms may be included in policy frames, but need not. Applied to the area of refugee policies, the following norms are identified:

- The *principles* of European integration, based primarily on the logic of the market place; national sovereignty; human rights; solidarity; in France Républicanism and the collective memory of colonialism, and in Germany, Rechtsstaatlichkeit and the memory of National Socialism;
- The *norms* of free movement of persons; international and national asylum norms and other relevant human rights norms; and the broader approach towards immigration as expressed in the conception of nationhood (ius sanguinis versus ius soli);
- The *European asylum frame*, comprising the factual definition of the underlying asylum "problem", the normative definition of "refugees", and the conception of international interdependence, including the dominant understanding about the scope and the limits of a common European refugee policy.

The impact of these normative factors is analysed through an investigation of political discourse. Language is the generating instrument of frames, the names assigned to specific problems concentrate the attention on certain elements and lead to the neglect of others (Rein/Schon 1991: 270). Thus, "in selecting certain terms over others", speakers "establish frameworks of meanings" through which they seek to understand events and to conceive respective policies (Chock 1995: 166). The analysis of these changing configuration of the asylum issue under the influence of Europeanisation is conducted through an investigation of textual material from the European institutions, national parliamentary debates in Germany and France, relevant ministerial documents and speeches, as well as a survey of major national newspapers in France (Le Monde, Libération) and Germany (Süddeutsche Zeitung, Frankfurter Allgemeine Zeitung). In addition, a total of 38 focused interviews were conducted with members of the Council of the European Union, the Schengen group, the EU Commission, the European Parliament, national parliaments, national ministries, political parties, as well as other international organisations and NGOs active in the field.

Conclusion

The Europeanisation of refugee policies is assessed through an institutional perspective that puts equal weight on the organisational and ideational dimension of the emerging European refugee regime. The institutionalisation of a common refugee policy implies both the reorganisation of institutional roles, routines, competences and resources and the development of common codes of meaning, referring to the normative and factual understandings guiding political action. The importance of ideational factors is reflected in the contested definition of refugee protection which has its basis in the tension between two fundamental norms of the modern state system: the universalism of human rights and the particularism of state sovereignty. This normative tension is mirrored in opposed philosophical perspectives on the question of protection, state-centric realism and liberal, individual-based idealism. Depending on which philosophical stance one adopts, refugees and refugee protection take on very different traits and, thus, different priorities emerge for policy-making. The discussion of these theoretical traditions not only helps to identify certain permanent normative orientations in contemporary discussions regarding the question of refugees which have to do with the issue of whether priority should be given to the state's sovereign interests or to the individual's rights, but also provide a background against which the contents of an emerging European refugee policy can be assessed. In particular, it is shown how much Europeanisation, by altering the institutional and ideational context of policy-making in the asylum field, impacts on the relationship between "realist" and "idealist" elements in French and German asylum policies and how far it leads to a common approach to refugee protection.

The analytical framework of the study builds on a combination of new institutionalism with the discourse-analytical concept of frames. The more organisational and the more ideational dimension of the emerging European refugee regime are not alternative explanations but two facets of the phenomenon of institutionalisation. On the one hand, Europeanisation changes the rules of policy-making in the multilevel arena, on the other hand, the practices and routines of political actors are always embedded in a structure of meaning which shapes cognitive perceptions, modes of reasoning and normative legitimations. In this process, particular actors may be empowered to the disadvantage of others, at the same time, particular perceptions and value judgements may be favoured vis-à-vis other problem definitions, thus limiting the range of policy options available. Applied to the process of Europeanisation, the development of a common refugee policy will depend from the degree of coordination between member state policies; agreement on the basic factual and normative definition of the refugee "problem"; the development of common procedural rules, normative standards, rights and obligations defining the admission, treatment, recognition, and eventually rejection and return of asylum seekers and refugees; the enforcement and expansion of these common instruments by supranational institutions of governance; and, ultimately, a sense of common responsibility and solidarity among the members of the European polity.

The parallels between this process of European political integration and the development of refugee policies in national polities are exemplified in the next chapter for the case of Germany and France. As the next chapter shows, the codification of an asylum right was directly linked to the development of modern liberal democracies and symbolises the recognition of an international responsibility for the protection of those basic rights which define the relationship between the individual and the state. Therefore, the Europeanisation of refugee policies touches an important aspect of the European state-building process, stressing the importance of pooling not only powers and responsibilities, but also the competence to define common values and normative accountability in the evolving system of multilevel governance.

Notes

[1]   The instrumentalisation of refugees for the purpose of "realpolitik" can have many faces. An example of this might be the conscious provocation of refugee flows in another country in order to drain its manpower skills or legitimacy and thus to destabilise its internal order. Furthermore, by encouraging the emigration of oppositional groups from another country and admitting them into one's own territory, states can actively support and empower these movements in their fight for power. Finally, as a foreign policy instrument, refugees can also be used as symbols as part of a propaganda campaign waged against unfriendly states.

[2]   This realist view on the refugee problem is implicit in the work of Aristide Zolberg (see Zolberg et al. 1989) and Gil Loescher (see Loescher/Monahan 1989); for an explicit conceptualisation of refugees and migration as a security problem see Teitelbaum/Weiner (1995); Weiner (1993).

[3]   Kant's argument for the abolition of state sovereignty is ambivalent, however. In contrast to these propositions for a sort of world-government in "The Idea for a Universal History with a Cosmopolitan Purpose" he argues in "the Perpetual Peace" for the establishment of a federation of free states which would gradually extend to encompass all the peoples of the world, thus forming an international state, his "Völkerstaat" (Kant, "The Perpetual Peace", printed in Reiss 1991: 41ff). For a discussion of the relationship between statist and cosmopolitan elements in Kant's thinking, see Hurrell (1990).

[4]   This assumption of the existence of universal values is contested in the literature as of carrying the risk of ethnocentrism. However, liberals agree on a core of universal rights which basically consist of the right to life and physical as well as mental integrity, see Hoffman (1994: 32) and Hurrell (1990: 203).

[5]   The term international regime is used in accordance with the widely accepted definition given by Stephen Krasner "as implicit of explicit principles, norms, rules, and decision making procedures around which actors' expectations converge in a given area of international relations" (Krasner 1983: 2). The establishment of the international and the domestic (French and German) refugee regimes after World War II is discussed in Chapter Two.

2 Post-World War II Refugee Regimes

"The formulation of refugee policy invokes a complex interplay of domestic and international factors at the policy-making level and illustrates the conflict between international humanitarian norms and the sometimes narrow self-interest calculations of sovereign nation states." (Loescher 1989a: 8)

As a phenomenon, refugee protection is as old as the history of mankind (Kimminich 1978). Its legal codification, however, is a product of this century and evolved in the context of the general move towards international cooperation after the Second World War. Indeed, it was directly linked to the establishment of the United Nations system. After having presented the issue of refugees from an abstract theoretical perspective, this chapter next turns to its normative conceptualisation as it has evolved in international and domestic legislation in France and Germany since 1945. After a discussion of the main normative foundations of the post-World War II international refugee regime, the second and third sections present the French and the German refugee regimes before Europeanisation. These sections set out with the normative roots of the national refugee regimes and recapitulate the major policy developments in both countries up to the late 1980s.

Increasing numbers of refugees from all over the world, the expansion of the causes of forced migration, and a general increase in public mobility and communications technology in the 1970s induced the transformation of asylum policies in Europe. Coupled with the general halt to economic immigration in 1973/1974, the right of asylum became - together with the right to family reunification - the most important legal means to enter Germany and France. In both countries, the early 1980s marked the globalisation of a hitherto primarily European asylum problem. This turnabout consisted both in a shift of the major regions from which asylum seekers and refugees originated, that is from formerly European countries to countries of the Third World, and in a transformation of the depiction of refugees from politically persecuted individuals to victims of generalised violence and civil war. Whereas in Germany, the politicisation of the asylum question began already in the late 1970s, later culminating in calls for an abolition of the constitutional asylum right, asylum policies in France remained relatively stable during this period, and the asylum right of the Constitution remained unquestioned. It is argued that, in the light of similar developments regarding the qualitative and quantitative evolution of the refugee issue in the two countries, these differences are mainly due to the early mobilisation of the *Länder* in the German federal polity and the broader scope of the foreigner discourse in France due to its greater self-awareness as country of immigration.

The International Refugee Regime

The international codification of refugee law must be seen in the context of the introduction of immigration controls in most European countries in the late 19th and early 20th centuries. During most of the 19th century, the emerging modern nation states followed a liberal open-door policy which essentially permitted uncontrolled and unrestricted immigration (Hathaway 1984: 348). This freedom of movement came to a halt with the rise of nationalism at the end of the century, when European governments began to introduce selective immigration laws which considered potential immigrants in the context of their possible contribution to the national well-being (Grahl-Madsen 1972: 17f; Hathaway 1991: 1). In the light of the massive refugee movements produced by the Balkan Wars (1912/1913), and later the First World War (1914-1918) and the Russian Revolution (1917), however, European states realised that they could not prevent these persons from transgressing borders and that some legal norms had to be found in order to regulate and formalise their move, stay or return. The codification of refugee law was thus an attempt to reconcile the reality of cross-border refugee flows and humanitarian needs with the principle of national sovereignty and control over the entry of persons into the national territory.

Principles

Basically, the general principles of international refugee protection centre around two issues: firstly, there is the relationship between humanitarism and sovereignty in the approach towards refugees and, secondly, there are the notions of international cooperation and solidarity in the relationships between states. These principles are re-traced in the following sections as they relate to the processes leading to the establishment of the international refugee regime, including the *travaux préparatoires* of the main international treaties and declarations constituting this regime, as well as its further development up until the late 1980s.

Human rights versus state sovereignty The codification of political asylum at the international level was embedded in the general move towards international cooperation and the implementation of universal human rights via the United Nations (UN) system. The international refugee regime thus emerged within the framework of the UN which, according to its charter, was set up with the purpose of solving, among other things, "humanitarian" problems and of "promoting and encouraging respect for human rights and fundamental freedoms without distinction as to race, sex, language, or religion" (Art. 1 (3) UN Charter; see also Art. 55c and 56).

Most of the work of the UN for refugees in the legal field emanated from the Commission on Human Rights. As early as 1947, it adopted a resolution[1] that defined refugees as persons whose country of origin no longer secured the protection of their basic human rights and who had lost the fundamental right to belong to a political community (Marx 1984: 152; Weis 1971: 35). The same resolution claimed "to examine at an early opportunity the question of the inclusion of the right of asylum of refugees from persecution in the International Bill of Human Rights or in a special Convention for the purpose."

Both the establishment and evolution of the international refugee regime are characterised by the difficulty of reconciling this humanitarian basis of refugee law with the general principle of national sovereignty. Basically, this principle expresses respect for the exercise of territorial supremacy and provides that this must be respected by other states. This principle is a basic pillar of classic international law which takes as subjects states rather than individuals (Marx 1984). The maintenance of this principle in international refugee law contrasts with a general development which, since the establishment of the UN, has seen "the internationalisation of human rights and the humanisation of international law" (Buergenthal 1997: 703). In contrast to this dynamic development, mainly in the fields of individual criminal law or minority rights (ibid: 717ff), the main subjects of refugee law are still states and not individuals.[2]

The tension between these two principles is best reflected in the unsuccessful attempts at implementing a subjective asylum right at the international level and the parallel evolution of a subsidiary protection mechanism based on the norm of *non-refoulement*. The first attempt to codify a subjective right to asylum at the international level by incorporating a binding obligation on states to provide protection took place in the negotiations leading to the adoption of the Universal Human Rights Declaration in 1948. While a first draft contained a right providing that "everyone has the right to seek and to be granted, in other countries, asylum from persecution",[3] the final version avoided the implementation of such a subjective right and underlined the primacy of state sovereignty by stating that everyone has the "right to seek and enjoy" asylum (Art. 14).

The same controversy is documented in the drafting history of the 1951 Geneva Refugee Convention (GC), which - together with its New York Protocol of 1967 - represents the primary source of international refugee law.[4] According to its preamble, this treaty is dedicated to the assurance of "fundamental rights and freedoms without discrimination" (Para. 1 Preamble GC) and that all states must recognise the "social and humanitarian nature of the problem of refugees and ... do everything within their power to prevent this problem from becoming a cause of tensions between States" (Para. 5 Preamble GC).

Although draft conventions submitted by France and the UN Secretariat contained an article on the admission of refugees,[5] the final version does not implement a subjective right of the person to be granted asylum but merely emphasises the right of the state to grant asylum. However, the real humanitarian limit to states' discretion over the admission or rejection of refugees into their territory must be seen in the (today customary) norm of *non-refoulement* in Article 33 GC, which generally prohibits the return of refugees to countries where their lives or freedoms would be threatened[6] (see Goodwin-Gill 1995: 4). Thus, although the international right of asylum is conceived of as a right of the state, in contrast to a right of the individual, this norm expresses the obligation on a state to admit onto its territory those who would otherwise fear serious human rights violations. The debates leading to the adoption of this norm (Weis 1995: 325ff; Goodwin-Gill 1996: 120) and its implementation in state practices reflect its central humanitarian orientation (Goodwin-Gill 1996: 117ff). This norm clearly expresses the primacy of the individual over the interests of the receiving state and thus represents the strongest humanitarian provision in the international refugee regime. Recognising the desirability of implementing a subjective asylum right, the signatories of the GC: "Expressed the hope that the Convention would have value as an example exceeding its contractual scope" (Recommendation E, Final Act GC).

In fact, both the domestic implementation of asylum laws (see below) and the further evolution of international refugee law reflect this endeavour to strengthen the regime. After the failure of the attempts to implement a subjective asylum right in the 1948 Universal Human Rights Declaration and the 1951 Refugee Convention, several attempts were made both by the

UN and the Council of Europe to adopt an international binding obligation on states to provide asylum to refugees. In the UN, this began immediately after the adoption of the GC. In 1957, France proposed a Draft Declaration on the Right of Asylum to the Economic and Social Council,[7] which after a decade of negotiations culminated in the Declaration on Territorial Asylum (DTA)[8] adopted by the General Assembly in 1967 (Goodwin-Gill 1996: 175f; Weis 1971: 38f). This was the last - unsuccessful - attempt to integrate a subjective asylum right into the UN system. As can be seen, the name was changed: the word "right" was deleted, in order not to give the impression that there is an individual right to asylum, and the word "territorial" was added instead. The Declaration recommends that states should base their asylum practice upon the principles declared, but reaffirms the prerogative of the state to grant asylum (Art. 1 DTA). Similar to the GC, Article 3 acknowledges the principle of *non-refoulement* and urges states to consider, if full asylum is not possible, other means of provisional protection. After the failure of this attempt, a draft convention on territorial asylum was prepared and submitted to a conference of plenipotentiaries in 1977 with the purpose of enhancing the scope of protection available to Convention refugees, however, this process ended in a stalemate (see Hathaway 1991: 14f).

A similar development also took place in the European context. Whereas the European Convention on Human Rights and Fundamental Freedoms of 1950 does not mention asylum at all, a first attempt to include asylum was made in a statement given by the Consultative Assembly of the Council of Europe to the Council of Ministers in 1961 which proposed the insertion of a substantive right to asylum in the second protocol of this European Convention. After the failure of this initiative, a second and final attempt was made through the Convention on Territorial Asylum adopted by the member states of the Council of Europe on 5 December 1977. Yet again, asylum was again confirmed as a prerogative of the state. In parallel with these unsuccessful attempts, however, the norm of *non-refoulement* was gradually strengthened; indeed, it now represents the crucial humanitarian norm of the international refugee regimes.

To sum up, refugee law is closely related to human rights law. Thus, as one United Nations High Commissioner of Refugees has put it: "this means that the interest of the refugee or asylum seeker as a human being should take precedence over the possible conflicting interests of states" (Jean-Pierre Hocké quoted in Skran 1992: 15). The asylum right is the answer of the international community to the fact that human rights are not yet observed everywhere and that efforts for the international protection of human rights have thus far only met with limited success (Weis 1971: 48). However, as the controversies regarding the implementation of a subjective right of asylum versus the right of states to grant asylum have shown, the clearly humanitarian motivation of this regime is based on a classic conception of international law which takes states as subjects rather than individuals and their rights.

International solidarity and cooperation The second group of principles constituting the international refugee regime refers to the relationship between states which are to be guided by the spirit of solidarity and cooperation. International action in refugee matters was from its very beginnings motivated by the aim to find common, cooperative forms of tackling the reality of refugee flows in the inter-war period.[9] These principles are expressed not only in texts, but also in the organisational structure of the international refugee regime.

As early as its first plenary session in 1946, the UN General Assembly was calling for international cooperation and solidarity in dealing with the refugee problem, recognising that it was "international in scope and in nature".[10] This is re-iterated in the preamble of the GC which states that a satisfactory solution to this international problem cannot be achieved without international cooperation (Para. 4 Preamble GC). Similarly, the 1967 DTA declares in its Article 2 that the plight of refugees remains a concern of the international community and, that where a state finds difficulty in granting asylum, other states "shall consider, in a spirit of international solidarity, appropriate measures to lighten the burden on that State". From this derives the sense that refugee protection is a matter for the international community, that is not just for the states therefore which are directly affected by an influx. Burden-sharing is thus an integral part of the regime (Skran 1992: 15). These principles are also reflected in the organisational structure of the international refugee regime. The regime is supervised and promoted by an international agency at the UN, the United Nations High Commission for Refugees (UNHCR). Ever since the 1970s, the UNHCR's activities have mainly dealt with refugee flows in so-called Third World countries, but this agency is mainly financed by the national governments of the richer First World countries of North America and Western Europe.

Beyond the UN context, the principles of solidarity and cooperation in refugee protection have been particularly promoted at the regional level under the auspices of the Council of Europe. In a 1967 resolution, its Committee of Ministers called for liberal admission policies in the member states and declared that "[w]here difficulties arise for a Member State in consequence of its action in accordance with the above recommendations, governments of other Member States should, in a spirit of European solidarity and common responsibility in this field, consider individually, or in co-operation, particularly in the framework of the Council of Europe, appropriate measures in order to overcome such difficulties".[11]

Norms

At the international level, these principles have found their expression in the norms of the 1951 Geneva Refugee Convention, together with its 1967 New York Protocol, as well as through other relevant treaties and declarations adopted in the framework of the United Nations and the Council of Europe. The crucial norms of refugee protection are on one side the formal right of asylum, which applies to a specified category of refugees, and secondary forms of international protection on the other, which derive from the norm of non-refoulement and other humanitarian considerations.

The right of asylum The norms of the international refugee regime, codified in the 1951 Geneva Convention, mainly regulate the status of refugees after its recognition and do not concern the organisation of status determination procedures. These are a prerogative of the sovereign nation states. Thus, the Geneva Convention is less concerned with the right of asylum than it is with the rights in asylum. Accordingly, the international refugee regime does not contain a subjective asylum right for the individual vis-à-vis the state or another international agency. The right of asylum is instead conceived of as the right of a state to grant asylum. This norm derives from the principle of sovereignty and the norm of non-interference in the domestic affairs of other states. With the codification of this right, states have agreed to respect each other's decisions in asylum cases and not to take the exercise of protection as a cause for tensions to develop in their relations.

According to Article 1A Geneva Convention, a refugee is defined as "any person who, owing to well-founded fear of being persecuted for reasons of race, religion, nationality, membership of a particular social group or political opinion, is outside the country of its nationality and is unable or, owing to such fear, unwilling to avail himself of the protection of that country". While this definition was originally limited to events which had occurred in Europe before 1951, these limitations were not applied by international refugee organisations and were officially deleted with the introduction of the New York Protocol in 1967.

Other forms of protection Due to the amplification and differentiation of the causes of involuntary migration in the latter half of this century, a second informal and less well implemented notion of "de facto-refugees" has evolved; this includes all sorts of human rights violations, such as generalised violence, civil wars or natural disasters. These alternative forms of protection are usually granted on the basis of group characteristics linked to national origin and political events without individual status determination procedures.

The existence of these two norms of international protection, the formal individualist refugee definition and the less formal group determination, can again be seen as a compromise between the humanitarian finality of the international refugee regime and the principle of national sovereignty.[12] While the principle of sovereignty is stronger in the formal asylum norm, this sovereignty finds its limits in the norm of non-refoulement which derives from human rights. This norm prohibits the return of persons to situations in which they would fear serious human rights violations (see above). Thus, the limited scope of Article 1A GC was compensated by this norm, which itself applies to a broader range of persons on general humanitarian grounds. With the evolution of the international refugee regime, the norm of non-refoulement was gradually strengthened and is now recognised as a norm of customary law, which means that it is binding universally on all states irrespective of their assent to the convention (Goodwin-Gill 1995: 4). This norm was also implemented in the European Convention on Human Rights and Fundamental Freedoms (Art. 3),[13] as well as in several international human rights treaties such as the 1966 International Convenant on Civil and Political Rights (Art. 31) and the 1984 UN Declaration against Torture and Other Cruel Inhuman or Degrading Treatment or Punishment (Art. 3). Furthermore, its application was extended to persons who present themselves at the frontier of the receiving country (and hence have not yet entered its territory) with the 1967 Declaration on Territorial Asylum (Art. 3 I DTA), which became widely implemented by Western European states (Weis 1971: 41).[14] This strengthening of Article 33 GC was accompanied by iterated, but unsuccessful, attempts to widen the formal refugee definition in order to adapt it to the changing causes of forced migration (see above).

In contrast, broader standards of refugee protection were implemented at a regional level in Africa and Latin America. In 1969, the Organisation of African Unity (OAU) adopted a "Convention governing the specific aspects of refugee problems in Africa"; this extends protection to all persons compelled to flee across national borders by virtue of any man-made disaster, whether or not they can be said to fear persecution (Art. 1(2) OAU Convention; see Hathaway 1991: 16). In Latin America, a similar definition was adopted in the Cartagena Declaration of 1984 (ibid: 19f). In Western Europe, the extension and promotion of refugee protection has been a constant concern of the Council of Europe, which has repeatedly called for an improvement in the treatment of "de facto" refugees.[15] However, it has not succeeded in attaining a formalisation of their status or their rights.

Notwithstanding the reluctance of Western states to formally widen the refugee definition, the scope of the international refugee regime has been extended by the international agency in charge of supervising and promoting international refugee protection, the UNHCR. This agency has gradually extended its mandate under a "good offices" doctrine to cover "persons of concern" or "persons in need of assistance" generally (see Glahn 1992; Goodwin-Gill 1996: 8ff).[16] These categories refer mainly to large groups of refugees - fleeing from civil war, generalised violence, ecological and/or economic disasters in the poorer parts of the world - who are either forced to leave their country or are internally displaced (Hathaway 1991: 13).

As a result of this double-tracked evolution, the international refugee regime encompasses two different categories of refugees with different rights and different degrees of institutionalisation. The first category are formal "statutory" refugees who fulfil the criteria of Article 1A GC and whose status is formally regulated by the Geneva Convention. This applies to persons whose migration is prompted by a fear of individual persecution on the grounds of civil or political status. The much larger group of "de facto" refugees, by way of contrast, is defined by general humanitarian considerations and is usually granted protection on a much more informal basis, but with a less secure legal status (see Hailbronner 1993a).

The German Refugee Regime

In Germany, the establishment of a refugee regime was directly linked to the creation of the Federal Republic in the aftermath of the Second World War. The asylum right in the Basic Law (*Grundgesetz*, GG) of the current German constitution has no predecessor in German history; neither the *Reichsverfassung* of 16.4.1871 nor the Weimar Constitution of 11.8.1919 included such a right. Accordingly, the principles, norms, and procedures regulating German refugee policies before the evolution of European cooperation have their origins in the broader ideational context in which the new West German state was created. The implementation of this asylum right in the Basic Law must be understood as a reaction from the founders of the Federal Republic to the experience of national socialism, especially their knowledge regarding the fate of millions of refugees who had not been able to find protection in another country. The importance of these considerations was furthermore supported by the fact that many of the members of the Parliamentary Council (*Parlamentarischer Rat*) in charge of elaborating the national constitution had themselves been political refugees during the Third Reich (see Bade 1994: 29; Münch 1993: 17).

The discussion of these normative foundations of the German post-World War II refugee regime is followed by a recapitulation of the main policy developments up till the late 1980s, when the constitutional asylum right came increasingly under strain.

Normative Framework

In the following, the principles and norms of the (West) German post-World War II refugee regime are established by analysing the drafting process of the original constitutional asylum right (Art. 16 II 2 GG) in the Parliamentary Council and the major normative developments from then up until the 1980s. According to a former president of the German Constitutional Court, Ernst Benda, a knowledge regarding the genesis of Article 16 II 2 GG is crucial for an understanding of the "continuous humanitarian duty of the country towards persecuted people regardless of short-sighted political considerations".[17] Against this background, the constitutional asylum right must be seen as firmly linked to the self-understanding of the new Germany (Bade 1994: 29).

Principles
The principles regulating German refugee policies up until the early 1980s are closely linked to the overarching principles of the Federal Republic. They are deeply rooted in the moral reorientation of the re-emerging German state and are an ethical reflection of the national socialism experience. These principles are characterised by a very strong humanitarian orientation, coupled with the emphasis on the "objective" rule of law against political arbitrariness. An account of the basic principles regulating the German post-World War II refugee regime, however, would be incomplete if one did not mention the broader principles regulating the German approach towards foreigners, which crystallise in the notions of *ius sanguinis* and the contention that Germany is not a country of immigration. In contrast to the "new" German values of liberalism and *Rechtsstaatlichkeit*, these principles have a long tradition and have developed from 19th century understandings of national belonging and ethnic unity which became translated into the concept of German citizenship.

Human rights versus sovereignty German refugee law is clearly rooted in the principles of human rights and liberalism. This is reflected in the fact that the right of asylum is included in the charter of fundamental human rights enshrined in the Basic Law (Art. 1-19) as a right of every individual irrespective of citizenship. It is part of the inalienable values of the Federal Republic. The primacy of these rights is underscored by Article 19 II GG, which states that "in no case may the essential content of a basic right be encroached upon". Furthermore, the inclusion of the asylum right in the charter of fundamental human rights signifies that the founders of the Federal Republic wanted to protect it from easy or quick transformation through simple legislative reform.

As interpreted by the Federal Constitutional Court, the Basic Law has established a value-oriented order based on human dignity as the "highest legal value".[18] The concept of human dignity, expressed in Art. 1 GG,[19] has been employed by the Constitutional Court as an independent standard of value by which to measure the legitimacy of the state's actions, as well as the uses of individual liberty (Kommers 1997: 203). In its interpretation of the constitutional asylum right, the Federal Constitutional Court has established a direct link between the protection of human dignity and asylum law. In its words, the principle of human dignity overlays ("*überlagert*") the asylum right (see Rothkegel 1994).[20]

The legislative debates preceding the adoption of the constitutional asylum norms document the primacy of humanitarian concerns among members of the Parliamentary Council. While the first drafts of this right did not exceed the obligations under international law and provided for the asylum right as a prerogative of the state, the deputies soon reached consensus about the formulation of asylum as a human right which any politically persecuted individual possesses vis-à-vis the Federal Republic.[21] The attempts of two deputies to add some limiting criteria to this asylum right - to individuals who have to leave their country because of their anti-fascist or anti-militaristic orientation,[22] for example, or the consideration that an unlimited asylum right might overburden Germany's intake capacities[23] - were immediately rejected in favour of a broad formulation. The underlying idea was that the asylum right should not be subject to political opportunism. Protection should be a question of generosity and also independent from political contentions.[24] As a consequence, asylum seekers must generally be allowed to enter German territory in order to have their claim examined; in doing so, any substantive limitation of the asylum right was rejected: "If we include limitations, the police at the border can do as they will. In this case, the constitutional preconditions for the asylum right have to be examined first. This examination lies in the hands of the border police. This makes the right to asylum absolutely ineffective".[25]

The debates in the Parliamentary Council reveal that - in the light of the existence of over 11 million non-German refugees in Europe after the end of World War II. (Wolken 1988: 23) - the deputies knew that this liberal attitude might place a burden on the country. This concern did not, however, prevent them from adopting the unlimited formulation of the constitutional asylum right unanimously on 8.2.1949.[26] This broad interpretation of the asylum right and the primacy of humanitarian commitments over political opportunism was later confirmed by the courts.[27] It was thus recognised that Article 16 II 2 GG had no immanent limits.[28] An exemption from this rule was only recognised in very exceptional cases; for example, where the security *of* the Federal Republic or public security *in* the country was being threatened. However, this exception was only to apply in the case of criminal activities being carried out by an asylum seeker and thus does not represent a limit on the asylum right, as such, but just as a general measure against crime (see Ulmer 1995: 41).[29]

The primacy of human rights in the German refugee regime is furthermore supported by a second general principle of the Federal Republic, the principle of *Rechtsstaatlichkeit* or "law state". With regard to refugee policy, this principle underscores the primacy of human rights and emphasises the role of the judiciary in guaranteeing the asylum right. The importance of the judiciary is reflected in the central role it plays with regard to the material interpretation of Article 16 II 2 GG and the originally extensive organisation of the judicial review procedure against any negative administrative status determination of asylum claims. The need to formulate a more precise interpretation of Article 16 II 2 resulted from its very open formulation which reads: "Persons persecuted for political reasons enjoy the right of asylum". Since the legislator itself restrained from fulfilling this requirement, it was accomplished by the courts through case jurisdiction. As a principle, the courts advocated an extensive interpretation of the notion of political persecution.[30] The availability of the full range of instances of judicial review for asylum seekers and refugees is a second expression of the *Rechtsstaat*-principle and derives from the inclusion of the asylum right in the charter of fundamental human rights in the German constitution (Article 19 IV GG).

To sum up, the principles of human rights clearly outweigh considerations over national sovereignty; the asylum right must not be limited by political considerations. The state was thus consciously deprived of the right to select the asylum seekers entering its territory. In turn, the asylum right became an integral part of the new West German political identity.

Ius sanguinis and "no immigration" The humanitarianism and cosmopolitanism expressed in the principles of human rights and *Rechtsstaatlichkeit* in the Federal Republic is countervailed by a very communitarian notion of citizenship and the self-understanding of Germany as a non-immigration country. These principles are deeply rooted in the national history of the country and have a strong impact on national self-understanding and the general attitude towards foreigners. The specific national concept of citizenship shapes the way in which the entry and stay of foreigners is perceived and thus affects the conceptualisation of refugee policies as being one specific form of immigration among others.

In contrast to the previously mentioned principles of human rights which were directly linked to the establishment of the Federal Republic after the fascist experience, the principle of *ius sanguinis* has a much longer tradition and goes back to the early 19th century (see Brubaker 1992: 119). In his ground breaking analysis of the German and French conceptions of nationhood and citizenship, Rogers Brubaker explains the evolution of this principle in the context of the German *Sonderweg*, that is the fact that the German nation emerged before the establishment of the nation state and that the idea of a nation was therefore originally not political or linked to an abstract idea of citizenship, but prepolitical and organic in the sense of cultural, linguistic or racial belonging (ibid: 1). This notion of *Volksgemeinschaft* or ethno-cultural belonging became codified in the citizenship regulations of the Wilhelmine era. Today's legal basis for German citizenship policies was established through the nationality act of 1913. This law is characterised by a strong duality: on the one hand, there is a remarkable openness towards ethnic Germans who have emigrated from Germany and, on the other, exists a remarkable sense of closure towards non-German immigrants (ibid: 3). Basically, this means that German citizenship could be acquired only by descent and not by territorial criteria, that is by birth or prolonged residence (ius soli). The Basic Law also recognises as Germans former citizens of the GDR and *Vertriebene*, that is persons who were "driven out" of Eastern Europe and the Soviet Union in the aftermath of World War II because of their German descent (Article 116 GG). In contrast, second-generation and even third-generation immigrants who are not of German descent could only acquire German citizenship only through naturalisation which, in Germany, is basically at the discretion of the state (ibid: 33).

The exclusive conceptualisation of citizenship was supported by the official rhetoric that Germany is not a country of immigration. This understanding was clearly expressed in the administrative regulations governing naturalisation which stated that the "Federal Republic is not a country of immigration (and) does not strive to increase the number of its citizens through naturalisation" ("*Einbürgerungsrichtlinien*" no. 2.3, quoted in Brubaker 1992: 77). As a consequence, naturalisation was not seen as routine, but was always an exception which, according to the supreme administrative court, "comes into consideration only in individual cases, in which it seems to be in the interest of the state" (ibid, quoted in Brubaker 1992: 174). These exclusive regulations were only released after the coming into power of the new coalition between the SPD and the Greens (since 1998) which passed a new law introducing the notion of *ius soli* for children of foreign parents who are born in Germany and requesting them to choose between their old and the German citizenship at the age of 23.[31]

Against this background, the liberal asylum right represented an exception to this denial of immigration. Voluntary immigration by non-Germans is, like their naturalisation, a prerogative of the sovereign state. In contrast to this exclusionary stance towards foreigners, which has its roots in the nationalist movements of the 19th century, the founders of the Basic Law underlined their commitment to the protection of persons in need of protection through the liberal formulation of Article 16 II 2 GG (original version) as a subjective human right. The logical linkage between the loss of citizenship and the asylum right is clearly reflected in the structure of the old Article 16 GG which - before its amendment in 1993 - included, apart from the right of asylum for non-German, politically persecuted persons (1) the protection of German citizens from denaturalisation, i.e. the withdrawal of the civil human right of citizenship and (2) a prohibition on extradition for any German in the sense of Article 116 GG. Accordingly, the right of asylum was seen as a substitute for the loss of citizenship rights in another country.

Norms

The legal norms regulating the German post-World War II refugee regime clearly reflect the principles of human rights and *Rechtsstaatlichkeit* in the protection or refugees. The principles of *ius sanguinis* and "non-immigration" only impact indirectly on German refugee policies through their influence on the general understanding of immigration and conception of the position of foreigners in the German nation state. This impact is illustrated in the political development of asylum policies in Germany up until the late 1980s (see below) and, more importantly, in the policy discourse which led to the incisive reform of the constitutional asylum right in 1993 (Chapter Four).

The right of asylum As mentioned above, the founders of the German Federal Republic formulated the right of asylum as an individual human right in Article 16 II 2 GG. This norm gives persons seeking asylum a legally enforceable claim against the sovereignty of the state; they can call for action from the state or demand that action is ceased or, indeed, employ both of these powers. This norm is also binding on the legislature, administration, and courts. The basic right of asylum therefore offers those suffering from political persecution protection against being refused entry into the country and against extradition to persecuting states; these rights are actionable and enforceable before German courts.

The open formulation of "political persecution" contained in Article 16 II 2 GG has been interpreted by the courts in the following manner. Firstly, it concerns, in principle, persecution by state actors.[32] Persecution by non-state agents is generally not recognised under this norm.[33] Furthermore, state persecution must be politically motivated, for instance on the grounds of race, religion, nationality, or membership of a particular social group or political opinion.[34] In order to find recognition under the asylum norm, any such persecution must prove a certain degree of intensity and particularity. General human rights violations which occur routinely in a particular system of governance, even if this includes torture,[35] do not thus automatically represent a case of political persecution in the meaning of Article 16 II 2 GG. This interpretation of the constitutional asylum norm is narrower than the refugee definition of Art. 1A GC in three respects: firstly, it requires a higher degree of objectivity of persecution and does not recognise the subjective "fear" of persecution; secondly, it does not apply to persons who are persecuted by non-state actors or in situations where no government is in force, for example due to civil war; and, finally, it does not apply to instances of persecution which have occurred after the person has left the country, the so-called "*Nachfluchtgründe*" (Wollenschläger/ Schraml 1994: 130).

While the drafting history of Article 16 II 2 GG demonstrates that this norm was consciously implemented as a subjective human right which exceeded the obligations deriving from international law (see above), it was surprisingly ignored during the first phase of German asylum legislation, up until 1965. Rather than taking the constitutional article as the legal basis for the right of asylum, the first legal regulation of the asylum procedure - the asylum decree of 1953 - did not refer to the Basic Law, but only to the Geneva Convention, as its legal basis (see Münch 1993: 38ff; Wolken 1988: 32ff). However, given that the vast majority of persons seeking asylum in the Federal Republic at than time were refugees from Eastern Europe, persons who, under the influence of the Cold War ideology, were seen to match the refugee definition of the Geneva Convention, this neglect of Article 16 II 2 GG did not really make any difference in the practice of asylum (ibid).

This situation changed in 1965 when a new Foreigners Act came into force; this recognised both Article 1A GC and Article 16 II 2 GG as legal bases for political asylum and provided for a common status determination procedure. Parliamentary consultations prior to the adoption of the act show that legislators were fully conscious of the scope of the subjective constitutional asylum right in contrast to international law and confirmed this special commitment to refugee protection through the formal insertion of Article 16 II 2 GG into procedural regulations.[36]

The strength of the constitutional asylum norms was further enhanced in the new asylum procedure code (*Asylverfahrensgesetz*) of 16. 6. 1982 which, in contrast to the 1965 Foreigners Act, referred only to Article 16 II 2 GG and assumed the inclusion of the refugee concept of the Geneva Convention in this norm. This development has led legal scholars to conclude that, until the early 1980s, the constitutional asylum norm was gradually strengthened both in legislation, jurisdiction and jurisprudence, and that it was independent of the "ups and downs of the asylum application numbers" (Kimminich, quoted in Bosswick 1997: 57).

Other forms of protection Similar to the norms of the international refugee regime, the German asylum policy is also characterised by the existence of "secondary" forms of protection which are not covered by the asylum norm of Article 16 II 2 GG. Those persons who are commonly referred to as de facto refugees by far exceed the number of asylum seekers who receive recognition under the constitutional right (Hailbronner 1993a: 19).

The first group of persons falling under these secondary forms of protection were refugees from Eastern European countries who, following a decree adopted by the Interior Ministry in 1966, were granted a general right to stay irrespective of their refugee characteristics (Hailbronner 1993a: 10f). A similar policy was applied with regard to quota refugees who were admitted under unilateral or multilateral relief programmes; examples of such protection measures were the admission of refugees from Chile, Argentina and Indochina in the 1970s. These persons were granted protection on the basis of general group determination criteria. A crucial difference between these protection measures and the formal asylum regime is that they are not regulated on the basis of legally codified rights, but are a clear expression of the will of the state according to its internal and foreign policy interests (see Münch 1993: 176; Hailbronner 1993a 27ff).[37]

Other forms of secondary protection have been developed in the light of the quantitative and qualitative transformation of the German asylum "problem", beginning in the mid-1970s (see below). These measures were a reaction to the fact that many of these persons, that is those who did not fulfil the specific criteria of the constitutional asylum right, were nevertheless in need of protection because of other humanitarian considerations. A first category of such de facto refugees would be persons who do not fulfil the criteria of Article 16 II 2 GG but who would be recognised under Article 1A Geneva Convention (see above). In German asylum law, these persons are usually granted the same rights and benefits as those persons recognised under the constitutional asylum right (Hailbronner 1993a: 26). Another category which neither falls under the refugee definition of Article 16 II 2 GG nor under Article 1 A GC are persons who cannot be returned because they might otherwise face serious human rights violations, torture or inhuman or degrading treatment according to Art. 33 GC, Art. 3 ECHR and Art. 3 UN Convention on Torture. The German Foreigners Act extended this prohibition to returning persons to countries where they would face the death penalty (§53 II AuslG) or other concrete dangers to life, body or liberty (§ 53 VI AuslG). In cases of generalised violence in the country of origin, such as wars or civil wars, the *Länder* can, in agreement with the Federal Interior Ministry, issue a ban on deportation. This form of de facto protection may be motivated by international law or humanitarian considerations or may follow the political interests of the Federal Republic (§ 54 AuslG). It is only a temporary measure, however, and must be regularly renewed if necessary. De facto protection has furthermore been granted to rejected asylum seekers for humanitarian reasons, for example on the basis of the length of their stay in the Federal Republic (Hailbronner 1993a: 22). These regulations were further formalised in 1993 in the context of a comprehensive reform of the German asylum law (Chapter Four).

To sum up, the development of a second, less formal, de facto-refugee regime in German asylum policies could be observed. Although these categories of refugees by far outnumber the number of persons granted asylum under the asylum right of the Basic Law, the rules regulating their admission and legal status have remained much more informal. Basically, these secondary forms of protection share two important characteristics. Firstly, they are not conceived of as enforceable rights, as with Article 16 II 2 GG, but as acts of "autonomous state sovereignty" (Hailbronner 1993a: 30) which offer the executive a very high degree of discretionary power. Secondly, owing to their low degree of formality, these measures still offer little legal or procedural safeguards to the individuals in question. These persons are usually not offered the right to stay, but are merely tolerated on a temporary basis due to the legal suspension of their deportation. Accordingly, their enforced return can be decided at any time by the responsible *Länder* government if the conditions in the country of origin are judged to allow it. The political developments surrounding this evolution of a secondary refugee norm as well as the increasing politicisation of the asylum question since the mid-1970s, is discussed in detail below.

Policy Developments: Emergence of the Asylum "Problem"

In the immediate post-World War II period, German refugee policy was marked by a high degree of liberalism and a generally generous attitude. Although the numbers of refugees were considerable and even if many of these mostly Eastern Europeans did not fulfil the formal refugee criteria, they were nevertheless admitted on an informal basis.[38] In fact, these refugees were actively welcomed as fighters for liberalism and democracy in the ongoing contest between communism in the East and the liberal democracies of the West. This generous attitude towards persons from communist countries was clearly expressed in the ministerial decision of 1966, which granted each of these persons an unlimited residence permit in the Federal Republic regardless of their legal qualification as refugees. Refugee policies were thus not only motivated by humanitarianism, but fitted well in the general foreign policy orientation of that time and were embedded in the ideological context of the Cold War (see Bade 1994: 30; Wolken 1988: 32ff).

This situation started to change in the mid-1970s following the general ban on labour immigration in 1973/74. The following sub-section begins by retracing the emergence and development of the asylum question as a "procedural problem" in policy discourse, before then examining its expansion as a "constitutional problem" in the mid-1980s.

Asylum as a "procedural problem"
The "asylum problem" first emerged in German political discourse in the mid-1970s. In this period, the numbers of asylum seekers started to rise again and their main regions of origin shifted from one which was primarily focused on Eastern Europe to the Middle East and Asia.[39] These refugees were often not recognised under the criteria of Article 16 II 2 GG. Although usually tolerated on the basis of secondary and less formal regulations as de facto refugees, the fact that these persons were not formally granted refugee status under the Basic Law implied that the recognition rates for statutory refugees went down; this also led to the perception that most of these "new" asylum seekers were bogus applicants (see Wolken 1988: 39). A second general change which impacted on the transformation of the asylum problem in Germany was linked to the general ban on foreign labour recruitment (*Gastarbeiter*) in 1974. While before that time, many refugees were able to enter the Federal Republic as economic

immigrants without having to go through the asylum procedure, after 1974 the only legal opportunity to immigrate was either through family reunification or via the asylum law. In addition, the ban on economic immigration intensified the need to develop other forms of protection for rejected asylum seekers who had previously been generally allowed to stay on the basis of immigration law. Finally, it is important to note that the main actors behind this politicisation of the asylum question were the *Länder*. Their mobilisation was in part due to an asymmetry between their increasing involvement in the granting of refugee protection and their limited voice in legislative processes; additionally, it was also the expression of hardening partisan opposition between a coalition government of social democrats and liberals at the federal level and the majority of CDU/CSU[40]-governed *Länder*.

One of the first reforms which had significant consequences for the further development of policy-making in this field was the decision to re-distribute all asylum seekers who, until that moment, had been centrally accommodated by the federal government during the status determination procedure, to the *Länder*. According to a ministerial decree in 1974, asylum seekers henceforth had to remain in the Land in which they first expressed their asylum claim.[41] This decision signified an increased financial and administrative responsibility in the asylum procedure for the *Länder* and local governments. Given that the numbers of asylum seekers in the various *Länder* varied significantly, this decision became a source of tension in the following years between these federal sub-units and the federal government (see Münch 1993: 65ff). These tensions intensified with the federal decision to exclude asylum seekers from the labour market during the first years of the determination procedure. As a consequence, asylum seekers became dependent upon local subsidies and thus placed a supplementary burden on the local infrastructure.

In the late 1970s, a series of administrative reforms followed concerning the entry and stay of asylum seekers, as well as their access to administrative and judicial review procedures. As was already mentioned, the subjective asylum right of Article 16 II 2 GG originally entailed a right of asylum seekers to enter the territory, a right to stay during the whole status determination procedure, and access to the full range of administrative and judicial review procedures. This new wave of procedural reforms began with an attempt in 1977 to establish a filter at the German border against "manifestly unfounded" asylum claims. An administrative decree provided for a sort of pre-screening strategy through which border authorities and the foreigner offices of the *Länder* would now be allowed to examine the potential unfoundedness of any application before its actual transmission to the central agency in charge of examining asylum claims, the Federal Office for the Recognition of Refugees (BAFl). This administrative practice was later rejected by the Federal Constitutional Court because it judged that this new procedure represented a violation of the core of Article 16 II 2 GG.[42] One year later, in 1978, a legislative amendment which was adopted which aimed at the acceleration of domestic asylum procedures through the abolition of the administrative review instance against negative decisions by the BAFl and the decentralisation of the judicial review procedure.[43] An attempt by the CDU/CSU to formalise a pre-screening competence at the German border and in the *Länder*'s foreigner offices did not receive enough support (see Münch 1993: 75). A second legislative reform was passed only two years later; it attempted to streamline the judicial review procedure (see Münch 1993: 80ff).[44] As an accompanying measure, visa requirements were introduced for the main countries of origin from which asylum seekers were coming (Wolken 1988: 47).

By the early 1980s, federal and partisan cleavages between the SPD/FDP[45] government and the CDU/CSU-opposition had developed a dynamic of their own and the asylum discourse became further dissociated from developments in the number of asylum seekers. This is indicated by the fact that, although the numbers of asylum applications following the 1980 reform dropped by more than 60%, the CDU/CSU and the *Länder* of Baden Württemberg and Bayern did not refrain from claiming restrictive reforms from the then ruling SPD/FDP government in the following years. Thus, rather than developments in the structure of the refugee "problem", the reasons for this ongoing discourse must be seen in the context of the 1980 federal elections and efforts by the CDU/CSU to come to power (see Münch 1993: 80 and 88f).

Before waiting for the results of the 1980 reforms, the conservative-led *Länder* introduced a reform proposal in the Bundesrat that included far-reaching measures regarding the entry and stay of asylum seekers.[46] In contrast with this restrictive initiative, the ruling SPD/FDP coalition only proposed limited reforms that were strongly oriented at the jurisdiction of the administrative and constitutional courts.[47] Holding a majority in the Bundesrat, the CDU/CSU immediately claimed that it would oppose this reform, which meant that the case was then transferred to a joint conference committee (*Vermittlungsausschuß*) for mediation. The resulting compromise took over many elements of the original initiative taken in the Bundesrat.

This reform led to the adoption of the Procedural Asylum Law (*Asylverfahrensgesetz*)[48] in 1982, replacing the procedural regulations of the Foreigners Act and the previous acceleration laws. The new regulations were designed to make staying in Germany more unattractive for asylum seekers and, thus, were aimed at reducing rising application numbers. This reform was a repeat attempt to limit the right of entry into the territory in cases of "manifestly unfounded"[49] asylum applications; through it expulsion proceedings could start immediately, appeals to the administrative court would be judged by a single judge, and a second appeal was only possible under certain circumstances.[50]

A renewed attempt to deny entry into West Germany of asylum seekers who were "safe from persecution"[51] in another country was made in 1987.[52] Accordingly, recognition of an asylum seeker as a refugee was impossible if the person had previously stayed in a safe state for at least three months. The extent of these reforms was limited however by the strict interpretation of the notion of "manifestly unfounded" claims by the courts, which thus limited their application to exceptional cases (Davy 1996: 71; Reermann 1992: 24).[53]

Summing up, while every asylum seeker had the possibility of having his or her claim examined before two administrative and three judicial instances (without counting the federal constitutional court) until 1978, the asylum procedure was gradually restricted to only one judicial review instance in most asylum cases. Beyond these measures, however, repeated attempts by the executive and the legislature to exclude certain "manifestly unfounded" claims from the asylum procedure were significantly hampered by the constraining rulings of the judiciary which, with reference to the norms and principles of the German asylum regime, upheld openness, liberality and *Rechtsstaatlichkeit*. Furthermore, despite this increasing politicisation, it is important to note that the political discourse did not as yet question the basic asylum right enshrined in Article 16 II 2 GG. This is documented in a quote from the then acting State Secretary in the Ministry of the Interior, C.-D. Spranger (CSU) who assured his listeners in 1983 that the CDU/CSU did not want to affect the constitutional asylum norm and that it shared the contention that the Federal Republic should remain open to political refugees.[54] The beginning of the dissolution of this normative consensus and the increasing questioning of Article 16 GG is summarised and analysed in the following sub-section.

Asylum as a "constitutional problem"
The position of the CDU/CSU started to change at the beginning of 1985, when its discourse became directed not only against asylum seekers who were seen as "manifestly" economically motivated ("*Wirtschafts-flüchtlinge*"), but also against those perceived as "real" refugees who were either recognised under the formal asylum norm or tolerated on a de facto basis. The lead in this process was taken at the local level by the then acting internal affairs senator from Berlin, Heinrich Lummer (CDU) and, once

again, the *Länder* of Baden-Württemberg and Bayern, both governed by the CDU/CSU. Deploring the "floods" of "*Asylanten*" arriving to abuse social funds,[55] the governments of Berlin, Baden-Württemberg and Bayern lodged a joint initiative in the Bundesrat in 1985 which foresaw incisive changes in the asylum law. The proposal expressed their clear intention to reduce the admission of asylum seekers by abolishing the protection of de facto refugees, excluding "manifestly unfounded" asylum claims from access to asylum procedures, and by limiting the asylum right to a period of two years.[56] The parliamentary debates on this initiative document two important changes in the political discourse: firstly, the entry of asylum seekers was increasingly being perceived as an illegal and criminal act; and, secondly, refugees fleeing civil war were increasingly being equated with "economic", and thus fraudulent, refugees.[57]

A taboo was slowly being broken shortly after, as individual conservative politicians began to question the constitutional asylum right of Article 16 II 2 GG. The lead was taken by the then acting Minister of the Interior, Friedrich Zimmermann (CSU), in the forefront of the 1987 federal elections. Claiming the need to damn up the "flood" of asylum seekers, Zimmermann invoked an amendment of the asylum right in the constitution as "the only solution".[58] Interestingly, this claim was right from the beginning linked to the "need" to harmonise the constitutional asylum right with the less far-reaching provisions of the other EC member states. The aim of developing a common European asylum policy was in fact part of the coalition agreement drawn up between the CDU/CSU and the FDP in March 1987 (Olms/Liehmann 1989). However, a delicate issue in this agreement was that, contrary to the views of the CDU/CSU and, in particular, those of Interior Minister Zimmermann, the FDP insisted on the fact that a comprehensive harmonisation of member state policies had to be accomplished before any eventual adaptation of German law - and particularly of Article 16 GG - could be taken into consideration. In contrast, the Interior Minister not only argued that the harmonisation of asylum policies in the European Community was imminent and that this made an amendment to the constitution "indispensable",[59] but also that Germany had to amend its subjective asylum right ex ante if it wanted to avoid being turned into the "*Reserveasylland*" of Europe, that is the country where all otherwise rejected asylum seekers would come to ask for asylum. This argument was taken over by the next Minister of the Interior, Wolfgang Schäuble, who maintained that, in the light of European integration, an amendment to the constitution had become "compulsive" ("*Zwang*", Schäuble 1989: 33) and that it was a necessary consequence of the Schengen Agreement.[60]

The call for a revision of the constitution intensified after the local elections to the Senate of Berlin in January 1989, which not only resulted in a majority for the opposition - the SPD and the Greens - but which also saw the right-wing Republikaner political party gain 7.5 percent of the vote and thus enter parliament (see Roos 1991a: 54). From that moment on, a second argument, besides that of a "European need", became consensual in the CDU/CSU; of course, this was the fear of right-wing extremism and xenophobia spreading, which would in turn threaten to destabilise the country. In the words of the Interior Minister, Wolfgang Schäuble, a reduction in the numbers of asylum seekers through a constitutional reform was imperative in order to ensure the subjective security of the people and the stability of the country (Schäuble 1989: 25). This securitisation of the asylum discourse was supported by a large increase in the number of asylum seekers ever since 1985 and was accompanied by a polemisation and deterioration of the political discourse. Whereas the increasing use of exaggeration, dramatisation and emotional depiction in the language of CDU/CSU politicians in 1987 and 1988 had provoked a large wave of protests in their own ranks,[61] the use of threats had become less controversial by the end of the decade.

Originally limited mainly to members of the CSU and only to individual members of the CDU, the calls for an amendment to the constitutional asylum right became increasingly popular throughout the whole CDU within the context of the 1989 legislature debates.

Nevertheless, a reform of Art. 16 GG still appeared to be out of reach. Despite weakening resistance inside the CDU/CSU, the strong opposition of their coalition partner - the FDP - and of the opposition - including SPD - made achieving the necessary 2/3 majority in the Bundesrat and Bundestag unrealistic. In 1989, the official position of the main political parties in Germany could be summarised as follows. The CDU/CSU was the only parliamentary group (*Fraktion*) in favour of constitutional reform. However, even within the group, their constituent parts were not fully consensual on this question. While the CSU favoured the transformation of the subjective asylum right into an institutional guarantee and the exemption of asylum seekers from the right to a full judicial review according to Article 19 IV GG, the CDU party was split both over the form and the content of such a reform. Consensus was reached merely on the argument that this reform was a "necessary consequence" of European harmonisation in which Germany would have to adapt its law to lower European standards. Related questions regarding immigration law or the development of a particular status for civil war refugees were not part of the agenda (CDU 1989; Knight/Kowalsky 1991). For the SPD and FDP, in contrast, these related questions were the focus of their attention; both

political parties called for a comprehensive European approach which
would include the right of asylum, immigration, and the integration of
resident aliens. In their view, the constitutional asylum right should not be
amended however (SPD 1989: FDP 1989).

This situation started to change in the 1990s when several
developments came together. On the one hand, there was the opening up of
the Eastern Bloc, the insecurities linked to German unification, increasing
unemployment, and fears regarding massive arrivals of refugees; these all
led to a dramatisation of the asylum discourse. On the other hand, the
contents of European cooperation in this field slowly entered into domestic
debates; the question of a constitutional revision was thus re-framed into
that of a commitment to a common European asylum policy according to
the guidelines of the Schengen Agreement and those of the Maastricht
Treaty. Before the development of this new level of European integration is
presented and considered in Chapter Three, the next section summarises
developments in the French refugee regime up until the end of the 1980s.

The French Refugee Regime

In contrast with the German asylum system which emerged in the context
of the new Federal Republic and which was very much influenced by the
experience of national socialism, the French refugee regime can look back
on a long tradition of the country as a "terre d'asile", one which has its
normative roots in the French Revolution of 1789. France's commitment to
the protection of the politically oppressed was to become a constant feature
during the 19th century and through the two World Wars (with the
exception of the Vichy regime, see below). Consequently, it became firmly
rooted in the national constitutions of the Fourth and Fifth Republics.

Normative Framework

As was mentioned above, the legal concept of refugee protection emerged
in the context of the French Revolution; it must be understood of as part of
the liberation project and "an essential element of the republican doctrine"
(Edouard Herriot, quoted in Weil 1995a: 34). The following paragraphs
examine the normative foundations of the French refugee regime with
regard to its leading principles, the norm of asylum, and other forms of
protection.

Principles
In line with the republican philosophy, the notion of asylum has been developed both as a human right, expressing the limits of political government upon the individual, and as a safeguard for the principle of the sovereignty of the people. This complementarity of humanitarianism and sovereignty in the granting of political asylum in France contrasts with the tensions which existed between these two principles in the evolution of the international and German refugee regimes, it also plays an important role in French policy discourse (see Chapter Four). A second prominent feature of the French refugee regime is the country's understanding of itself as a country of immigration and the adoption of the principle of *ius soli* as the legal basis for granting citizenship.

Human rights versus sovereignty The rights proclaimed in the Declaration of Human Rights of 1789 expressed that the natural rights of the individual are antecedent to society and unalienable. As such, the Declaration mentioned liberty, property, security, and the right to resist oppression. The notion of refugee protection derives directly from three of these rights. Firstly, it expresses the need to recognise the liberty of thought and opinion - at that time, especially of a religious nature - and the right to express these. The corollary of liberty is security, namely the fact that nobody should be arbitrarily detained or punished. This principle follows from the idea of the rule of law and the notion that all executive power must be bound by law. The concern that a government may impinge upon these natural rights is expressed in the affirmation of the right to resist oppression.

Drawing on these ideals, the refugee was seen as a combatant for liberty. Asylum was a major issue for some revolutionaries (Noiriel 1991: 33). A poignant example of the considerations from that time is quoted by Gérard Noiriel with reference to the debates in the Constituent Assembly of 19.2.1791. When considering a request from the Austrian government for France to extradite an alleged counterfeiter, one delegate of the Assembly inferred that the proposition touched on one of the most important questions of public law. He believed that

> "in principle it is true that a nation should always render fugitive criminals to a foreign power that reclaims them, but this should not be done on the simple request of a minister, on an arbitrary requisition... All the despots of the neighbouring states, and you are surrounded by them, would reclaim through their ministers all the friends of humanity, all those persons who have committed no other crime than preaching liberty... I thus beg the Assembly to consider if this is not the moment when France can become the asylum of all

the friends of liberty." (quoted in Noiriel 1991: 33, own translation)

From that moment on, the right of asylum became a stake of the revolutionary struggle. Robespierre himself became one of its most influential proponents, claiming that asylum was the most important issue of public law because the determination of reciprocal rights and duties of nations was at stake (ibid). These considerations led to the adoption of an asylum right in the first constitution of a French republic - the Constitution Montagnarde of 24.6.1793 - which, however, never entered into force. In its Article 120, this constitution declared that the French people "give asylum to foreigners banned from their countries in the name of liberty".

After 1793, this universalist orientation gave way to growing nationalism, but France was still to become the major destination country for political refugees fleeing from upheaval in Italy, Spain, Portugal and Poland during the first half of the 19th century. It was mainly under the Monarchie de Juillet and the Second Empire that the country established its identity as "terre d'asile" (Noiriel 1991: 37ff). The granting of asylum was seen as a sovereign act and as an exercise of humanitarianism (ibid: 40).

Although a new wave of nationalism at the end of the century entailed the development of measures aimed at protecting the domestic labour market from certain groups of economic immigrants, France's asylum tradition was not affected. This was manifested in its relentless admission of members of ethnic minorities fleeing from the newly emerging nation states in Turkey, Iraq, the Ukraine and the Balkans in the early years of the 20th century and in its admission of refugees after World War I. Despite the adoption of an increasingly restrictive stance towards labour immigration in the wake of the economic crisis of the early 1930s, this special commitment towards refugees was generally upheld[62] In fact, France was the major refugee receiving country in the inter-war period (Norek/Doumic-Doublet 1989: 21; Weil 1995a: 36). This was supported by the emergence of numerous private associations assisting refugees and France's active promotion of international cooperation in this matter. In its self-understanding as *the* "pays des droits de l'homme" (Noiriel 1991: 141), however, this international engagement was from its very origins two-sided: while aimed at the general improvement of refugee protection in Europe, French foreign policy in these matters has always been very much concerned with the protection of national sovereignty. Thus, any transfer of competence to international actors was opposed and the independent national exercise of protection defended (Noiriel 1991: 141ff). The preservation of sovereignty was justified through the idea that no foreign or international agency could exceed French humanitarianism (ibid). In this sense, the exercise of human rights policies towards refugees was seen as an exercise of sovereign power rather than a challenge to it.

After World War II and the rupture of the Vichy regime between 1940 and 1944,[63] the French government immediately resumed its international and domestic human rights orientation towards refugees. These principles are reflected in the preamble to the 1946 Constitution, which was taken over in the current Constitution of the Fifth Republic adopted in 1958. This expresses that: "The French people solemnly proclaims its attachment to Human Rights and the principles of national sovereignty as they have been defined in the Declaration of 1789, confirmed and completed by the Preamble of the 1946 Constitution". Among these human rights, § 4 of the Preamble provides that: "Everyone persecuted because of his actions on behalf of liberty has the right of asylum in the territories of the Republic". With its incorporation into the Preamble of the French Constitution, the asylum right became part of the general and fundamental principles of the French Republic and became binding on the executive, legislature, and the courts.

Ius soli and immigration According to Patrick Weil, one of the most respected French immigration experts, France has been a country of immigration since the 13th century (Weil 1995a: 26). Official efforts to control the entry of foreigners did not start before the mid-19th century, when an economic need for immigrants began to contrast with the strengthening notion of nationalism which legitimated increased intervention by the state in these matters. First of all, restrictions on the access of immigrants to certain professions were introduced, together with the requirement to carry passports and identity cards at the turn of the century (Noiriel 1991: 89ff). Since then, an official immigration policy has taken shape which considers immigration as a solution to the economic and demographic problems in France (Weil 1995a: 26ff). This line of policy was made explicit in 1945, when General de Gaulle declared France to be a country of immigration with his signature of the ordinance of 2.11.1945 (Weil 1995b: 277). Despite repeated attempts to close the borders to labour migration ever since the economic crisis of the mid-1970s, legal and illegal immigration has continued to be a reality in France.

This long tradition of immigration in France was linked to this country's colonial policy and was accompanied by the development of a citizenship regulation; this has allowed for the full integration of immigrants, both through naturalisation and by territorial principles. In contrast to the German concept of citizenship, which is based on ethnic descent, the French tradition is much more influenced by the principle of *ius soli* by which citizenship is attributed by birth on the territory. While this principle was clearly dominant throughout the Ancien Régime, the attribution of citizenship by descent emerged only in the 19th century with the rise of nationalism (Weil 1995b: 291). Today's citizenship law consists of a combination of *ius sanguinis* and *ius soli*, which was first established in the nationality law of 1889. With this concept, France adopted an expansive definition of citizenship, one that "automatically transforms second-generation immigrants into citizens, assimilating them - legally - to other French men and women" (Brubaker 1992: 3).

Norms
As in the German case, the category of norms is limited to the concept of the right to asylum or other forms of protection as shaped by the general principles of the refugee regime. Again, the question of citizenship and immigration is not directly included, but must be seen as part of the broader ideational framework guiding refugee policies.

The right of asylum As mentioned above, the current constitution of the Fifth Republic includes the right of asylum as a right of the individual in §4 of the Preamble: "Everyone persecuted because of his actions on behalf of liberty has the right of asylum in the territories of the Republic". With this formulation, the founders of the constitution clearly resumed the liberal tradition of the 1789 Revolution; it is directed against despotic governments and extends protection to those who struggle against them.

Beyond its implementation in the constitution, the domestic formulation of the asylum norm was deeply enmeshed in efforts to set up a refugee regime at the international level. This parallelism of international negotiations and domestic legislation resulted - somewhat similarly to the first years of refugee protection in Germany - in the establishment of two parallel, partly overlapping and partly differing, conceptualisations of the asylum right; one derives from the constitutional provision and one is based on the 1951 Geneva Convention. While a first attempt to include asylum seekers in the general provisions concerning immigration regulated in the ordinance of 1945 on the entry and stay of foreigners was turned down by the Council of State (*Conseil d'Etat*) invoking the need to provide particular regulations for this group of persons (see Weil 1995c), their situation was regulated by the refugee-specific law of 25.7.1952 and the decree of 2.5.1953. These two regulations implemented the provisions of the 1951 Geneva Convention and do not mention the constitutional asylum right. As a consequence, asylum seekers were (until 1998, see Chapter Four) granted asylum on the basis of the refugee definition of Article 1A Geneva Convention which is broader than the notion of persecution due to "actions on behalf of liberty" as laid down in §4 of the Preamble (see Legoux 1995;

Norek/Doumic-Doublet 1989: 36; Tiberghien 1984). Since the interpretation of Article 1A GC in France includes the subjective fear of persecution and considers the possibility of protection elsewhere, it exceeds the scope of Article 16 II 2 GG in Germany (Classen 1993: 229).

In contrast to the Geneva Convention, the role of the constitutional asylum norm has long remained unspecified. Although the Constitutional Council (*Conseil Constitutionnel*) recognised the constitutional status of the 1958 Preamble,[64] this norm has some time been neglected both in administrative and judicial status determination procedures.[65] However, this did not really affect asylum practice since France traditionally followed a very liberal asylum policy, which, in accordance with § 4 Preamble (Norek/Doumic-Doublet 1989: 38), accorded every asylum seeker the right to enter the national territory (ibid: 32; Hailbronner 1989: 69; Classen 1993: 232) and to stay until the end of the status determination procedure was reached (Classen 1993: 227; Norek/Doumic-Doublet 1989: 32). This practice, which was first informal, was confirmed and codified with a circular from the French prime minister in 1985 (Oellers-Frahm 1992: 33).

To sum up, it can be asserted that despite some confusion about the binding nature of § 4 of the Preamble, the French asylum norm largely corresponded with the German regulation. It provided for the right to have an asylum request examined, and, for this purpose, it allowed the asylum seeker both to enter the territory and stay for the duration of the procedure. From a substantive point of view, however, the French norm was broader than the German since it granted refugee status according to the criteria of the 1951 Geneva Convention, which in turn exceeds the interpretation of Article 16 II 2 GG in Germany.

Other forms of protection Similar to the international and German refugee regimes, this formal asylum norm has been complemented by secondary and less formal forms of refugee protection. This has, however, occurred on a more limited basis and only started to be formalised in the second half of the 1980s.

Two categories of persons can be distinguished as those who receive protection on the basis of secondary policies: firstly, refugees accepted on a quota basis as a function of humanitarian and foreign policy considerations and, secondly, rejected asylum seekers who are allowed to remain.

The admission on a quota basis outside the formal status determination procedures mainly concerned refugees from South-East Asia (Indochina) during the 1970s.[66] Influenced by its colonial past, France took the lead in the admission of these refugees; they were selected "sur place", on the basis of general group determination criteria (see Norek/Doumic-Doublet 1989: 39 and 86ff). This quota policy was totally separate to the regime guiding the admission of asylum seekers at France's frontiers or in its territories and must be seen as a foreign policy measure and expression of the sovereign will of the state (Legoux 1995: 196).

The second category of non-statutory refugees are de facto refugees whose asylum applications have been definitively rejected by the competent authorities but who, nevertheless, are allowed to stay on the national territory. Their numbers have been much less important than in Germany. This can be explained by several factors. Firstly, it is important to note that, given that the formal definition of a refugee in France exceeds the criteria applied in Germany, recognition rates of asylum seekers in France have generally been much higher. This indicates that more categories of refugees have been able to find recognition under the formal asylum norm in France than they have in Germany. While this includes primarily persons with a subjective fear of persecution, another example of persons in this category are those who fear persecution by non-state actors.[67] Although instances of generalised violence and civil war were excluded from the formal asylum norm in 1976,[68] Luc Legoux has shown that these persons were formerly included under the formal refugee definition and constituted the majority of statutory refugees in the 1950s and 1960s (Legoux 1995: 39 and 103ff; see also Tiberghien 1984). A second possible explanation for the relative unimportance of de facto refugees may result from the fact that the French labour market has traditionally been much more open towards foreigners than has been the case in Germany, so that rejected asylum seekers could nevertheless construct an existence as economic immigrants.

Thus, while officially rejected de facto refugees were thus able to find other forms of protection in practice, their situation was slightly more formalised with a circular from the interior minister of 17.5.1985 and specified by the circular of 5.8.1987. Accordingly, the rejected asylum seeker might be exempted from an obligation to leave the country because (a) of particular family or other personal reasons which proved that the respective persons were already well integrated into French society, and (b) as a result of humanitarian considerations concerning the situation in the country of origin which indicated that a risk regarding the security or liberty of the persons existed in the case that he or she was returned (Hailbronner 1993a: 62f). The first category of persons could be exempted from the obligation to leave the country only in exceptional cases. The decision about their right to stay was taken at the local level by the prefect through the exercise of that official's discretionary powers.[69] In the second case, the prefects were asked to consult the Ministry of the Interior, which then decided on the import of the situation extant in the country of origin (ibid, see also Norek/Doumic-Doublet 1989: 99ff).

As in Germany, these persons were "tolerated" on a very informal basis and did not enjoy the legal and social advantages granted to formal refugees. A formal law on temporary protection for refugees fleeing instances of generalised violence was passed only in 1998 in France, five years after a similar reformed was adopted in Germany (see Chapter Four). The status of these persons is regulated on a temporary basis only and must be regularly renewed. To sum up, the emergence of this secondary regime again demonstrates the strengthening of sovereignty elements because it moves protection away from an enforceable human right protected by the courts to a discretionary act to be exercised by the executive.

Policy Developments: Questions of Integration and Nationality

In comparison with the early politicisation of the asylum issue in Germany, the evolution of the French refugee regime up until the end of the 1980s shows a very high degree of continuity and stability. In the literature, it is generally acknowledged that the liberal tradition of the 1789 Revolution was upheld until then and that in contrast to immigration policy, which was always subject to political, demographic and economic considerations, the asylum right remained largely sheltered from political disputes (Norek/Doumic-Doublet 1988: 38; Vincent 1987: 485; Weil 1995a: 36).

The sustenance of liberalism, not only at the level of principles and norms, but also at the level of procedures, is particularly interesting considering the parallel development of refugee flows in France and Germany. In the first years of refugee protection after World War II, both countries received very high numbers of refugees who came exclusively from European countries; in France, these refugees came mainly from Spain (as a consequence of the civil war), as well as from Central and Eastern Europe.[70] Although the Spanish refugees especially, but also many Eastern Europeans, did not fulfil the criteria of individual persecution, they were nevertheless granted formal refugee status (Legoux 1995; Tiberghien 1984). After a strong decline in the numbers of refugees between 1960 and 1974, the situation started to change significantly in the mid-1970s after an official halt was enacted on economic immigration with the closure of the labour market; before this change this method had allowed many persons, including potential refugees, to enter the country legally and to stay without claiming asylum (Norek/Doumic-Doublet 1989: 84f; see also Weil 1995a). In contrast with Germany, however, where the asylum system - apart from family reunification - became the only legal means of entering the country, France continued to recruit temporary labour on a regular basis (Farine 1993:12). More than that, many persons continued to enter the country illegally. Coupled with the well-established practice of regularising illegal immigrants, this form of immigration developed, as in Southern European countries like Italy or Spain, what were very nearly structural features (see Foot 1995; Manfrass 1989). The main legal source of immigration in France at that time was family reunification; indeed, this amounted to 60% of the total immigration. Asylum seekers, in contrast, made up only 20% of all legal entries (Wihtol de Wenden 1994: 256). Of course, these differences with Germany have their origins in the long tradition of France as an immigration country and its special ties with its former colonies, especially those in Northern Africa.

Given these important differences in the historical background of the foreigner issue in Germany and France, the attention paid to asylum seekers in the latter's political discourse has always been relatively small, despite an active and generous asylum policy. In contrast to Germany, where the aim of restricting the constitutional asylum right had already entered political discourse by the mid-1980s, in France this call only emerged only in 1993, unexpectedly at that, and was nearly exclusively justified through the need to implement the various European agreements. During the 1970s, 1980s and most of the 1990s, France's political discourse mainly centred on the more general questions of voluntary, legal and illegal immigration, integration, and citizenship. This discourse began to take shape during the economic recession of the 1970s and evolved from what was initially a purely economic question - centring on the role of immigration in the economy and its influence on the labour market and social policy - to a question of national identity and citizenship by the 1980s (Hochet 1988; Krulic 1988; Kastoryano 1996; Schnapper 1991, 1998; Silverman 1992; Wihtol de Wenden 1994). While this evolution reflects the enlargement of the "immigrant problem" from a purely economic to a social and political predicament, it is important to note that the category of refugees and asylum seekers remained largely screened from this politicisation and did not emerge at the top of the political agenda before Pasqua's reform proposals were made known in 1993.

Immigration as an "economic" and "social" problem
The economic thematisation of foreigners in the 1970s initially concentrated mainly on illegal immigration and its perceived strain on the labour market and on social benefits. This departure from the earlier "laissez-faire" policy was promoted by President Giscard d'Estaing's (UDF) conservative government[71] which started to return immigrants to their home countries in 1978 before these policies were annulled in the last instance by the Council of State for breaching the French liberal tradition (Weil 1995a: 179ff). The introduction of the immigration question into the public and political discourse was partly supported by local officials and

administrators who had become increasingly involved in the implementation of policies aimed at the better integration of immigrant populations into local structures through housing, social benefits and schools. Despite their limited impact on decision-making, these local officials contributed significantly to the emergence of anti-immigrant sentiments both in the public and political discourse. They coined the slogan of a "threshold of tolerance", basically meaning that the increased number of immigrants was putting a strain on local social structures.[72] According to Martin A. Shain, this local mobilisation in the 1970s prepared the ground for the xenophobic and racist discourse of the Front National (FN) a decade later (Schain 1996).

Despite this increasing politicisation of immigration, the generous attitude towards asylum seekers and refugees was upheld. Political insurgencies and upheavals, especially in South America and Indochina, led the French government to admit significant numbers of refugees on a quota basis.

When President François Mitterrand and his Parti Socialiste (PS) came into power in 1981, immigration and integration rose to the top of the political agenda. Under Mitterrand, the unfolding immigration discourse received a strong ideological component and a deeply symbolic value (Hochet 1988; Wihtol de Wenden 1987, 1994). Notwithstanding the ongoing arrival of economic migrants and the increasing numbers of asylum seekers in a time of economic recession and growing unemployment rates, he redefined the question of immigration from an economic issue to one of human rights, actively promoting the rights of resident aliens in France. The most spectacular measure was the regularisation of over 200,000 "clandestins" in 1981 and 1982, as well as the granting of the right of association to immigrants in 1983 and local voting rights in 1983. At the institutional level, the power of the legislature was strengthened vis-à-vis the executive through the transformation of hitherto purely administrative circulars and decrees into laws. The discretionary power of the administration in this field was further weakened through the enhanced competency of the judiciary, particulary in expulsion cases. According to Patrick Weil, these measures aimed at countering police practice ("les pratiques policières") and the reestablishment of the law state ("l'etat de droit"). Furthermore, these measures were to underline the traditional values of the left, that is solidarity, internationalism, and the fight against any form of exploitation (Weil 1995a: 216ff). At the discursive level, the PS advocated a multicultural society and coined the slogan "the right to be different" ("le droit à la différence").

This turnabout was supported by the relative independence of Mitterrand's PS from the mainly communist local governments which, as in

Germany, followed a more anti-immigrant stance. This liberal approach was primarily concerned with policies directed at the integration of resident aliens; it did not however relax the restrictive stance on illegal entry or border controls, as was reflected in the Law of 27.5.1982. Although this law did not become relevant in practice, it provided the possibility of rejecting asylum seekers at the border if it was clear that their quest was manifestly unfounded. Accordingly, if the border police (*Police de l'Air et des Frontières*) was of the opinion that a claim was clearly unfounded, it was not allowed to simply return the claimant but was required to refer the case to the Ministry of the Interior, which would then decide what to do about the admission or refusal of the person onto French territory after consultation with the Ministry of the Exterior and the UNHCR (see Norek/Doumic-Doublet 1989: 40; Oellers-Frahm 1992: 31). This decree thus established a sort of prescreening procedure independent of the regulations concerning the lodging of an asylum request within the territory. However, its importance was significantly diminished given that the vast majority of applications in France are placed from inside the territory. Furthermore, the possibility of refusing entry was hardly ever applied in practice (Hailbronner 1989: 69; Norek/Doumic-Doublet 1989: 40). Given this lack of implementation, the importance of the law was in regard to its status, as it meant that provisions on the entry of foreigners at the border were for the first time not issued through an administrative circular but via a regular law, thus increasing transparency and democratic control.

The efforts to counter the restrictive trend developed under Giscard d'Estaing came to an end in 1983 with the dramatic success of Jean-Marie Le Pen and his Front National (FN) at the local elections. From that moment on, the FN succeeded in expanding upon the question of immigration in both the public and political discourse. Concentrating on immigrants from the former colonies in Central and North Africa, the main theme of the FN was the redefinition of these people from an economic to a social problem; they were thus constituted as a threat to French identity and the nation state (see Silverman 1992: 70ff; Weil 1995a: 110ff). The emergent catch-word of this spreading racist discourse was that of the "non-assimilables" - the designation of certain immigrants mostly of Muslim origin - whose integration or better assimilation into French society and republican values was said to be impossible due to cultural, religious and ethnic difference (Silverman 1992: 71f). In turn, this securitarian discourse of the FN became the focal point for traditional parties as well, leading to a shift of those on the Right further to the right and a destabilisation of the Centre and the Left (see Schain 1996; Schor 1996; Tuppen 1991: 54 ff).

This polemisation of the political discourse paralleled the growth of social movements both of immigrant and non-immigrant origin, thus leading to social disturbances including riots and strikes in the summers of 1981 and 1982, as well as marches for equality in 1983 and 1984 on one side, and the publication of anti-immigrant studies and increased anti-immigrant violence on the other (Silverman 1992: 140ff; Wihtol de Wenden 1994: 73). Given the long-lasting presence of immigrants in France and their crucial role in the national economy, this mobilisation also included economic actors, particularly employers, who opposed these restrictions on illegal labour. Furthermore, many pro-immigrant associations were created in this period, thus fuelling their interests into the political arena (Schain 1990: 260).

Despite this heated environment, the mid-1980s were also a time when a basic consensus was reached between the traditional parties; this consisted of the aim of enforcing the closure of borders and the fight against illegal entries while putting increased efforts into the integration of resident aliens (Schain 1996: 182f; Weil 1995a: 285ff; Weil 1995b: 276f). This consensus however, which was largely kept undercover, was stronger with regard to the closure of borders than it was with regard to integration, as the subsequent debate on the nationality code revealed.

This debate reached a preliminary climax with Charles Pasqua's 1986 proposal to abolish the automatic granting of citizenship to second generation immigrants, thus turning it into a discretionary act. This proposal provoked heavy protests across the political spectrum apart, of course, from the FN, who had already previously expressed this idea. In order to calm this polemicisation down and rationalise the discourse, a *Commission de la Nationalité* was set up under the lead of Marceau Long with the task to reflect upon the citizenship law and the integration of second generation immigrants. The Commission concluded in 1988 that French citizenship should be revalued through a voluntarist conception, thereby strengthening the civic and cultural aspects of French nationhood (see Favell 1998: 55ff; Guiraudon 1994; Silverman 1992: 140ff; Weil 1995a: 440ff). The conclusions of the Commission was the preliminary peak of a strident debate which went straight to the core of French identity and France's tradition as a country of immigration. The Pasqua proposal was dropped, but it re-emerged, together with measures regarding asylum seekers, five years later in 1993.

Immigration and refugees
As was previously mentioned, the foreigner discourse in France during the 1980s was mainly concerned with continued immigration from former colonies and questions of integration and citizenship. Nevertheless, the

restrictive turn in French immigration policy under the Government of Jacques Chirac and Interior Minister Charles Pasqua did not completely exclude the category of asylum seekers: far-reaching reforms were worked out, but they did not hold up in the face of opposition both from the PS and from within parts of the ruling RPR/UDF coalition.

The ground for Pasqua's restrictive proposals was laid with a significant institutional reform which consisted of the suppression of the specialised Ministry for Immigration Affairs which had been set up under the PS and which had been charged with the coordination of measures in this field. This reform gave an unprecedented degree of autonomy to the Interior, Foreign, and Social Affairs Ministries. It also paved the way for the subsequent strengthening of the Interior Ministry's role. Together with the above-mentioned reforms, the new Minister of the Interior began to question the situation of asylum seekers. Events which were related to the expansion of this discourse included the observation in 1984-1985 that the number of rejected asylum seekers exceeded, for the first time in the OFPRA's (*Office Français pour la Protection des Réfugiés et Apatrides*)[73] history, that of recognised refugees (Legoux 1995). Another reference included the terrorist attacks in Paris in 1986, the authors of which were identified as Islamic refugees by the FN and parts of the RPR (see Tuppen 1991: 60ff). This terrorist "threat" constituted a central element in the subsequent attempt to securitise the asylum question; Pasqua immediately called for radical measures in the field of asylum policies, including the abolition of the suspensive effect of appeals in front of the *Commission de Recours des Réfugiés* (CRR) and the introduction of asylum regulations into the ordinance of 2.1.1945 regarding the entry and stay of foreigners. This proposal foresaw as an obligation the lodgement of asylum claims at the border before entering French territory, contrasting sharply with the fact that over 95% of all asylum applications in France are lodged inside the country. This re-organisation of asylum procedures was to be coupled with the introduction of pre-screening measures at the border, which would thus have allowed the immediate return of certain categories of persons (Doumic-Doublet 1989: 104f). In addition, Pasqua called for the imposition of sanctions on air, sea and land carriers enabling the entry of persons who did not possess the required entry documents (ranging from a visa, passport, and living allowance, as well as a return ticket). Although these sanctions were not to apply to asylum seekers whose claim was not manifestly unfounded, they would nevertheless have placed a heightened level of responsibility on transport companies who would have had to decide whether or not to transport a person who was without the required documents.

These reform proposals, which would have signified a fundamental transformation of the French asylum regime, yielded large waves of protests not only from the opposition, but also from within the RPR/UDF coalition, and from a public invoking their pride in, and the normative commitment of, France as a "terre d'asile" (Weil 1995a: 295). Faced with this opposition, Pasqua withdrew his proposals and the controversy over asylum seekers came to a halt (ibid). Instead, Pasqua passed a bill that generally re-enforced the power of the executive and the police by restricting entry conditions, and introducing the possibility of immediate expulsions in cases of "absolute urgency" by the *préfectures* if the person concerned was seen as threatening public order (law of 17.9.1986). This measure weakened the impact of the judiciary, which was hitherto responsible for expulsion measures, and widened the competencies of the Interior Ministry which at the local level is represented by the prefect.[74] This reform was coupled with a very strict application in pertinent *circulaires* by the Ministry of the Interior, thus widening the discretionary powers of the prefects vis-à-vis the judiciary (Weil 1995a: 298).

In summation, the opposition to the Pasqua proposals and the conclusions of the Commission des Sages put a preliminary end to the controversies regarding immigration. In the 1988 elections, no political party (apart from the FN) put this issue on its electoral programme and the aim of avoiding any new polemics and thereby containing Le Pen's FN became a priority of the elected PS government of Prime Minister Rocard and President Mitterrand. Sticking to the above mentioned consensus reached in 1984 which combined restrictive entry policies with the enhanced integration of aliens inside the territory, the Pasqua law of 1986 restricting the conditions for entry and the facilitation of expulsions was not fully abolished, but several circulars were released allowing for its liberal implementation and the role of the judiciary was again strengthened vis-à-vis the police (Weil 1995a: 302).

In the late 1980s, asylum seekers were not a primary concern. This is reflected in the fact that, although their numbers reached an unprecedented peak of over 61,000 in 1989, the political reaction was not to call for restrictions but the strengthening of status determination procedures. The OFPRA's budget was doubled and its staff significantly increased.[75] Although the introduction of speedier procedures raised protests from refugee advocacy associations, this reform was praised by the UNHCR as a "model in Europe" (Le Monde of 2.7.1991). In the aftermath of this reform, which allowed an application to be processed within only three months, the numbers of asylum applications decreased significantly and status determination procedures were relieved.[76] This acceleration led the French government to abolish in October 1991 the right of asylum seekers to work during the status determination procedure. At the same time, it was decided to regularise, under the condition that they had found regular employment, the stay of over 25,000 rejected asylum seekers whose status determination procedure had exceeded the period of two years.[77]

Comparing this relative stability of France's asylum policy with the widening asylum discourse in Germany, one expert concluded in 1989 that asylum policy was not likely to become Europeanised. The French concern with preserving sovereignty was too strong and the foreigner discourse too complex, dealing more with questions of voluntary immigration, integration, national identity and citizenship than with institution of asylum (Manfrass 1989: 176). This conclusion was supported by the so-called Vetter Report on European asylum policies issued by the European Parliament in 1987, according to which French officials declared that the country did not have a "refugee problem".[78]

Conclusion

This review the domestic determinants in the asylum policies of France and Germany in the 1970s and 1980s reveals an intriguing development. Despite a similar normative commitment to human rights principles, a comparable quantitative and qualitative transformation of the asylum issue, and similar economic developments, policy responses in France and Germany differed significantly during the latter period. These differences concerned the construction of the asylum "problem" in the political discourse, the evolution of the asylum norm (in Germany, the salience of a secondary *de facto* system of protection; in France greater stability of the formal asylum norm), and restrictions of the asylum procedure (increasingly restrictive reforms in Germany versus the stability of procedures in France).

Summing up, two important dynamics were identified as being behind these different developments: firstly, there were differences in the normative framework of refugee policies, implying a much broader scope in the immigration discourse and the relative secondarity of the asylum question in France; and, secondly, there were differences with regard to the institutional configuration of the discourse arenas and particularly the importance of federalism and partisan politics in Germany.

With regard to normative factors, the relative stability of the French liberal tradition in the 1980s, in contrast to the restrictive turn which took place in Germany, was linked to France's self-understanding as an immigration country and its colonial past. Together with the principle of *républicanism* and the civic concept of citizenship, these factors provided that the presence of aliens was inherently part of the national identity. Not only did this broader normative framework imply a broader mobilisation of public and private actors, it also raised a wider range of issues in which the asylum question was to play only a minor role. This discourse concentrated on the continued entry of voluntary illegal immigrants, but was gradually widened to encompass a broad range of issues ranging from the questions of integration and multiculturalism to the very concept of French nationality and the idea of citizenship; these questions were directly linked to the colonial past and the national understanding of France as a country of immigration (Weil 1995b: 277). In normative terms, the securitisation of immigration in France is based on two axes: a civic and an ethnic one. The civic semantic is linked to the republican understanding of the French nation and problematises migrants in particular in view of a perceived lack of political loyalty and affiliation to the French political system. The ethnic perspective, in turn, perceives of migrants primarily with regard to their cultural background, their traditions and religion. This is the semantic of the "non-assimilables", that is persons in particular from the former colonies in central and north Africa, whose cultural, ethnic or religious difference would impede assimilation to the unversalist and herewith also homogeneous understanding of the French society (Targuieff 1991; Schnapper 1998; Silverman 1992). In this complex, and politicised discourse, the question of asylum seekers was secondary and was largely restricted to the issue of effective border controls against illegal immigration and the acceleration of status determination procedures. Until 1993, one can say that the perception of asylum seekers was still very much shaped by the ideals of republicanism and France's role as "terre d'asile", thus closer to an idealist policy frame.

As was mentioned before, these differences cannot be explained with through the "objective" representation of the foreign population in these two countries alone, especially if one considers that Germany also had de facto become an immigration country with the presence of "Gastarbeiter" and the arrival of their families dating from the 1970s. However, Germany's understanding of itself as not being a country of immigration and the principle of *ius sanguinis* impeded a comparable extension of the foreigner discourse and, indeed, facilitated a narrow concentration on the continued entry of asylum seekers and refugees as an "anomaly" in a "non-immigration" country. Within this German asylum discourse, normative reflection centred on the experience of national socialism and the special respon-sibility of the German nation in relation to the protection of universal human rights. Originally promoted across all political parties, these normative orientations were no longer consensual by the end of the 1980s. Influenced by the principle of *Rechtsstaatlichkeit*, declining recognition rates for asylum seekers were more and more interpreted by conservative politicians as signs of an abuse of asylum procedures and threats to the rule of law - thereby neglecting the fact that many of these rejected asylum seekers, although not fulfilling the narrow persecution criteria of the constitutional asylum right, were nevertheless granted protection on other humanitarian grounds as de facto refugees. The second discursive axis in the securitisation of asylum seekers in Germany was less based on identity politics (such as the immigration discourse in France) than on economic arguments such as increased competition on the labour markets and welfare losses. In contrast to the French immigration discourse, the German asylum discourse was thus not about the place of immigrants in state and society, but concentrated more narrowly on a perceived loss of control over the entry of foreigners into the territory and the resulting strains on the judicial system and public expenditures.

The second dynamic that lies behind these divergent developments in Germany and France refers to institutional factors and in particular to the vertical and horizontal differentiation of the discourse arena. In contrast to the strong involvement of federal units in Germany (*Länder* and local governments), local governments and the *départements* in France only played a subordinate role. In Germany, the salience of the asylum issue in the political discourse was significantly shaped by the federal division of the country and the significant impact of the *Länder* on policy-making through the Bundesrat. The activism of the *Länder* was spurred by partisan politics and the fact that during most of the social-liberal coalition, the conservative opposition held the majority in the Bundesrat. The mobilisation of the *Länder* was also the result of a discrepancy between their crucial involvement in the implementation of asylum policies on the one hand and their limited financial support from the Bund and their limited voice in decision-making on the other. In addition, their opposition to government policy was fuelled by the unequal distribution of asylum seekers and by increasing competition among the *Länder* against any additional admissions.

Conversely, the politicisation of immigration policies in France was promoted by different institutional settings. The French immigration discourse was strongly influenced by the electoral successes of the xenophobic Front National, which developed into the crucial point of reference for both socialist and conservative politicians, and by the activities of the alternating political leaders. The problematisation of immigrants started with Giscard d'Estaing in the 1970s, before being appeased by a liberal turn under President Mitterrand in the first half of the 1980s, it re-emerged during the latter's cohabitation with Prime Minister Chirac, before being again appeased with the return to power of the PS government in 1988. These trends document the dominant role played in French asylum and immigration policies by the political leadership and the significant degree of autonomy held by Heads of State in shaping policy. This autonomy was aided by the general preponderance of the executive in the French polity and the fact that large chapters of immigration and asylum regulations were not regulated by laws, but by administrative circulars and decrees.

In the face of such important differences, the numbers of common concerns shared between France and Germany with respect to foreigner issues in the early 1990s appear to be rather few. Indeed, these can basically be reduced to one, that is the aim of limiting the entry of new foreigners into their respective countries, this aim became consensual in France and Germany during the 1980s. Still, this consensus did not yet include the question of asylum seekers. While the abolition of new entries focused on the category of presumably "bogus" asylum seekers in the German political discourse, it concentrated on the more general question of illegal immigration and family reunification in France and did not really question the access of asylum seekers to status determination procedures.

Which course did the Communitarisation of refugee policies follow considering these important differences in the configuration of the asylum "problem" in France and Germany at the beginning of the 1990s? How far does this Communitarisation lead to an approximation of asylum policies in both countries in the sense of Europeanisation? These questions are analysed in the following chapters.

Notes

[1] U.N. Doc. E/600 para. 46, quoted in Weis (1971: 37).

[2] This general principle has partly been softened by the activities of the UNHCR vis-à-vis refugees, mainly in the main regions of origin where individuals are addressed directly (see Goodwin Gill 1996: 32 ff).

[3] Art. 12 Draft Universal Declaration on Human Rights, UN Doc. E/800.

[4] In the following, "Geneva Convention" (GC) refers to both the 1951 treaty and 1967 protocol.

[5] See Ad Hoc Committee on Statelessness and Related Problems, Memorandum by the Secretary-General: UN Doc. E/AC.32/2 of 3.1.1951, quoted in Goodwin-Gill (1996: 175).

[6] Art. 33.1 GC reads: "No Contracting State shall expel or return ("refouler") a refugee in any manner whatsoever to the frontiers of territories where his life or freedom would be

threatened on account of his race, religion, nationality, membership of a particular social group or political opinion".

[7]   ECOSOC, Official Records, 22nd Session, para. 109-112.

[8]   UN General Assembly, Resolution 2312 (XXII), adopted on 14.12.1967.

[9]   In the League of Nations, refugee assistance programmes depended especially on their financing by two Great Powers, Britain and France, and on their widespread popularity among the smaller countries of both Western and Eastern Europe (Skran 1992: 15).

[10] UN General Assembly, Resolution 6 (1) of 12.2.1946.

[11] Art. 4 Council of Europe Resolution (67) 14 of 29.6.1967. On the role of the Council of Europe in promoting cooperation among European states see Chapter Three.

[12] The tension between these two principles is also reflected in the literature. Two contrasting interpretations of the reasons for the implementation of individual criteria for persecution in the GC, in contrast to broader group characteristics, are given. From one perspective, these criteria were seen as providing a more open basis for the protection of all kinds of refugees who were violated in their basic human rights (Goodwin-Gill 1996: 19; Holborn 1975: 65ff); from the other, this refugee definition was "to make the status of refugees exceptional, so as to preclude overwhelming numbers" (Zolberg et al. 1989: 25; see also Hathaway 1984).

[13] Also Art. 8 (the right to private and family life) and Art. 13 (the right to an "effective remedy before a national authority") of the Convention provide protection against refoulement.

[14] The applicability of Article 33 GC at the frontier is also recognised in the legal literature (see Goodwin-Gill 1996: 123ff).

[15] Parliamentary Assembly of the Council of Europe, Recommendation no. 773 of 1976; Committee of Ministers Recommendation R (84) 1 of 1984.

[16] For a definition of these terms see UNHCR, Doc. WGSP 15 from 4.12.1990, 5ff

[17] "Die Kenntnis der Enstehungsgeschichte ist eine wichtige Voraussetzung für eine sachliche Erörterung der gegenwärtigen aktuellen Probleme. Sie kann dazu beitragen, die humanitäre Verpflichtung zur Hilfe für verfolgte und unterdrückte Menschen nicht von kurzsichtiger Tagesopportunität abhängig zu machen, sondern sie als eine im Wandel der Verhältnisse beständige Aufgabe des Landes zu begreifen, das auch heute noch Anlass hat, sich der in seinem Namen begangenen Verfolgung zu erinnern" (Ernst Benda quoted in Kreuzberg 1984: V).

[18] BVerfGE 50, 160 (175).

[19] Article 1 GG, I. "The dignity of man shall be inviolable. To respect it shall be the duty of all state authority."

[20] BVerfGE 62, 123 (124); see for the relationship between Art. 1 GG and Art. 16 II 2 GG BVerfGE 54, 341 (356).

[21] The *travaux préparatoires* of the constitutional asylum norm (Art. 16 II 2 GG) are printed in Kreuzberg 1984.

[22] See Stenographischer Bericht, Ausschuß für Grundsatzfragen, 23. Sitzung, 19.11.1948; printed in Kreuzberg (1984: 36).

[23] See Stenographischer Bericht, Hauptausschuß, 18. Sitzung, 4.12.1948; printed in Kreuzberg (1984: 39); and Stenographischer Bericht, Hauptausschuß, 44. Sitzung, 19.1.1949; printed in Kreuzberg (1984: 45).

[24] See Stenographischer Bericht, Hauptausschuß, 18. Sitzung, 4.12.1948; printed in Kreuzberg (1984: 39 and 46).

[25] This was the view of von Mangold, a member of the Parliamentary Council; see Stenographischer Bericht, Hauptausschuß, 18. Sitzung, 4.12.1948; printed in Kreuzberg (1984: 40); also see Stenographischer Bericht, Hauptausschuß, 44. Sitzung, 19.1.1949; printed in Kreuzberg (1984: 50).

[26] See Kurzprotokoll der 47. Sitzung des Hauptausschusses, printed in Kreuzberg (1984: 60).

[27] BVerfGE 57, 193 of 4.2.1959 and Ernst Benda, former president of the Federal Constitutional Court, in (Kreuzberg 1984: v).

[28] BVerwGE 49, 202 (204).

[29] BVerwGE 49, 202 (208f); 56, 216 (235). The subsequent inflation of the term "security" to a general assumption of threat is documented in Chapter Four.

[30] BVerfGE 9, 175-180. The court argued that the notion of persecution in the Basic Law exceeded that of the Geneva Refugee Convention (ibid: 181).

[31] The new citizenship and nationality law passed the two chambers of parliament in May 1999 and entered into force as of 1 January 2000.

[32] See BVerfGE 74, 51 (64); 76, 143 (158); 80, 315 (335, 345); 81, 58 (65). For a detailed discussion of the material substance of Article 16 II 2 GG, see Ulmer (1995: 35 ff); Hullmann (1997).

[33] Indeed, it has only been recognised in very exceptional cases where persecution could be attributed to the state because it did not have the will or ability to offer protection; see BVerfGE 67, 317 (318f); 54, 341 (357); 80, 315 (335, 340).

[34] This moves Article 16 II 2 GG closer to the refugee definition of Article 1A GC, see BVerfGE 9, 174 (181); 54, 341 (356); 80, 315 (343).

[35] BVerfGE 81, 142 (150ff).

[36] See BTDrs. 4/3013 of 26.2.1965.

[37] "Gesetz über Maßnahmen für im Rahmen humanitärer Hilfsaktionen aufgenommene Flüchtlinge" of 22.7.1980 together with §33 AuslG; accordingly, any decision to admit

quota refugees is taken by the Interior Ministry in accordance with the agreement of the *Länder*.

[38] The numbers rose from 1,906 asylum seekers in 1953 to 11,664 in 1969 following the upheavals in Czechoslovakia and went again down to 5,595 in 1973.

[39] This phenomenon is documented in the following numbers:

Year	total asylum seekers	%Eastern Europe	%Middle East	%Asia
1970	8,645	85.5%	4.8%	0.5%
1973	5,595	51.3%	6.0%	1.5%
1975	9,424	30.5%	37.5%	2.7%

(quoted in Heine 1978: 410ff).

[40] CDU stands for the conservative party (Christlich Demokratische Union) and CSU for its Bavarian sister party, the (Christlich Soziale Union).

[41] Decree of the Standing Conference of Interior Ministers (Ständinge Konferenz der Innenminister der Länder) of 14.9.1974.

[42] Amendment of the *Verwaltungsvorschrift zur Durchführung des Ausländergesetzes* (AuslVwV) of 29.3.1977, Gemeinsames Ministerialblatt 1977: 121, rejected through BVerfGE 56, 216 (241f).

[43] Gesetz zur Beschleunigung des Asylverfahrens (BGBl. 1978. I, S. 1108) and Zweites Gesetz zur Beschleunigung der Verwaltungsgerichtsordnung (BGBl 1978 I., S. 1107); for a comprehensive account, see Wolken (1988: 46ff).

[44] Zweites Gesetz zur Beschleunigung des Asylverfahrens of 23.8.1980, BGBl. 1980 I, S. 1437. The main provisions of this law were the introduction of single judges in the judicial review procedure and the introduction of a joint appeal procedure against any negative status determination or order to leave the country.

[45] SPD stands for the social-democratic party (Sozialdemokratische Partei Deutschland) and FDP for the liberal party (Freie Demokratische Partei).

[46] The lead was taken by Baden Württemberg with the initiative BRDrs 432/80 of 10.7.1980; it was followed by Reinland-Pfalz, BRDrs 432/1/80 of 10.11.1980, and Hessen, BRDrs 540/80 of 15.10.1980.

[47] BTDrs 9/875 of 7.10.1981.

[48] Asylverfahrensgesetz (BGBl 1982 I., S. 946).

[49] That is, *"unbeachtliche"* and *"offensichtlich unbegründete"* asylum claims; the first category includes cases where the asylum applicant has already found protection from persecution in a third country or when the new claim is only a repetition of an already negatively received application.

50 The criteria of unfoundedness was fulfilled if the foreigner had "manifestly" already found protection in another country ("offensichtlich ... bereits in einem anderen Staat Schutz vor Verfolgung gefunden", § 2 I; § 7 II, §§ 10 and 11 AsylVfG of 1982.

51 That is: "bereits in einem anderen Staat vor Verfolgung sicher", § 2 I AsylVfG 1982 in the version of November 1987.

52 Gesetz zur Änderung asylverfahrensrechtlicher, arbeitserlaubnisrechtlicher und ausländerrechtlicher Vorschriften (BGBl. 1987 I, S. 89).

53 See BVerwGE 69, 289 (292); BVerfGE 71, 276 (296); and BVerwGE 79, 347 (351ff). The court recognised the notion of "safety from persecution" only in cases where flight had ended in a third country and thus there was no connection between flight from the country of origin and entry into the Federal Republic.

54 The German quote is: "Ich möchte mich an dieser Stelle nachrücklich zu dem in der Verfassung verankerten Grundrecht auf Asyl bekennen. CDU und CSU haben nie einen Zweifel daran gelassen, daß dieses Recht unangetastet bleiben muß. Auch in schwierigen Zeiten ... hat die Union die Überzeugung vertreten, daß die Bundesrepublik Deutschland für politisch Verfolgte offen bleiben muß" (Spranger, quoted in Roos 1991a: 51).

55 "Asylanten-Schwemme" (Lummer, quoted in Die Welt of 31.12.1984) and "Sozialhilfetourismus" (Lummer, quoted in Kantemir 1985: 25). The German word "Asylant" has a pejorative connotation and entered into the political discourse in the context of the debates on an abuse of asylum procedures in the 1970s. On the semantics of this word, and more generally for a linguistic approach to the asylum-discourse in Germany, see Klein (1995).

56 Initiative of the Land Berlin from 15.2.1985 (Bundesratsdrucksache 91/85), together with the joint initiative by Baden-Württemberg and Bayern from 26.2.1985 (Bundesratsdrucksache 99/85).

57 This emerging perception is well documented in the following quote taken from a decision of the Bundesrat: "Nach Auffassung des Bundesrates kann es nicht angehen, daß der Bundesrepublik Deutschland bei jeder Krise in einem Staat der Dritten Welt oder durch neue Erfindungen von Schleuser-Organisationen die Gefahr droht, von Asylbewerbern überflutet zu werden, die der schlechten wirtschaftlichen Lage oder einer Bürgerkriegssituation in ihrem Heimatland entkommen wollen" (Resolution of the Bunderrat, BRDrs 91/85:3).

58 See Zimmermann in Bayernkurier (the leaflet of the CSU party) of 9.8.1986.

59 See the publications of the Interior Ministry, Der Bundesminister des Innern (1986), (1987) and the following quote from Interior Minister Zimmermann on 7.1.1987, quoted in Wolken 1988: 285f: "[Es] müssen in der nächsten Gesetzgebungsperiode die Grundlagen für ein einheitliches Asylrecht in Westeuropa geschaffen werden. Dafür ist eine Grundgesetzänderung unabdingbar".

60 See also the Answer of the Federal Government to a small query ("kleine Anfrage") from Deputies Anretter et al. and the SPD group in the Bundestag "Die Folgen des Schengener

Übereinkommens und der Vollendung des Binnenmarktes", BTDrs. 11/3594 of 30.11.1988, and the Report of the Federal Government "Europa der Bürger", BTDrs. 11/6297 of 23.11.1990.

[61] See the protests of a group of CDU deputies entitled "Christlich-Soziale Positionen für eine rationale und ethisch verantwortbare Asylpolitik" in 1987, in which they condemned the inducement of xenophobia and aggression in the German people and the undermining of the constitutional right of asylum through the use of exaggerated and emotional language, while calling for a return to more sober and accurate language (quoted in Nuscheler 1995: 134). One year later, this call was reiterated by the youth organisation of the CDU, the "Junge Union" (see FR of 3.11.1988), as well as by economic associations, the churches and NGOs (see Bade 1994: 32).

[62] In 1938, the then ruling Front Populaire established, for the first time in history, a clear distinction between the economic immigrant and the political refugee who benefited from particular access to the labour market and were protected against expulsion (Noiriel 1991: 115, footnote 1; Weil 1995a: 48; idem 1995b: 81). The efficiency of these safeguards was demonstrated in the admission of thousands of Spanish refugees fleeing from civil war in 1939 (ibid).

[63] During the Vichy regime, many of the refugees staying in France again became potential persecutees and were often deported to the Reich; see Weil (1995a: 54ff).

[64] Conseil Constitutionnel, Decision 71-44 DC of 16.7.1971.

[65] For example, when assessing the compatibility of a decree from 27.5.1982, on the entry of asylum seekers at the border, with §4 of the Preamble, the Council of State decided that this paragraph had no direct impact (see Norek/Doumic-Doublet 1989: 36f). In another decision concerning a law from 10.1.1980, amending the conditions of entry and stay regulated in the decree of 2.11.1945, the Conseil Constitutionnel did not even mention this paragraph (Decision 79-109 DC of 9.1.1980; see Oellers-Frahm 1992: 29).

[66] These dramatic refugee flows were caused by the takeovers in Vietnam and Cambodia by the troops of General Giap in Saigon and the Khmer Rouge in Phnom-Penh; as a consequence, millions of refugees also fled to Thailand, Malaysia, the Philippines and Singapore.

[67] Commission de Recours des Réfugiés (CRR), Decision of 3.4.1979 and Council of State, 27.5.1983; see Norek/Doumic-Doublet (1984: 52f).

[68] Commission de Recours des Réfugiés, Decision of 13.7.1976; see Norek/Doumic-Doublet (1984: 53).

[69] Law of 9.9.1986 on the return of foreigners.

[70] According to Legoux (1995: 45ff), the refugees staying in France during these years numbered between 200,000 (figures provided by the Ministry of the Interior) and 300,000 (figures from the OFPRA). The numbers of new applications for asylum per year are estimated at between 15,000 and 20,000. As this divergence shows, it is very difficult to rely on statistical material in estimating the scope of the asylum problem. Nevertheless,

the methods of statistical data collection became more precise, especially from the mid-1970s onwards.

[71] The Gaullist RPR (Rassemblement pour la République) and more centrist UDF (Union Démocratique Française) coalition was in power between 1974 and 1981.

[72] Interestingly, these local officials were mainly from the communist party - the PCF (Parti Communiste Français) - which governed the majority of the cities with large immigrant populations.

[73] Office Français pour la Protection des Réfugiés et Apatrides; this is the administrative agency in charge of examining asylum requests in the first instance.

[74] The préfectures are the local representatives of central government and are attached to the Interior Ministry; their tasks include pursuing the national interest, public order and administrative control over local collectivities (Tricot/Hadas-Lebel/ Kessler 1995: 418f).

[75] A similar, although more limited, reform had already occurred in 1985. Together with the strengthening of its resources, the OFPRA also accelerated the status determination procedures. While this acceleration was criticised for introducing "T.G.V. Procedures", thus not providing enough time for the thorough examination of claims, this reform did not question the right of asylum as such and, instead, rather strengthened existing structures.

[76] The decrease of asylum applications is not only related to the dissuasive effect of this reform on unfounded asylum applications, but also to changes in the main countries of origin of asylum seekers in France; see Legoux (1993 and 1995).

[77] See LM 2.7.1991; 11-12.7.1991; 20.7.1991. This regularisation of rejected asylum seekers was the first since that of 1981 and 1982 under President Mitterrand.

[78] European Parliament, Committee of Legal Affairs and Citizens' Rights, Report on the right of asylum, Rapporteur: H.O. Vetter, Doc. A2-227/86/B of 23.2.1987, § 15 (see Chapter Three).

3 The Communitarisation of Refugee Policies

"The work programmes ... have been drawn up pragmatically: harmonisation has not been regarded as an end in itself but as a means of reorienting policies where such action makes for efficiency and speed of intervention." (The Ministers responsible for immigration 1991)

"The European Council reaffirms the importance the Union and Member States attach to absolute respect of the right to seek asylum. It has agreed to work towards establishing a Common European Asylum System, based on the full and inclusive application of the Geneva Convention, thus ensuring that nobody is sent back to persecution, i.e. maintaining the principle of non-refoulement." (European Council 1999: § 13)

Forty years after its legal codification, the post-World War II refugee regime has gone through dramatic transformations. Throughout the Western world, the issues of asylum and migration have now gained the status of high politics. The collapse of the old bipolar system, the persistence of ethnic and political conflicts all over the world, and growing economic disparities, as well as increasing numbers of refugees and asylum seekers, are among the most prominent factors in the growing perception of the refugee "problem" as a threat to national stability and security.

At a time when most Western states are trying to limit their exposure to the flows of undesired migrants, asylum and immigration matters have made their way on the European agenda and are now and integral part of EU policy-making. Almost fifteen years after the beginning of intergovernmental cooperation, the establishment of a common European asylum system has become a priority of European Union politics. This priority has its legal base in the Treaty of Amsterdam, which defines common asylum and refugee policies as central elements in the development of an "area of freedom, security and justice" (Title IV EC). Its political background rests with the enduring politicisation of asylum seekers in the member states and the recent experiences with massive refugee flows in the context of the Yugoslav crisis.

Which role can the European Union play in the field of refugee policy, and how does this role relate to traditional refugee regimes in the member states? This chapter analyses the emergence and evolution of European cooperation in asylum and immigration matters with a focus on its institutional and ideational determinants. This analysis provides the basis upon which this study investigates the impact of this cooperation on the domestic policies followed in Germany and France in Chapter Four. In analysing the emergence and evolution of European cooperation right from the mid-1980s through to the year 2000, this chapter argues that the prospects for establishing a common European asylum system are significantly constrained by the institutional legacies of past cooperation. These institutional legacies have two dimensions. Firstly, the Communitarisation of asylum and immigration matters is marked by the dominance of transgovernmental cooperation structures which concentrate authority within the national executives to the detriment of supranational institutions and traditional international fora competent in refugee matters. Secondly, whereas recent developments under the Amsterdam Treaty point at a possible reorientation of European refugee policies, transgovernmental cooperation has framed asylum seekers and refugees in strongly "realist" terms which conflict with the calls for a comprehensive European asylum policy based on the common humanitarian tradition and the principles of the Geneva Convention.

This chapter is divided into three sections. Section one discusses, by way of introduction, earlier efforts at harmonising European refugee and asylum policies within the framework of the Council of Europe. In the mid-1980s, cooperation in these matters shifted away from the Council of Europe and instead entered onto the agenda of intergovermental fora composed of EU member states. The second section examines this "first generation" of cooperation among EU member states that dated up until 1992. This includes the negotiations leading to the two hitherto most important intergovernmental agreements, namely the Schengen and the Dublin Conventions. Thereafter, a third and final section opens with the introduction of asylum and immigration as "matters of common interest" in the third pillar of the Maastricht Treaty, thus launching a new generation of cooperation, and ends with the nearly full Communitarisation of this cooperation in the Amsterdam Treaty of 1997.

Prologue: Activities of the Council of Europe

Long before the EU started to deal with the question of refugees and asylum seekers, European states sought to harmonise their national policies within the framework of the Council of Europe. Although the ECHR does not include an asylum right (see Chapter Two), the issue of refugee protection has been on the agenda of the Council of Europe right from its very beginnings. Already in 1953, the Parliamentary Assembly of the Council issued a Resolution, according to which the refugee issue was recognised as a common European problem which had to be dealt with in cooperative manner by all member states of the Council of Europe (Council of Europe 1953). In accordance with its distinguished humanitarian mandate, these efforts have concentrated on improvements in the situation of asylum seekers both during national status determination procedures and after their recognition as refugees; the codification of a formal status for de facto refugees who, although not recognised under the formal persecution criteria, are nevertheless tolerated on humanitarian grounds; and, finally, the enhancement of cooperation among its member states in the spirit of European solidarity and burden-sharing (Leuprecht 1989).

General Framework of Cooperation

Two specialised committees have been set up to deal with asylum and refugee matters in the Council of Europe, one working for the Parliamentary Assembly and the other subordinate to the Council of Ministers.

The Committee on Migration, Refugees and Demography (CDMG) is the main intergovernmental organ of the Council of Europe dealing with questions of international migration. Its general mandate is to follow the development of European cooperation concerning migration, especially with regard to the integration of immigrants in host societies, and the situation of refugees (Council of Europe 1996). The Committee prepares reports, resolutions and recommendations for the Parliamentary Assembly of the Council of Europe, a consultative body made up of delegates from the national parliaments. On the basis of the work prepared by the CDMG, the Parliamentary Assembly has issued several recommendations in the field of asylum seekers and refugees that have focused on the elaboration of appropriate instruments for the protection of de facto refugees, the situation of recognised refugees in a host country, questions related to specific groups of refugees in their regions of origin, and the harmonisation of admission policies and status determination procedures. Although non-binding, these recommendations have significantly shaped the work done by the Committee of Ministers, the decision-making body of the Council of

Europe; the Committee of Ministers is composed of the foreign affairs ministers of the member states and the permanent representatives of those countries.

One of the first initiatives in asylum matters was the proposal to include a provision on the asylum right into the Second Protocol to the ECHR in 1961. This aim, however, was dropped. It was recognised that even the member states which had enshrined an asylum right in their national constitutions "hesitate to submit their decisions regarding asylum to the international control system instituted by the Convention" (CE Doc 1986: 9, quoted in Uibopuu 1983: 65). Instead of implementing a formal asylum regulation, the Council of Europe re-oriented its efforts towards the strengthening of Article 3 ECHR "which, by prohibiting inhuman treatment, binds contracting Parties not to return refugees to a country where their life or freedom would be threatened" (Council of Europe 1965). The first important, and legally binding resolution of the Committee of Ministers "on asylum to persons in danger of persecution" was adopted in 1967. Apart from iterating the norm of non-refoulement, it provided that governments "should act in a particularly liberal and humanitarian spirit in relation to persons who seek asylum on their territory" and that they should cooperate "in a spirit of European solidarity and of common responsibility in this field", particularly within the framework of the Council of Europe (Council of Europe 1967). Shortly after the failure of the UN conference on territorial asylum in 1977, the Committee of Ministers adopted a "Declaration on Territorial Asylum" which was to affirm the positive attitude of its member states towards refugee protection (Council of Europe 1977). In order to underline this commitment, a second and more specialised committee for refugee matters was set up, the Ad Hoc Committee of Experts on the Legal Aspects of Refugees (CAHAR). This committee - which is composed of governmental experts in the fields of asylum and refugee policy (mainly from its member's interior and justice ministries), recognised experts in the field of refugee law and protection, and, as observers, representatives of the UNHCR and the Holy See - began its work in April 1977. Its tasks were comprised of the pursuit of an intergovernmental dialogue on the situation of the system regarding refugee protection in the aftermath of the failed attempt to implement an international subjective asylum right at the 1977 UN conference; and the examination of the above mentioned recommendations of the Parliamentary Assembly for the adoption of eventual conventions or other legal instruments. Following the "liberal and humanitarian spirit" of the member states of the Council of Europe (Council of Europe 1996: 26), this body thus elaborates the juridical instruments adopted by the Committee of Ministers (that is, its conventions and recommendations). Part of its remit is to find concrete solutions with regard to the harmonisation of domestic asylum policies. The next section briefly summarises what have been the main results of this cooperation.

Early Attempts at Harmonisation

Throughout this time, the Council of Europe's efforts have followed a humanitarian approach to the refugee problem in Europe; it has generally been aimed at strengthening and harmonising the implementation of the international refugee regime. Applying the frame analytical model developed in Chapter One, these efforts are closely related with the idealist or humanitarian perspective on refugee protection. Their unit of concern is the individual refugee and that person's rights in regard to the state; the focus on their human right to be granted protection establishes a clear distinction between refugees and voluntary migrants. Furthermore, one of its main purposes is the strengthening of cooperation and solidarity among European states and with countries of origin or transit; finally, it can be said that the measures proposed all belong to the field of low politics. Apart from repeated appeals to improve the situation of recognised refugees in their host countries, the main contribution of the Council of Europe has consisted of its elaboration of common principles for a harmonised approach towards de facto refugees and national asylum procedures in general. Another main area of concern has been its attempt to establish a system of regional cooperation based on the "first country of asylum" concept.

The harmonisation of procedural standards and de facto policies

As early as 1976, the Parliamentary Assembly of the Council of Europe raised the issue of de facto refugees; although not recognised under the formal refugee definition, the latter are, because of humanitarian reasons, unable or unwilling to return to their countries of origin. In a recommendation, the Assembly noted the existence of considerable numbers of such refugees and observed that their situation required some sort of harmonisation and regularisation. In particular, it claimed that the provisions of the Geneva Convention should, as much as possible, also be applied to these refugees, particularly with regard to residence and work permits, social security, and expulsion. In addition, this recommendation invited the member governments to apply the refugee definition of the Geneva Convention liberally in order to encompass a broad range of refugees (Council of Europe 1984). The need to harmonise the national policies towards de facto refugees was again underlined in another

Parliamentary Assembly Recommendation in 1988 (Council of Europe 1988).

Another focal point in the activities of the Council of Europe has been the harmonisation of formal status determination procedures in the member states. Its aim has been to establish common guidelines for the examination of asylum claims. A recommendation of the Parliamentary Assembly in 1976 (Council of Europe 1976) started from the observation that individual refugee and asylum claims were decided in a very disparate manner in the single member states, a fact reflected in the important differences existing between the recognition rates of the countries. This implied that an asylum seeker who was granted formal refugee status in one country would not necessarily be recognised in another. These concerns led to the adoption of common procedural standards in the form of a (non-binding) recommendation by the Committee of Ministers in 1981 (Council of Europe 1981). Recalling the "liberal and humanitarian attitude of member states ... with regard to asylum seekers", the list of these principles reflected the Council of Europe's aim to establish high standards of refugee protection throughout Europe. Among these principles, it includes the right of the applicant to remain in the territory of the state while his of her demand is being examined, referral of the decision to a central and independent agency, impartial and objective judgement including the possibility of a review procedure, and clear instructions to border officials against refoulement. Exceptions to this enshrined right to remain on a country's territory during the status determination and review procedures were allowed only in very limited cases, basically in cases where sufficient evidence was given that the claim was fraudulent or that it had no connection at all with the criteria laid down by the Geneva Convention (Uibopuu 1983: 76). The impact of this recommendation was limited however: firstly, it was not legally binding; and, secondly, the enumerated principles were so general that they constituted hardly the basis for the harmonisation of national asylum procedures (see Gerber 1984: 114; Hailbronner 1989: 28).

A more thorough harmonisation of domestic asylum laws was sought with another recommendation from the Parliamentary Assembly in 1985 (Council of Europe 1985). This recommendation documented a re-orientation of the hitherto liberal and humanitarian refugee policies of the member states. In particular, the development of restrictive attitudes was criticised: "the number of refugees in Europe compared with the total number of aliens in Europe does not justify the restrictive attitudes of the receiving countries" (Article 3). In order to counter these tendencies, the resolution proposed the harmonisation of the substantive recognition criteria and status determination procedures in a "liberal way" (Article 6 ii b). Furthermore, it called for the enhancement of cooperation between the member states and increased burden-sharing on the basis of existing international conventions, recommendations and resolutions (Article 5 iii). Finally, the recommendation raised the problem of so-called "refugees in orbit", that is those who are not able to find a state willing to examine their claim or to offer protection. In order to fight this phenomenon, it proposed the elaboration of a system of responsibility allocation based on a harmonised definition of the notion of "country of first asylum". These claims were outlined in a further recommendation from 1988 (Council of Europe 1988) which, recalling that the granting of asylum is "a humanitarian act based on the principles of political freedom and human rights" (Article 1), called for the full preservation of the right to asylum "as one of the generous liberal traditions of democracy" (Article 6). It also called for the adoption of a coherent European refugee policy in a spirit of burden-sharing and solidarity; in turn, this policy would be monitored by a permanent body in the framework of the Council of Europe and the UNHCR (Articles 7 and 10). These propositions aimed not only at the preservation and improvement of protection standards in Europe, but were also intended to prevent that "certain measures taken or envisaged in some member states [might] increase the burden laid on the other member states of the Council of Europe" (Article 3).

The notion of "country of first asylum"
The proposition of the Parliamentary Assembly to establish a system of allocating responsibility based on a harmonised notion of the "country of first asylum" is particularly important from the point of view of the Communitarisation of refugee policies among EU member states from 1985 onwards. Although it did not lead to political agreement over this concept, cooperation in the framework of CAHAR can still be seen as a sort of forerunner to the key provisions of the Schengen and Dublin Conventions adopted by EU member states in 1990, as well as the notion "safe third country" laid down in a 1992 resolution (see below). Although not investigated to a great extent, knowledge about the work in CAHAR allows us to highlight the flexible scope of this concept between restrictiveness and generosity and, thus, to understand and identify the ideational shift which has occurred with the EU intergovernmental context more deeply. Furthermore, a brief discussion of the endeavours in the framework of the Council of Europe has already indicated a crucial characteristic of this concept, namely its inherent redistributive logic; together with the call for higher protection standards, this significantly hampered the prospects of an agreement in the more heterogeneous framework of the Council of Europe.

The endeavour to adopt a harmonised notion of the "first country of asylum" concept must be understood in the context of attempts by the international community to establish a system for the allocation of responsibility in the examination of asylum claims. These endeavours date back to the United Nations Conference on Territorial Asylum in 1977 which sought a general improvement in international protection standards, inter alia through attempts to implement an international subjective asylum right (see Chapter Two). In order to enhance states' commitment to refugee protection, particularly to ensure that every asylum seeker has the chance to have their claim examined, one draft article of the UN Conference proposed that "asylum should not be refused by a contracting State solely on the ground that it could be sought from another state". An exception to this was only legitimate "where it appears that a person requesting asylum has a connection or close links with another state, the contracting state may, if it appears fair and reasonable, require the asylum seeker first to request asylum from that state" (Hailbronner 1993b: 59).

This initiative was aimed at combating the phenomenon of "refugees in orbit", defined as "persons who, although they have not been placed in immediate jeopardy by being rejected at the frontier or otherwise sent back to the country where they are liable to persecution, are not granted asylum, still less refugee status, in any country in which they make an application for asylum. As a result, they are shoved from one country to another in a constant quest for asylum" (Melander 1978: 71, own translation). This phenomenon was provoked through the expanding practice of some member states who excluded some categories of asylum seekers from refugee status including those who failed to lodge their claim within a certain period after they had left their country or origin or after they had entered the potential host country; or those who had spent some time in a third country, where they were safe from refoulement, before claiming asylum in another state (ibid: 72ff).

The above mentioned draft article of the UN Declaration on Territorial Asylum was taken over by Conclusion No. 15 of the UNHCR Executive Committee in 1979. This conclusion on "refugees without an asylum country" basically aimed at the adoption of common criteria according to which responsibility for the examination of an asylum claim could be allocated in a "positive manner" (Jackson 1984: 67). This means that an asylum application should generally be admitted, unless the applicant has already found protection from persecution elsewhere (ibid: 68). In a case where, in exercising its responsibilities, a country was confronted with a massive arrival of asylum seekers, other states would be requested to help in a spirit of "equitable burden-sharing". Finally, in regard to the respective asylum seeker, the conclusion stressed that that person's intentions should be respected as far as possible.

These questions became a central concern in the work of the CAHAR. Noting important differences in the practices of the member states with regard to the concept of "protection elsewhere" or "first country of asylum", it advocated the adoption of a harmonised definition. From the beginning, these efforts were first oriented towards liberal and humanitarian principles, and secondly, with the aim of finding a balance between the interests of the asylum seeker and those of the first and second countries of asylum.[1] The overarching motivation was to avoid the production of "refugees in orbit" (Uibopuu 1983: 73; Kimminich 1984: 58). In a first draft from 1981, the following rules were included: as a general rule, every asylum application should be examined, unless the applicant has already been granted asylum in another country or has strong links with that country. These links might be based either on close family relations, a working permit, or the fact that the asylum seeker had already handed in an asylum application in that country.[2] Subsequently, a fourth exception to the obligation to examine an asylum claim was introduced, that is when the applicant had legally resided for more than 100 days on the territory of another contracting state (Gerber 1984: 116).

When the draft was passed on to national governments, it became clear that no political consensus could be found on these provisions. In 1984, it was shelved due to opposition from several member states. The underlying problem was the major differences that existed between the traditional transit countries (especially Italy and Austria) and the countries of asylum (in this case, mainly Germany and the Scandinavian countries). As transit states for many of the asylum applicants seeking entry into Europe, Italy and Austria felt that the terms of the draft agreement would mean that they would end up with the responsibility of examining the bulk of asylum requests in Europe. After the failure of this first draft, a new initiative was launched at the end of 1986 in order to try to finalise an agreement on the question. This new initiative followed political pressure, particularly from West Germany (Rudge 1989: 213). At the same time, however, cooperation in these matters shifted away from the humanitarian platform of the Council of Europe and of the UNHCR to new intergovernmental fora composed of (selected) EU member states. This shift considerably weakened the endeavours of the CAHAR in the following years; indeed, the aim of reaching an agreement within the framework of the Council of Europe finally petered out. Instead, a system of responsibility was adopted by EU member states through the 1990 Schengen and Dublin Conventions.[3]

"First Generation" Cooperation Among EU Member States

As previously mentioned, in the mid-1980s a shift in the locus of European cooperation regarding refugee matters can be observed, away from the humanitarian framework of the United Nations and the Council of Europe to newer intergovernmental fora composed of the EU member states' representatives. The Communitarisation of refugee matters has been centred in two partly overlapping, and partly differing intergovernmental fora: (i) the Ad Hoc Group on Immigration, regrouping representatives of all (at that time twelve) member states, and (ii) the Schengen group, which originally contained only five member states - France, Germany, and the Benelux countries. In 1990, these two groups adopted two partially corresponding international agreements, the Schengen Implementation Agreement and the Dublin Convention, which established the basic pillars and guidelines for the further elaboration of common asylum and immigration policies in the European Union.

In the following, the emergence and evolution of this first generation cooperation is retraced; this cooperation prepared the ground for the introduction of asylum and immigration as "matters of common interest" in the Maastricht Treaty on the European Union of 1992 and their subsequent transfer to the first pillar in the 1997 Amsterdam Treaty. The first sub-section deals with the EU-specific institutional dynamics let loose by the Single European Act of 1986, which itself provided the context for the inclusion of refugee issues on the EU's agenda. Thereafter, in the next two sub-sections, the actual handling of the issue in the intergovernmental fora is investigated, the emphasis being on the specific institutional structures which regulated this cooperation. The next sub-section then scrutinises the ideational structure of this cooperation and analyses the cognitive frame according to which the issue of refugees is perceived and defined in the relevant texts of the intergovernmental negotiations, before the final sub-section briefly summaries first generation cooperation.

The European Integration Project and Migration: General Remarks

The question of migration has been part of the European integration project ever since the establishment of the European Communities in the 1950s (Geddes 2000; Guild 1999). In the language of the EC Treaties, however, this question has not been referred to as "migration" but, rather, as the "freedom of movement for persons". Indeed, this is one of the four freedoms to be established alongside freedom for services, capital, and goods.[4] This freedom provides for the abolition of any discrimination regarding employment, as well as social and fiscal benefits based on nationality towards the workers of any of the member states. Accordingly, the European Commission - but also the European Parliament and the European Court of Justice (ECJ) - has taken a very active role in the promotion of free movement and equal treatment for citizens of the member states (see Butt Philip 1994; Callovi 1992). These endeavours have been invigorated by organisational reforms of decision making-processes at the European level through the 1986 Single European Act; the latter introduced qualified majority voting in the Council and strengthened - although only slightly - the role of the European Parliament. In addition to the rights of EU citizens, the supranational EU institutions have also been active in questions relating to the improved integration of legally resident third country nationals. This broadening of the scope of supranational activities occurred in the context of the general ban on labour migration issued by most member states in the early 1970s. The initiative was taken by the European Commission with its proposition of an "Action Programme in favour of migrant workers and their families" in 1974. Many of these propositions were approved by the Council of Ministers; in a resolution of 9.2.1976, it encouraged the member states to adopt common labour migration policies in consulation with the Commission. In 1985, the Council adopted a resolution regarding a European Commission proposal on "Guidelines for a Community Policy on Migration" which articulated the Community's goal of attaining "equality of treatment in living and working conditions for all migrants, whatever their origin" (Commission 1985b). The situation of non-Community workers was later subject to a ruling of the ECJ on 9.7.1987 in which it advocated a Community competence in these matters.[5]

In contrast to the high degree of Communitarisation regarding the economic migration of citizens from the member states and the active stance taken by EU organs with regard to legally resident third state nationals, issues relating to the admission of third state nationals and refugees did not enter the European agenda until the mid-1980s (Geddes 2000; Guild 1999). From the European integration perspective, their political salience was directly linked to confirmation of their aim to realise the single market project and to abolish internal borders through Article 8A of the Single European Act of 1986. In the wake of this decision, the European Commission proposed an elaboration of common rules in its White Paper of 1985 on the residence, entry and access to employment of third-country nationals, as well as the harmonisation of asylum policies (Commission 1985a). Furthermore, it announced a Decision based on Article 118 EC Treaty aimed at the harmonisation of national legislation on foreigners. According to this Decision, member states would be required to give the Commission and the other member states information, in good time, on "draft measures which they intend to take with regard to third-country workers and members of their families, in areas of entry, residence, and employment, including illegal entry" (Commission 1985c).

This initiative, however, was refuted by several member states on the grounds of sovereignty considerations. The governments of Germany, France, the Netherlands, Denmark and the United Kingdom appealed the Commission Decision before the ECJ, arguing that migration policy regarding nationals from non-member states exceeded the scope of the Commission's competence. The Court ruled partly in favour of the Commission and partly in favour of the Governments. Denying the Commission's competence to influence the contents of national policies and consultations, it nevertheless accepted its authority to set up the framework for such consultations. Such a framework was set up through a new decision issued in 1988, but it has remained largely ineffective due to the opposition of the member states regarding its utilisation (Callovi 1992: 357; Niessen 1996: 23ff; Papademetriou 1996: 21ff).

The unwillingness of the member states to develop a Community competence in asylum and immigration matters was also manifested in the negotiations which led up to the adoption of the Single European Act. These issues arose in the context of disputes regarding how Article 8a SEA providing for - inter alia - the free movement of persons should be interpreted. Disagreeing about the core question, whether this provision only applied to citizens of the member states or to third state nationals as well, the member states' governments adopted a general declaration in which they reaffirmed their national rights with regard to immigration from third countries, terrorism, crime and the trafficking of drugs (adopted in Luxemburg on 9.9.1985). Despite their clear refusal of sovereignty transfers in these matters, the member states' governments added a political declaration to the SEA at the same time, in which they agreed to cooperate intergovernmentally on exactly these matters.

Thus, it appears that cooperation was approved, but only outside of the formal Community framework and without the involvement of its supranational organs. This attitude was confirmed in 1988 when the Council of Ministers rejected a - for the moment - final Commission initiative proposing the harmonisation of asylum and immigration policies (Commission 1988); the Council invoked a lack of community competence in these central matters of national sovereignty (see Lobkovicz 1990: 97).

Faced with this opposition, the Commission took on a more pragmatic stance and concluded that it was best to leave the field to the discretion of the member states. By that time, in fact, cooperation between member states had already been advanced by two intergovernmental fora outside of the Community framework, that is the Schengen- and the Ad Hoc Group on Immigration.

The Transgovernmental Track: Schengen, Trevi, and the Ad Hoc Group on Immigration

Instead of pursuing the harmonisation of domestic asylum policies within the humanitarian framework of the Council or Europe or the supranational system of the European Union, EU member states chose to cooperate at a purely intergovernmental level. This cooperation originated in two partly parallel processes, the Schengen agreement and the Trevi process, the latter of which was taken over by the Ad Hoc Group on Immigration. While "Schengen" began as the initiative of a limited number of EU member states in 1985, "Trevi" or the Ad Hoc Group on Immigration could look back on a longer "tradition" of consultations, beginning in the mid-1970s, among the interior ministries of all the member states. These processes have led to the institutionalisation of what has been coined as structures of "intensive transgovernmentalism" (H. Wallace 2000), structures which challenge our knowledge about the dynamics of European integration and the application of the Community method of policy-making (den Boer/Wallace 2000). A knowledge of the emergence of this intensive transgovernmentalism in asylum and immigration matters - that is until their introduction in the Treaty on the European Union of 1992 - is of crucial importance in understanding two persevering characteristics of this policy field: firstly, the perseverance of intergovernmental elements in the current framework of cooperation and; secondly, the limited scope of refugee protection engendered by this cooperation.

Trevi and the ad hoc group on immigration: the inflation of internal security

The "Trevi"[6] process relates to the beginnings of EU-wide cooperation among European interior ministers which can be traced back to the mid-1970s. The Trevi group was founded at the European Council in Fontainebleau in 1976, but without any contractual basis outside of the Community's framework. Its primary task was the coordination of home and justice affairs in the field of internal security and public order.

The establishment of this group coincided with the growth of intergovernmental consultations among EU and other European and non-European countries on internal security matters. At that time, in the 1970s, the two main common threats perceived in the field of internal security were terrorism and drugs trafficking. Several partly overlapping fora were set up to deal with these matters, all of which featured Germany and France as members.[7] The Trevi group, in contrast, gathered together the EU member states exclusively. Similar to the other intergovernmental fora, the initial focus of this last group was on the fight against terrorism and the exchange of information on this subject among the member states. Whereas the group met only irregularly and without much impetus in the first years of its existence,[8] its scope was quantitatively and qualitatively expanded in the mid-1980s; at that stage it was extended to deal with organised crime, drugs, police cooperation, and immigration.[9] In 1986, the "Ad Hoc Group on Immigration" was formally split from the Trevi structure. With regard to refugees, its primary task was stated as the elaboration of common measures against the abuse of asylum procedures (Hailbronner 1989: 21).

Apart from an increased level of political awareness regarding issues related to asylum seekers and refugees in several member states (in particular, the Schengen countries), this qualitative expansion received an impetus with the confirmation of the prospect of internal border controls being abolished through in the Single European Act. More specifically, three developments seem to have supported the creation of the Ad Hoc Group on Immigration. Firstly, the need to harmonise national immigration and asylum policies was recognised; this had been raised by the European Commission in its White Paper on the Internal Market, while the consent to do so had been announced in a Declaration attached to the Single European Act. The fact that this cooperation was proposed at a purely intergovernmental level, however, in a forum composed nearly exclusively of representatives of the interior ministries, points to a second dynamic: namely a counter-reaction by the interior ministries to the prospect of an increasing Community competence being developed in their domains through the Communitarisation of the "interior" (see Bigo 1992: 27). A third development which supported the introduction of asylum and immigration matters onto the agenda of the Twelve was the progress of cooperation in another intergovernmental forum, that is the Schengen Group, and the dynamic levels of interaction between this burgeoning group and the larger - and slower - Ad Hoc Group on Immigration.

"Pilot project", "motor" and "laboratory": the Schengen process
The Schengen process is a typical example of differentiated integration initiated by a limited number of EU member states (den Boer 1997; Meijers et al. 1991; Nanz 1994; Pauly 1993 and 1994). It was launched as a Franco-German initiative in 1984 through which Chancellor Helmut Kohl and President François Mitterrand agreed to the gradual abolition of controls at their common borders (Agreement of Sarrebrücken of 13.7.1984). Shortly afterwards, the Benelux decided to join this initiative; this move led to the adoption of the First Schengen Agreement on the Gradual Abolition of

Checks at the Common Borders on 14.7.1985 (printed in Pauly 1993: 187ff). In the period which followed, this initiative was to become a pilot project, a sort of "laboratory" negotiated between a limited number of member states, which would serve as an example of EU-wide cooperation. In doing so, Schengen became the prototype of differentiated integration.

When the first Schengen Agreement was signed in 1985 by France, Germany, and the Benelux, it was presented as a measure promoting the realisation of the Single Market among a core of motivated member states. While this general vision might well have guided the top-level approach represented by Kohl and Mitterrand, a closer look at the negotiation process shows that the agreement was initiated for several divergent reasons. In particular, two other motives appear to have been behind this conscious decision to accelerate the abolition of internal borders. The first motive was the level of enduring strikes among customs officials and truck drivers in France who were protesting against the long queues at Europe's internal borders. The Sarrebruck Accord of 1984 reflected France's aim of finding a solution to the impediment of the free circulation of goods provoked by these strikes. Secondly, the adhesion of the Benelux was - at least partly - also supported by the goal of finding a new role for its secretariat by enlarging the provisions of the 1960 Benelux Accord (Bigo 1996: 113ff). This interpretation is underscored by the fact that the first Schengen Agreement was signed by the Ministers of Transport and External Affairs, with the exception of Germany which was represented by the *Bundeskanzleramt* (the Federal Chancellery) and the ministry of the interior. In addition, the treaty was used as a chance to promote joint intergovernmental approaches to common transnational challenges such as organised crime, terrorism, illegal immigration, and asylum seekers. At the initiative of the German interior ministry, an annex was added to the treaty which linked the abolition of internal border controls to the necessity of elaborating "compensatory measures" for the safeguarding of internal security. This annex initiated a dynamic process of cooperation, particularly among the interior ministries of the Schengen countries which, culminated in the adoption of the Second Schengen Agreement Applying Schengen I on 19.6.1990. While the 1985 treaty only contained three articles referring to illegal immigration, issues relating to third country nationals later constituted the main part of the 1990 agreement.

The Institutional Structure of "First Generation" Cooperation

The polity of concentric circles
The institutional structure of intergovernmental cooperation until the Maastricht Treaty was a polity of concentric circles centring around a core

of EU member states composed of France, Germany and the Benelux, as well as broader circle grouping all member states in the Ad Hoc Group on Immigration and Trevi. This overlapping structure of differentiated membership has played a crucial role in the diffusion of policy approaches among Western European countries. As was indicated in the section on the early years of European coordination in the framework of the Council of Europe, its broad and heterogeneous membership significantly hampered the adoption of common measures in the field of refugee policy. Gathering a small number of "like-minded" EU member states together, countries which faced similar situations with regard to the percentage of third country nationals living in their respective territories and a comparable intake of asylum seekers, the Schengen initiative turned into a motor for EU-wide, and later pan-European, approximation in refugee matters. Despite repeated applications, the traditional emigration and transit countries - Italy, Portugal and Spain, which had opposed harmonisation in the Council of Europe - were not allowed to adhere before conclusion of Schengen II, thereby avoiding any possible conflicts of interest.

In contrast to these differences with regard to country membership, the two intergovernmental groups converged significantly in relation to their internal differentiation. Both were differentiated in a three-level operational structure. At the top level, the decision-making body consisted of the member states' ministers of justice and home affairs. Their sessions were prepared by a group of senior officials at the middle level (in Schengen this was the "Central Group"), which gathered leading ministerial officials (usually heads of departments) together. The third and lower level was the most influential one with regard to the specific contents of cooperation. It contained different working groups which consisted of ministerial and police officials (see Rupprecht/Hellenthal 1992: 150). These working groups developed a large degree of autonomy and must be seen as the actual drafters of the 1990 Schengen and Dublin Agreements. At this level, the links between the two intergovernmental fora were very strong, since the majority of members of the Schengen working groups also represented their countries in the parallel groups of the Ad Hoc Group on Immigration.

Another strong parallel in the composition of the two fora concerned the professional backgrounds of their key members. While the Schengen initiative was launched at the top political level by the Heads of States, backed up by the foreign and transport ministries, it was gradually taken over by the interior ministries. In Germany, this shift, at first informal, from the Federal Chancellery to the Ministry of the interior was formally accomplished after the signature of the 1990 agreement. Below this top level, the coordination of the Schengen process in the Central Group was firmly in the hands of this latter ministry, more precisely within its policing department. In France, by way of contrast, the Central Group was represented by the foreign affairs ministry, which, however, had little impact on the contents of the negotiations process at the working group level as it was nearly exclusively made up of members of the interior ministry. This corresponded with the composition of the Ad Hoc Group on Immigration. Nevertheless, at the top ministerial level, the ministers of these sectors began to meet as the "Ministers of Immigration".

Both the Schengen and the Ad Hoc Group on Immigration were divided into several sub-groups which reflected the scope of their actions. Here the main difference between the Schengen pilot project and cooperation between the Twelve may be observed; in the latter, by comparison, was narrower on many significant points. In contrast to the ad hoc group, Schengen evolved into a comprehensive project of policy coordination in the field of internal security and freedom of movement; it encompassed four steering groups dealing with "police and security", "movement of people", "transport", and "customs and movement of goods". Within the group on the movement of people, four sub-groups - dealing with asylum, visas, migration (admission and expulsion), and external borders - were created. The scope of the Ad Hoc Group on Immigration corresponded widely to this steering group and was itself differentiated into several sub-groups dealing with external borders, visas, exchange of information, false documents, admissions, deportation, and asylum (see organigrams in Bigo 1996: annexes).

In short, one can say that, with regard to asylum and immigration, the mandate of the intergovernmental groups was restricted to the elaboration of common high standards of control at the external borders, tight entry conditions for third country nationals, the fight against illegal immigration and, with regard to asylum, the fight against bogus applications. In addition, these measures were linked to the overall aim of safeguarding internal security and combating all forms of serious deliquency, including serious forms of crime, terrorism, and drug-dealing. [10]

Relations with supranational and national actors
Both intergovernmental processes were launched outside the Community framework and with no formal linkage to the provisions of the EC treaties. Accordingly, the supranational EU institutions had no competencies in these negotiations. While the European Commission was only allowed in as an observer after the drafting of the Second Agreement of the Schengen group in 1990, it was allowed to follow the work of the Ad Hoc Group on Immigration, though without the right to issue initiatives, right from the beginning. The European Parliament, as was the case for the national

parliaments, had no formal rights in these processes; indeed, neither was it to be informed nor heard/consulted on particular issues. This also applied to the European Court of Justice which did not receive the competence of judicial control over the outcomes of the intergovernmental processes. Less clear were the links between the intergovernmental fora, especially the Union-wide Ad Hoc Group on Immigration, and the Council of Ministers. Although formally independent, the Council's secretariat was used by the ad hoc group for administrative purposes.

Beyond their relations with EU institutions, the links between the two parallel intergovernmental fora themselves deserve attention. Given the overlapping personal composition of the two groups, the Schengen actors were able to engage in double-tracked activities, and, thus, could pass on their ideas to other member states. In this sense, this core of "like-minded" states was able to act as a "laboratory" and "motor" which could serve as an example for EU-wide cooperation. In particular, the system of the rotating presidencies among the participating states every six months allowed the Schengen group to introduce their proposals onto the agenda of the Twelve. Accordingly, the provisions of the Second Schengen Agreement, largely drafted by September 1988, were simply taken over by the almost identical Dublin Convention signed on 15.6.1990 by each of the twelve member states (see draft Schengen Treaty printed in Hailbronner 1989: 214ff). Thus, cooperation in asylum and immigration matters became a prototype of the differentiated integration process which was being promoted by a core of member states. At the same time, however, the maintenance of these intergovernmental fora was a means of avoiding the development of any Community competence over these sensitive matters of national sovereignty.

Finally, the review of inter-organisational relations also concerns the links between the ministerial actors in the intergovernmental groups and their domestic polities. Here, dominance by the interior ministries, particularly at the expert level, led to remarkable tensions not only with the European Parliament and national parliaments, but also within national bureaucracies. Within the national administrations, the steady gain in importance by the interior ministries was unpleasantly felt among other ministries - such as external or social/labour ministries - because they had to accept a loss of influence over questions of immigration which had formerly fallen within their domain. In Germany, this increased dominance by the interior ministry at the working group level even caused some tensions to develop within the Federal Chancellery, which, in pushing for an early abolition of internal border controls, was more sceptical about the necessity of "compensatory measures". In general, it turned out that the bureaucratic actors acted less favourably on the early introduction of measures for the free movement of people but, rather, delayed it with an elaborate set of multiple additional and partly counteracting measures which were deemed necessary for the safeguarding of internal security after the abolition of internal border controls. From the point of view of bureaucratic politics, the elaboration of these measures clearly reflected the concern of the interior ministries to Europeanise their internal security and public order domain; their aim was to maintain their organisational field of activity, particularly control over the entry of foreigners into their territories.

The rules of technocracy, secrecy and urgency
The rules operating in the intergovernmental groups were those of technocracy, secrecy and urgency. The rule of technocracy must be understood in contrast to political modes of decision-making and conflict-resolution. Contrary to political action - which is usually characterised in modern democracies by the setting of general future goals; the open debate over the different means of achieving these ends; the taking of collectively binding decisions in democratic ways; and the possibility of judicial control over these decisions - the term "technocratic" refers to the rule of non-political bureaucratic experts acting outside of the public space (see Curtin/Meijers 1995). After a degree of political prompting at the outset in the case of Schengen, presented as a pilot project personally launched by the Heads of State, both intergovernmental processes were ultimately pushed and shaped at the working group level that was composed of experts from the respective national ministries. Strongly linked with the notion of technocracy is the relative closeness of the intergovernmental groups with regard to members and participation. It has already been mentioned that the relevant negotiations took place in working groups primarily composed of representatives from the interior ministries. This homogeneity of actors is striking when compared to other international fora dealing with refugee issues. In contrast to the CAHAR group in the Council of Europe (see above) for example, neither academic/professional experts nor the UNHCR as the watchdog of the international refugee regime were allowed to assist with the sessions. The UNHCR was informed of the intergovernmental agreements only after their drafts were completed. While the Ad Hoc Group on Immigration offered this organisation the opportunity to express its concerns at the end of 1989, the Schengen group waited until May 1990 before doing so.

This closeness was accompanied by a very high degree of secrecy regarding the activities of the intergovernmental fora. Between 1985 and 1988, the intergovernmental groups acted in nearly total secrecy. Indeed, below the level of ministers, all members, agendas, protocols or decision-making procedures were kept strictly confidential. Neither the European Parliament, nor the national parliaments were informed about the proceedings from the intergovernmental negotiations (see Curtin/Meijers 1995).

Finally, the intergovernmental groups acted under a strong sense of urgency. The deadline of "Europe 1992" - later symbolically postponed to 1.1.1993 - eased the adoption of quick decisions, simplified the agenda and favoured a technical pragmatism, which in the end avoided the thematisation of more political or philosophical questions related to civil liberties, sovereignty, or the humanitarian tradition of most member states. The next section analyses the contents of cooperation in these intergovernmental fora and extracts the ideational frame that underlies their conception of the refugee question.

Towards a Securitarian Frame

As has already been suggested in the previous sub-sections, cooperation in refugee issues evolved along two partly contradictory paradigms: on the one hand, there was the communitarian objective of the free movement of persons and, on the other, the technocratic concern with safeguarding internal security and bureaucratic assets as determined by the organisational self-definition of the actors involved. It was not the quantitative or qualitative evolution of the refugee "problem" or the aim of attaining the harmonisation of national asylum policies which stood out at the beginning of this intergovernmental cooperation but, rather, the prospect of the abolition of internal border controls and the perception that the resulting consequences might undermine the control of cross-country movements in and into the Union.

In order to understand the content of this cooperation and its specific approach to the refugee question, this sub-section analyses the texts and extracts the cognitive frame according to which the refugee issue has been perceived and defined in the intergovernmental negotiations. For several reasons, an identification of this cognitive frame is crucial in understanding changes in the integrative principles of refugee policies. Firstly, it allows the unveiling of the deeper logic underpinning the development of common refugee policies in the Union independent from external conjunctures. This claim is supported by the fact that the main elements of the European asylum frame were already established in 1988 with the draft Schengen II Agreement, that is well before the opening up of the Eastern borders and widespread apprehension regarding a "global refugee crisis". Secondly, knowledge of this ideational core not only allows conclusions to be drawn on the scope and contents of subsequent policies, but it also increases the sensibility for questions of national sovereignty versus international cooperation and European integration in general and, from a more normative point of view, highlights some of the fundamental challenges underlying international refugee policies at the intersection between human rights and national sovereignty.

The principal texts examined are the First and Second Schengen Agreements (1985 and 1990) and the Dublin Convention of 1990 which basically contains the Schengen Agreement's asylum provisions. In order to give a more complete picture of this first generation cooperation, a second sub-section examines the counter-frame as expressed in the reports and decisions of the European Parliament in that period.

The intergovernmental frame: the Schengen and Dublin conventions
Freedom of movement and border controls The starting point and central concern of the Schengen and Dublin Conventions are not refugees, but the questions of freedom of movement and territorial borders in the European Union. The primacy of free movement and the "European" political finality are strongest in the First Schengen Agreement of 1985. Its preamble clearly states the aim of achieving an ever closer union between the peoples of the member states and to affirm their solidarity through the establishment of free movement for persons, goods and services (§2 and §3 Preamble). Accordingly, the vast majority of articles concentrate on the reduction of control measures at the internal borders. Only 3 out of 33 articles deal with questions related to third country nationals and propose, only "if necessary", the harmonisation of relevant legislation.[11] No mention is made of refugees or asylum seekers.

The main Schengen Agreement of 1990, which fixes the conditions for the implementation of the more general political aspirations laid down in the 1985 treaty, clearly shifts the emphasis away from freedom of movement towards the strengthening of controls and questions related to internal security. Whereas Schengen I focuses on borders from the point of view of their abolition, Schengen II can be read as a re-confirmation of the function of borders for state sovereignty and security through the establishment of alternative control mechanisms in a territory and the implementation of heightened control standards at external borders. Although its preamble mentions the Single European Act, this reference to the communitarian norm of free movement was inserted at the last moment and only following pressure from the European Commission (Bolten 1991: 15). This shift away from the liberal norm of free movement is best documented by the fact that only one out of 142 articles stands for the introduction of free movement (Art. 2 I);[12] however, this provision is significantly weakened by the possibility of re-introducing border checks for reasons of "public policy or national security" (Art.2 II). Accordingly, the remaining articles contain so-called "compensatory measures" which are regarded as necessary for the safeguarding of internal security and public order. Indeed, the emphasis on state sovereignty is strengthened even further by the use of a high number of exception clauses and the vagueness of many articles.

In contrast to Schengen I, which concentrated on free circulation within the common territory and called for enhanced cooperation particularly against drugs trafficking and other forms of criminality (Art. 8, 9, 18 and 19) but only "if necessary" on issues relating to third state nationals, the latter formed the main body of the Second Schengen Agreement. Title II of the Treaty on the "Abolition of checks at internal borders and movement of persons" contains only one article relating to internal free movement (Art. 2, see above) but has 36 articles relating to third country nationals.[13] Setting strict conditions for the crossing of external borders,[14] the biggest consensus among the contracting parties was manifested in questions relating to the fight against illegal immigration and the intake of asylum seekers, which was in fact where the most detailed and far-reaching provisions were adopted – although the question of asylum seekers and refugees was not even mentioned in Schengen I. More sensitive issues, such as long term (economic) immigration, residence permits, citizenship issues or substantive asylum law, were not touched.

The importance attributed to refugee issues is clearly reflected in the levels of parallel cooperation among the twelve member states in the Trevi and the Ad Hoc Group on Immigration. While, as mentioned above, cooperation among the interior ministers of the member states began by focusing on the fight against terrorism and later drugs trafficking, by the end of the 1980s the most significant and tangible output consisted of the adoption of an international convention on who had responsibility for examining asylum claims, the Dublin Convention of 1990.

Refugees and illegal immigrants As far as the general content of first generation cooperation in internal affairs can be interpreted as an attempt to safeguard and even to strengthen some basic functions of territorial borders as one of the most tangible expressions of state sovereignty, the specific provisions relating to asylum seekers move this issue away from their traditional humanitarian framework and underline the primacy of the state. The question of refugees is subsumed under a whole variety of migratory movements which converge in their border-crossing quality (including it with terrorism, crime, drug trafficking, and illegal immigration). The general perspective which guides this cooperation on cross-border movements is that of safeguarding - or even strengthening - the ability to control the entry of foreigners into the territory in an area without internal borders. The overall aim is to prevent the irregular movement of persons which, following this line of argument, would be facilitated by the abolition of border controls inside the Union.

As a result of this agglomeration of cross-border movements, the issue of refugees has moved much closer to the phenomenon of illegal immigration. Many provisions in fact apply to both groups without discrimination: for example, strict entry requirements, cooperation in visa matters, and the imposition of carrier sanctions on carriers who enable the entry of persons who do not fulfil these requirements (Schengen II and Draft External Borders Convention).

Chapter 7 of Schengen II and the Preamble of the Dublin Convention open with a reaffirmation of the contracting parties' obligations under the Geneva Convention of 1951 and its New York Protocol of 1967 (Art. 28). No reference is made to other relevant human rights provisions, such as the Universal Declaration on Human Rights or the European Convention on Human Rights, regularly mentioned in the texts issued by the Council of Europe and the UNHCR. Article 29 I of the Schengen Agreement confirms that the contracting parties "undertake to process any application for asylum" lodged within their territory. This commitment is immediately weakened in paragraph 2, however, which provides that this does not entail the right of asylum seekers to enter or stay in the territory: "Every Contracting Party shall retain the right to refuse entry or to expel any applicant for asylum to a Third State on the basis of its national provisions". The emphasis on states' sovereign discretion over the entry and stay of asylum seekers on their territory is further emphasised by the fact that no reference is made to the norm of non-refoulement which prohibits the return of persons in need of protection (see Chapter Two).

The cornerstone of the two agreements with regard to asylum seekers is the introduction of a responsibility rule for the examination of asylum claims among the contracting parties and the determination of criteria for assessing this responsibility. According to Article 29 III SA and Article 3 II DC, only one contracting party - normally the country which the asylum seeker reaches first - shall be responsible for processing an application.[15] With this rule, the contracting parties agree to examine the asylum application of persons falling under their responsibility and, correspondingly, to refer other claimants who do not fall under these categories to the responsible state. This is a significant departure from the traditional system of refugee protection which bound every individual state to provide protection under the Geneva Convention.

Despite this fixing of one single responsible state for the examination of an asylum claim in the common territory, neither the Schengen or Dublin

Conventions question state sovereignty. Both contain a clause safeguarding the sovereign right of any contracting party to examine an application, even when it is not determined as being responsible (Art. 29 IV SA and Art. 3 IV DC). Furthermore, these treaties explicitly refrain from affecting substantive or procedural aspects of refugee law: applications shall be processed "in accordance with ... national law" (Art. 32 SA and Art. 3 III DC).

While Schengen II does not specify the aim behind this system of responsibility determination, the Preamble to the Dublin Convention makes reference to the problem of refugees in orbit and claims to provide a guarantee that an asylum application will be examined in one of the member states so that applicants "are not referred successively from one member state to another without any of these states acknowledging itself to be competent to examine the application for asylum" (Preamble DC). With this, the Dublin Convention alludes to the attempts to fight the phenomenon of refugees in orbit made in the Council of Europe before cooperation in asylum matters shifted to the intergovernmental fora composed of EU member states (see above). While this determination of state responsibility was commonly referred as "country of first asylum" rule in the Council of Europe, meaning that the applicant should have spent a certain amount of time in the responsible country and should be de facto safe from persecution, the intergovernmental negotiations in Schengen and the Ad Hoc Group on Immigration document a semantic shift of this concept to the notion of "first host country", thereby indicating a departure from the principle that the applicant should actually already have found protection or asylum in the responsible country in order to be sent back.

The review of the drafting process of the Dublin Convention, the parallelism of Schengen II and the contents of these agreements all points to another dynamic behind this intergovernmental cooperation: namely, the aim to reduce the number of asylum applications in the contracting countries (i) by implementing strict requirements for entry into the territory and re-enforcing control standards and (ii) by abolishing the possibility of multiple asylum applications by one asylum seeker in different member states, that is the so-called "asylum shopping" phenomenon.

Certain considerations support this interpretation. First of all, the mandate of the Ad Hoc Group on Immigration which elaborated the Convention is unambiguous: namely the fight against bogus asylum applications and illegal immigration. No mention was made of the aim to improve protection standards in Europe (as in the Council of Europe's mandate). Secondly, the review of the drafting process demonstrates that, at first, the negotiations in the ad hoc group only referred to the problem of "asylum shopping", the reference to the problem of "orbit" situations was only introduced at a later stage. The secondary nature of the problem of "orbit" situations is further supported by the fact that it is not even mentioned in the Schengen Convention, which provided the blueprint for "Dublin". Thirdly, the broader framework of restrictive entry regulations, the system of redistribution, the weakness of the responsibility rule, the lack of reference to relevant human rights provisions, and particularly the norm of non-refoulement all underscore the intention to reduce the numbers of asylum seekers. The clearest evidence of this is the third country provision of Article 3 V DC and Article 29 II SA which authorise the contracting parties to send back any applicant to a third country in accordance with their national regulations regardless of their responsibility under the agreements, later harmonised under the third pillar (see below). In addition, a closer examination of the texts shows that they omit to answer the question whether the responsibility to examine a claim includes the obligation to admit the applicant on the territory. Furthermore, neither the Dublin nor the Schengen Conventions provide for an obligation to grant asylum once an application has been positively determined. Taken together, these observations not only bear out the danger of further orbit situations inside the Union, but they also manifest the limits of the responsibility rule which is formally restricted to the examination procedure and which neither extends to the admission of the asylum seeker on the territory nor to that person's protection after the determination of their status. Fourthly, this protectionist attitude is further documented by the total lack of reference to the problem of de facto refugees who, by the end of the 1980s, already represented the majority of persons in need of protection in the member states (see Chapter Two). This fact is particularly intriguing, especially given that this group of persons would also fall under the category of cross-border movements, so that the "abolition of borders - irregular movements - control" problematique would also apply to them. The fact that these persons, whose status is fragile and mostly informal, are excluded from the system of responsibility allocation only demonstrates the reluctance of the member states to strengthen their commitment towards these persons, to formalise their policies and, ultimately, to restrict their margin of sovereign discretion.

Cooperation and competition The third category in the asylum frame refers to the conceptualisation of international interdependence and the relationship between states in refugee protection. Here, the intergovernmental texts show an intriguing combination of cooperation and competition. The aim to strengthen cooperation is at the heart of the intergovernmental process; indeed, it is stated both in the Preambles of Schengen II and the Dublin Convention, and in the introductory notes to the Palma Document. In substance, this cooperation extends to the joint effort to strengthen external borders, the functioning of the responsibility system based on the "first host country principle", and the exchange of information for the functioning of this system.

Behind these cooperative regulations, however, lies a perception of the refugee problem as a zero-sum game in a border-free Europe. As previously mentioned, the driving force behind the intergovernmental processes was the fear of a loss of sovereignty and control capacity over cross-border movements after the abolition of internal border controls foreseen for 1992. In this line of reasoning, the abolition of border controls means that the refugee policies of one state (similar to policies regarding illegal immigration, drugs, crime and terrorism) directly affect the problem-constellation and the relevant policies of any other contracting party. In a border-free Europe, asylum seekers would - like other categories of unwanted migrants, such as illegal immigrants, drug traffickers, criminals, terrorists - move freely from one country to another and would be able to submit several asylum claims in several countries, thereby contributing further to the congestion of domestic asylum procedures. In this way, liberal admission policies in one state would immediately "threaten" the other parties through the arrival of these persons onto their territory.

Based on this perception of refugee protection as a zero-sum game, the responsibility provisions contained in the Schengen and Dublin Conventions set up a system of negative redistribution for the handling of asylum claims. Responsibility for handing an asylum claim is placed on the state which first enables the entry of an asylum seeker into the common territory. Considering that most asylum seekers reach Western Europe either by boat or by land from the South and the East, this rule puts a considerable burden on the countries possessing an external border of the Union in this direction, thereby modifying traditional refugee flows which tended to find their final destination in the centre of Western Europe - France, Germany and the Benelux. The treaties do not mention the possible redistributive effects of the responsibility criteria. The competitive character of these is enhanced by the complete lack of reference to solidarity among the member states and the possibility of burden-sharing, values which are at the core of the normative framework of international refugee law (see Chapter Two) and which are regularly mentioned in the texts of the Council of Europe. The possibility of over-burdening a particular member state as a consequence of this redistributive mechanism is nevertheless hinted at in the Dublin Convention adopted by the twelve member states, that is both traditional transit and receiving countries. Articles 16-18 provide for the possibility of a revision of the treaty "if a member state experiences major difficulties as a result of a substantial change in the circumstances obtaining on conclusion of this convention" (Art. 17 DC). In particularly serious cases, the affected state may also be authorised to suspend its obligations under the treaty (ibid). These provisions do not, however, include support from the other contracting parties.

A securitarian approach With the introduction of the refugee question onto the agenda of the Ministers of Internal Affairs meeting - inter alia - in the Schengen and Ad Hoc Group on Immigration, this issue was shifted from a humanitarian "low politics" arena into a "high politics" one concerned with cross-border threats to internal security. The basic assumption behind this cooperation is that the abolition of border controls would lead to a quantitative and qualitative increase of the asylum "problem" in the member states, thereby threatening not only their internal stability and security but also the process of European integration.

Refugees were presented as a threat to the internal security of both the member states and European integration including freedom of movement in the Union. This threat is not only constructed by the thematic linkage of the problematique with that of serious forms of delinquency, presenting cooperation as a necessary "compensatory measure" for the safeguarding of internal security after the abolition of internal border controls, but also by the nearly exclusive focus of these negotiations on the fight against bogus asylum applications ("asylum shopping", see above). It has thus led to a strong approximation of the policy options adopted for refugees with those against illegal immigrants. This particularly concerns the provisions of the relevant texts on the conditions for entry, visa requirements, expulsion and readmission, or the imposition of carrier sanctions. However, the amalgamation of these issues is also reflected in the establishment of a central database, the "Schengen Information System" (SIS, see Title IV SA), which has as its purpose the maintenance of "public order and security" (Art. 93 SA). These provisions are again relevant for EU-wide cooperation too, since they provide the blueprint for a similar "European Information System" (EIS) established among the Twelve (now Fifteen). Once more, the text does not distinguish potential refugees from other personae non grata,[16] a category which may, as it stands, also include rejected asylum seekers.

Within this securitarian "high politics" logic, the intergovernmental texts preserve a very technical stance which, by reducing the problematique of asylum seekers to the question of border controls, at the same time supports the de-politicisation of the issue. The technical appearance of the texts on the one hand promotes the impression of the existence of "easy" solutions to a complex problem and, on the other, expresses a limited ambition in these matters, since the treaties do not touch substantive matters of refugee law but indicate that they are to be restricted to the measures necessary in fulfilling the goal of European integration.

The counter frame of the European Parliament
During the "first generation" of intergovernmental cooperation in asylum matters, the European Parliament issued several documents; these expressed a view of the asylum "problem" contrary to that contained in the intergovernmental texts examined above and comprise of the so-called "Vetter-Report" of 1987 on the right of asylum (EP 1987a), the subsequent Resolution on the right of asylum of that year (EP 1987b), and the Resolution on the asylum policy of certain member states three months later (EP 1987c). The following paragraphs briefly summarise the main elements of this counter frame in order to underline the specificity of the intergovernmental negotiations.

Refugee regimes in the member states In contrast to the intergovernmental texts analysed above, the Report and Resolutions of the European Parliament on asylum do not insert themselves in the context of the Single Market Project and freedom of movement, but take the situation of refugees and asylum seekers in the member states as their point of departure. They aim at providing generous general principles regarding their treatment and also "guarantee the right of asylum" through "humane and constitutionally acceptable" procedures (EP 1987b: §10). The texts take the existing principles and norms of international human rights law and refugee law in particular as their starting point. The problematique of borders, control and territory is not raised. The Single Market Project is only mentioned once in the Resolutions and then not in very prominent places. Here, both texts claim that the internal market requires the adoption of "common legal and social standards for asylum seekers" (EP 1987b: § M; EP 1987c: §6). The forthcoming abolition of internal border controls is not mentioned, as such; accordingly, the problematique of common external borders - their control and entry conditions - is not raised either.

The rights of refugees In not questioning the norm of state sovereignty, the texts of the European Parliament still underline states' obligations under international law and emphasise the human rights dimension of the policy field. This human rights context is clearly reflected in the exhaustive enumeration - in the Introduction to the Vetter Report and in the Preamble to the Resolution of 12.3.1987 - of relevant human rights treaties and soft law adopted by the Council of Europe and the UNHCR (Excom), as well as the endeavours of NGOs. This Resolution then states explicitly in § L that "all measures adopted in regard to the right of asylum must take as their starting point respect for human dignity, the Convention on Human Rights of the Council of Europe, the UN Declaration of Human Rights and the guidelines adopted by the European Parliament on the drawing up of a European policy on human rights".

This emphasis on the human rights dimension of asylum is dominant throughout the texts. Calling in the first paragraph on the "moral and historical responsibility of the Member States ... towards asylum seekers and refugees" (EP 1987b: §§A-C), the Resolution of March 1987 and the Vetter Report contain normative and procedural safeguards for the admission of asylum seekers, the examination of their claim, and their general treatment. These safeguards correspond to those included in the subsequent resolution of June 1987, which basically contains a critique of the negotiation of restrictive policies in the Trevi Group[17] and their application in domestic policies. The texts call for liberal entry policies and respect for the norm of non-refoulement; they condemn the imposition of restrictive visa requirements and the rejection of asylum seekers at the border, as well as their detention in airports (EP 1987a: §§ 26-40; EP 1987b: §1a,b; EP 1987c: §§A-F). They also call for the asylum seeker to be allowed to stay on the territory during the whole procedure (EP 1987b: §1), respect for the procedural safeguards and the rule of law in the examination of asylum claims - which shall be in accordance with those provided by the Excom of the UNHCR (EP 1987a: §§ 41-47; EP 1987c: §§ 3-4) - and also request humane reception policies (EP 1987a: §§ 75-84). Furthermore, in calling for a harmonisation of substantive asylum law, the European Parliament urges the member states to extend the criteria of the Geneva Convention to recognition of refugees according to the broad refugee definition proposed by the Organisation of African Unity (see Chapter Two) and that they should also include persecution because of sex or sexual tendencies in that criteria (EP 1987a: §§ 51-74). Finally, the texts include the question of de facto refugees as well and claim that these "must be treated as recognised refugees during their stay in the country" (EP 1987a: §§59-50). The texts do not deal with the question of "bogus" asylum applications.

Summing up, it is possible to say that the texts do not question the sovereign right of states to grant asylum, but they clearly underline the humanitarian dimension of the policy field by summoning both the moral or ethical responsibility of the member states so that they respect human rights and the rule of law in status determination procedures.

International solidarity The European Parliament texts emphasise cooperation in three regards: firstly, they appeal for stronger solidarity and cooperation with the countries of origin of asylum seekers; secondly, they require the Communitarisation of refugee issues; and finally, they stress the need to cooperate in an open fashion with other organisations on these issues. The rationale behind this cooperation is that "an international problem cannot be dealt with by national provisions, because this only means that the problems are passed on to another country" (EP 1987a: §§ 3,16). Thus, the European Parliament shares the vision of a zero-sum game that the intergovernmental groups have, but takes this as a reason for claiming far reaching cooperation, burden-sharing, and ultimately Communitarisation.

The need to cooperate closer with the countries of origin is expressed in the first paragraphs of the 1987 March Resolution and in the Vetter Report. These texts mention the colonial burden in these countries and the necessity for enhanced economic and political cooperation. They call for greater solidarity with these countries and stress that "only a small proportion" of the world's refugees actually come to the Community (EP 1987b: § H; EP 1987a: § 12).

With regard to European integration, the European Parliament supports a much more far reaching Communitarisation of the policy field, one which clearly exceeds the degree of coordination aspired in the intergovernmental negotiations. In this regard, it advocates the adoption of a future Commission directive on the harmonisation of asylum laws and calls for the appointment of a Community spokesman on asylum questions (EP 1987b: §8; EP 1987c: §7). Furthermore, by raising several questions of substantive and procedural asylum law, it clearly promotes a thorough harmonisation of asylum policies in Europe. Taking into account the different situations pertaining in the single member states, the European Parliament strongly advocates the introduction of a burden-sharing mechanism which could be based on the Community budgetary scale (EP 1987b: §5; EP 1987a: §§ 13: 87-93).

Finally, the European Parliament stated that this Communitarisation of refugee policies should not be detached from the existing human rights framework, but that it sould operate in close cooperation with traditional actors in the field, such as the UNHCR (and the Excom), the Council of Europe, NGOs, and individual experts.

A humanitarian approach In these texts, refugee policy is clearly conceived of as a matter of low politics. At no point is the arrival of asylum seekers mentioned as a threat to the country taking them in or the European Community. In putting the emphasis on the safeguarding of high legal and procedural standards in status determination procedures, the texts also stress the social situation of asylum seekers during the procedure and call for the humane harmonisation of reception policies. In addition, they contain several provisions aimed at the reduction of refugee producing circumstances. These exceed the borders of the Union and include, in particular, enhanced economic and political cooperation with the countries of origin in order to stabilise their economies and to guarantee the protection of human rights (EP 1987a: §§ 97-99; EP 1987b: §§ B-E). The questions of illegal immigration or bogus asylum seekers are not addressed.

Summary

To sum up, the first phase of cooperation in asylum matters evolved in the context of the re-affirmation of the Single Market Project in the mid-1980s and was directly linked to the issue of abolishing internal border controls. In a nutshell, the line of reasoning of the intergovernmental frame is the following: the general cause of the "problem" leading to cooperation was seen as the abolition of border controls and, more specifically with regard to refugees, the increase of bogus asylum applications in the member states. The consequences of this problem would have been a loss of control, a further increase in bogus asylum applications, and the resulting destabilisation of the countries taking refugees. Thus, the proposed measures suggested the elaboration of alternative control mechanisms, basically meaning the strengthening of external borders and the adoption of the single responsibility rule. At the normative level, a moral appeal was being made on the one hand to the legal norm of Art. 8a (freedom of movement) and with this to the overarching principle of European integration; on the other, a strong appeal was being made for the safeguarding of the principle of state sovereignty and internal security. In this context, the appeal to the legal core of refugee law was rather weak; only the 1951 Geneva Convention is mentioned, no other human rights treaties were. However, while very close to a "realist" perspective, this frame includes a strong "idealist" element with the principle of (regional) cooperation among EU member states.

The frame expressed by the European Parliament, like that of the Council of Europe and the UHNCR, contrasts sharply with this. The causal problematique was not primarily a question of European integration, but rather the increasing levels of disparity between the (rich) industrialised nations and the countries of origin, as well as the other causes of refugee flows. A second cause expressed most clearly in the 1987 June Resolution regards the increasingly restrictive attitudes of the member states. The consequence of all this is the increasingly precarious situation of refugees and asylum seekers; the measures proposed were, on one side, more generous admission and protection policies in the member states, and on the other the fight against refugee producing circumstances. While the factual dimension is thus very distinct from that of the intergovernmental frame, some parallels exist at the normative level, in particular the call for cooperation; however, the latter differs both in intensity and scope from that of the intergovernmental frame. Cooperation is not limited to the idea of freedom of movement within the Union but is framed in the context of the legal norms and principled beliefs of the international refugee regime.

How did the subsequent Communitarisation of refugee policies actually evolve, especially when considering these opposite frames on the European refugee "problem"? The next section analyses the introduction of asylum and immigration matters into the framework of the European Union through the Maastricht and Amsterdam Treaties and examines the relationship between "realist" and "idealist" elements in the development of a common "European" refugee policy.

"Second Generation" Cooperation: Towards a "European" Refugee Policy?

Although originally of limited scope, intergovernmental cooperation in asylum and immigration matters set free a far reaching dynamic which led to the gradual Communitarisation of the policy field, finding a preliminary end with its inclusion in the EC Treaty with the Treaty of Amsterdam signed in 1997. This gradual Communitarisation of asylum and immigration policies took some time and was not uncontroversial. Already one year after signing the Schengen and Dublin Agreements, the Ministers responsible for immigration issued a report for the European Council meeting in Maastricht (The Ministers responsible for immigration 1991) which listed two main reasons for pursuing cooperation. Firstly, it was recognised that the treaties called "in themselves...for more thorough harmonisation". It was noted that the rule of exclusive responsibility, which prescribes that the contracting states recognise the grant or refusal of refugee status by the responsible party, required a certain degree of equivalence regarding both status determination criteria and confidence in each other's asylum policies (ibid.: footnote 97). The second reason given for pursuing cooperation relates to the external development of the refugee "problem" and the perceived consequences of the opening up of the Eastern Bloc. In this regard, the report states that "the pressure of immigration on most member states has increased significantly in recent years" and that "a strictly national policy could not provide an adequate response" (ibid: 13). With this, the intergovernmental actors officially detached their cooperation from the context of free movement so that it became an aim in itself.

In the two Intergovernmental Conferences leading to the Maastricht and Amsterdam Treaties, discussions on asylum and immigration matters centred around two issues. The first aspect related to the institutional framework of this cooperation and the different possibilities of bringing the intergovernmental groups closer to the Community method. The second aspect concerned the contents of this cooperation. In this respect, the above mentioned Maastricht report established a work programme which advocated a "pragmatic" approach "re-orienting policies where such action improves efficiency and speed of intervention" (ibid). At the same time, however, it warned that "if the harmonisation process were initiated without defining basic principles, harmonisation might be carried out at the lowest level" (ibid: 15). Eight years later, in the aftermath of the Kosovo refugee crisis, it seems that the EU Heads of State recognised the danger of an emerging "fortress Europe". Meeting at the European Council in Tampere (Finland), they called for a common European asylum system that should be firmly rooted in a "shared commitment to ... human rights" and be based on "the full and inclusive application of the Geneva Convention" (European Council 1999).

How then did second generation cooperation evolve? Did asylum matters become firmly incorporated into the Union structure? Were the securitarian elements of the intergovernmental frame "softened" through a recourse to humanitarian norms? This section approaches these questions in three steps. The first sub-section deals with the organisational reform of the cooperation process under the Maastricht Treaty. A discussion of the main measures adopted under the third pillar and during the first year after entry into force of the Amsterdam Treaty follows in a second sub-section, including the main proposals issued by the supranational organisations. The last sub-section scrutinises the latest reforms to this institutional framework adopted in Amsterdam 1997 and investigates the degree, to which transgovernmental structures prevail under the current framework of policy-making in the EU.

Institutionalising the "Third Pillar"

In the forefront of the Maastricht negotiations at the end of 1991, the intergovernmental practice came under increasing criticism from both political actors and public opinion. This was linked to the ratification procedure of the Schengen Convention in the national parliaments and the subsequent publication of its contents. Preceded by earlier critiques presented by the European Parliament against the undemocratic and secretive mode of operation of the intergovernmental groups (EP 1987a; EP 1987b; EP 1987c), several national parliaments complained about their lack of involvement in and information regarding these processes. The clearest attack came from the Dutch Parliament which made ratification conditional on the introduction of democratic control through formal consultation procedures and increased transparency; indeed, it also pressed for a guarantee of full judicial control over these intergovernmental policies and harmonisation of procedural and substantive standards (de Boer 1992: 674; Cruz 1991). As intergovernmental treaties, neither the Schengen nor the Dublin Convention are subject to the ECJ's jurisdiction. These concerns were also strongly voiced by NGOs dealing with humanitarian issues as they feared both a devaluation of humanitarian standards and the rule of law through these proceedings.

These criticisms did not however really affect the institutional reforms in the context of the Maastricht negotiations. In April 1991, the Luxemburg Presidency submitted a draft treaty proposing a so-called "temple" structure. This proposal suggested that the traditional *acquis* of the EC could co-exist alongside two intergovernmental pillars - one for Common Foreign and Security Policy (CFSP), the other for Justice and Home Affairs (JHA) - which would remain outside the institutional and jurisdictional framework of the central Community institutions (Council 1991). This model, which basically contained the formalisation of the first generation structure within the framework of the EU, was not uncontroversial. At the Luxemburg Summit in June 1991, German Chancellor Helmut Kohl called for the adoption of a common immigration and asylum policy under the auspices of the supranational institutions. This initiative was supported by the Netherlands; indeed, upon assuming the Council's Presidency in July 1991, it proposed a "tree" model in which justice and home affairs would be included within existing Community structures. Facing opposition from Denmark, the United Kingdom and France, however, this second proposal was finally dismissed to the advantage of the former.

As a result, the intergovernmental structure of first generation cooperation in the Ad Hoc Group on Immigration was largely taken over, the Schengen Group remained outside the formal EU structure. Asylum and immigration matters were introduced as "matters of common interest" - together with the crossing of external borders, the fight against drugs and fraud, judicial cooperation in civil and criminal matters, customs cooperation and police cooperation in the fight against terrorism, drugs trafficking and other serious forms of international crime - in Title VI of the Treaty on European Union of 8.2.1992. This "third pillar" on Justice and Home Affairs covered the broad range of cooperation matters which were originally raised as a counter-reaction to the prospect of internal borders being abolished. Asylum and immigration were not separated from internal security issues and were thus included as law enforcement matters alongside criminal and police related issues.

Linking up with the earlier analysis of first generation cooperation, it can be said that the EU Treaty brought few innovations while basically formalising the previous intergovernmental structure. Herewith, the structure of intensive transgovernmentalism was introduced into the Union's framework, which differs from the Community method in the following respects. Firstly, the polity of concentric circles of first generation cooperation was maintained. Although the Schengen Group was enlarged to include all member states with the exceptions of the United Kingdom and Ireland, it remained outside from the official EU institutions. The Commission was represented in the K.4 Committee and acted as an observer at the steering and working group level (see below). This internal differentiation corresponded to that of the first generation, but added two additional political levels. Now referred to as Steering group I on Asylum and Immigration, the former Ad Hoc Group on Immigration including its sub-division into working groups was taken over. Two additional levels were introduced just below the Ministers responsible for immigration through the K.4 Committee and the COREPER.[18] Set up with the task of not only coordinating the work of several intergovernmental fora dealing with asylum and immigration issues, but also dealing with cooperation within and among national ministries, the introduction of the K.4 Committee was meant to decrease the autonomy of particular bureaucratic actors at the working group level and increase communication and transparency inside the ministerial structure. These changes, which were aimed at meeting some of the deficiencies in the earlier structures, soon turned out to be too cumbersome and time consuming however to allow for substantive progress. Accordingly, they constituted a major point of debate at the Intergovernmental Conference revising the Maastricht Treaty in 1996.

While concentrated in the third pillar, cooperation in asylum and immigration matters was also touched on by some of the provisions in the first and second pillar. With regard to the first pillar, the main provision was the introduction of a Community competence in visa matters (Art. 100c EC); the second pillar concerns the external relations of the EU, thus including relations with those countries from which migrants and asylum seekers originate, as well as the relations with transit countries.

The most important effect of the introduction of the third pillar into the EU structure with regard to inter-organisational relations was the formalisation of the links between the intergovernmental actors and the supranational institutions. According to Article K.3 EU, the Commission received the right of co-initiative, while the European Parliament should be regularly informed and consulted on principal aspects. The Council retained the right to issue decisions (by unanimity) and to adopt joint positions and actions, as well as conventions. In practice, however, the initiatives of the Commission were hardly ever taken on board and the European Parliament constantly complained about the violation of its right to be informed and consulted.

While maintaining a strong intergovernmental character, this institutional framework contained several dynamic elements. One was the possibility of giving the ECJ the jurisdiction to interpret and arbitrate disputes arising from community policies on the basis of a Council decision (Art. K.3 EU). A second was the possibility of qualified majority voting in the Council for the adoption of joint actions or conventions (ibid). Finally, the most far-reaching provision was the possibility of transferring competence over most "matters of common interest", including asylum and immigration, to the Community's first pillar by a unanimous Council decision on the initiative of the Commission (Art. K.9 EU). In a "Declaration on Asylum", added on Germany's behest to the EU Treaty, priority was given to asylum policies; the Council agreed to consider, by the end of 1993, the possibility of applying the so-called *"Passerelle"* regulation which contained the possibility to transfer asylum and immigration matters to the first pillar. By the time of the Treaty's revision in 1996, however, none of these possibilities had been invoked.

A second effect of the inclusion of these "matters of common interest" in the Maastricht Treaty was the deepening of the tight relations that existed between the cooperation at the level of the Twelve with that of the Schengen Group. After all EU member states with the exceptions of the United Kingdom and Ireland had joined the Schengen Group and had ratified the Schengen Convention, cooperation in asylum and immigration was taken over by the Twelve. Their focus was on the implementation of the Dublin Convention which would, once in force, make the parallel provisions of Schengen II obsolete. The Schengen Group nevertheless remained important with regard to the implementation of the Schengen Agreement which finally entered into force on 26.3.1995. In addition, this group continued to promote and cooperation especially with regard to the crossing of external borders, readmission agreements and the trafficking of migrants.

Finally, in relation to the domestic polity, the establishment of the K.4 Committee was aimed at improving communication and transparency inside and between ministries, as well as introducing stronger political authority over these bureaucratic processes which would not only be able to propose solutions but also to resolve differences when necessary (Coordinators' Group 1992). This additional political level proved particularly useful for the member state fulfilling the role of the presidency by allowing it to introduce its own priorities onto the agenda; however, it also contributed to additional tensions with the other supervisory body, the COREPER.

Confronted with the above-mentioned critique from other political actors and NGOs, the Ministers responsible for immigration raised the possibility in their report of breaking up their technocratic, closed and secretive mode of operation by increasing transparency, by stepping up the briefing of the European Parliament and the national parliaments, and by establishing contacts with the external organisations concerned. However, these possibilities were not really applied and the work of the intergovernmental groups remained largely inaccessible both to other political groups and to private actors.

Components of a Common European Refugee Policy

As was previously mentioned, the second generation of cooperation in asylum and immigration matters departs from earlier endeavours through the fact that it allegedly detached itself from the problematique of free movement and recognised cooperation in these matters as an aim in itself. This was already indicated by the "Declaration on Asylum" included in the Final Act of the Maastricht Treaty; it stated that "the Council will consider as a matter of priority questions concerning Member States' asylum policies, with the aim of adopting, by the beginning of 1993, common action to harmonise aspects of them". Six years later, the ministers responsible for immigration iterated this objective in the Amsterdam Treaty, and the aims of defining minimal standards for the admission and recognition of asylum seekers and refugees were enshrined in the first pillar of the Union. Still two years later, in October 1999, these goals were again expressed in a hitherto unprecedented vigour by the EU Heads of State and Government meeting at the Tampere European Council, who urged for the establishment of a common European asylum system.

The achievements and failures of cooperation in the EU framework are discussed in the following sub-sections. It is shown that, after an initial phase of strong activism, the pace of cooperation calmed down significantly after the adoption of common restrictive measures and once the impetus for substantive harmonisation faded away. Limited cooperation evolved instead with regard to refugees from the former Yugoslavia, however, member states have shown a strong reluctance towards a formalisation and harmonisation of temporary protection and the idea of burden-sharing. In sum, common European refugee policies so-far have developed on the lowest common denominator, blurring the distinction between refugees and (illegal) immigrants and establishing a system of negative redistribution among member states and the neighbouring eastern and southern European countries. These characteristics are mirrored in the last sub-section which, turning to the positions of the European Parliament and the European Commission, briefly summarise the main elements of the more "humanitarian" counter-discourse of these supranational institutions.

The initial drive: the fight against abusive asylum claims
The new impetus for common action documented in the Maastricht negotiations rapidly led to results. Even before the Treaty entered into force, the Ministers responsible for immigration issued several resolutions and conclusions on asylum. These measures were the direct continuation of first generation cooperation in the Ad Hoc Group on Immigration and were aimed firstly at the implementation of the Dublin Convention and secondly at the adoption of restrictive measures reducing the potential for abusive asylum claims in the member states.

The clearing houses A first step in the realisation of the work programme presented at the Maastricht Summit was the establishment of a Clearing House (CIREA)[19] for the gathering and exchange of information on asylum seekers in the second half of 1992. In particular, this information is to focus on the sources of migration pressure in sending countries and transit countries, and on member states' policies and procedures. This measure stands in the context of the implementation of the Dublin Convention and is meant to provide for the obligatory exchange of information expressed in Article 14 DC. A related development was the elaboration of a computerised fingerprint identification system for asylum seekers (EURODAC), with the express purpose of fighting multiple asylum applications (so-called "asylum-shopping") and thus assuring the single responsibility rule of the Schengen and Dublin Conventions. In parallel with this Clearing House on asylum seekers, a second Centre for Information, Discussion, and Exchange on the Crossing of Borders and Immigration (CIREFI) was set up with the task of assisting the implementation of tight external border controls; subsequently, it was also to assist member states in the fight against illegal immigration and in improving expulsion procedures. Under the Amsterdam Treaty, the Commission has decided to improve the exchange of statistics and information on asylum and immigration through the setting up of a (virtual) European Migration Observatory.

The London Resolutions and Conclusions The next step in the realisation of the Maastricht programme followed soon after with agreement being reached on two resolutions and a conclusion introducing simplified procedures for "manifestly unfounded applications for asylum" at a meeting in London on 31.11/1.12.1992. These measures were formally adopted at the Edinburgh Council in December 1992. Their ideational background is illustrated by a declaration approved that same day which invokes the "danger" and "destabilising effects" of uncontrolled immigration on host societies (European Council 1992).

Basically, the so-called London Resolutions and Conclusions aim at reducing access to domestic asylum procedures for certain categories of persons, that is those seen as not being "in genuine need of protection within the member states" (Council 1992). The first *Resolution on manifestly unfounded applications* (RMUA) applies to cases where "there is clearly no substance to the applicant's claim to fear persecution in his own country"[20] or in the fact that "the claim is based on deliberate deception or is an abuse of asylum procedures".[21] In these cases, member states may apply accelerated procedures which do not include a full examination and in which review procedures may be more simplified (§§ 2-3 RMUA). In addition to these cases, the first London Resolution mentions the category of persons falling under the second *Resolution on a harmonised approach to questions concerning host third countries* (or "safe third countries", RSTC), where "an application may not be subject to determination by a member state of refugee status" (§ 1(b) RMUA). Thus, in contrast to the first London Resolution on manifestly unfounded claims which aims at the prevention of abusive applications through the reduction of procedural guarantees for certain categories of asylum seekers, this second London Resolution applies to all asylum seekers who want to submit an application in a member state irrespective of whether or not they may be regarded as refugees. In principle, this latter resolution takes up the system of responsibility determination contained in the Schengen and Dublin Conventions, which is based on the rationale that an asylum claim must be examined by the first country with which the applicant has had contact. It makes direct reference to the Article 3 (5) of the Dublin Convention which confirms the right of every contracting party to send back an asylum seeker to a third country before examining their application according to national legislation; furthermore, it states the wish "to harmonise the principles under which they [the member states] will act under this provision" (Preamble RSTC). The criteria for applying this rule are fulfilled when the third country respects the norm of non-refoulement (Art. 33 GC) and does not expose the applicant to torture or inhuman or degrading treatment (§§ 2(a)(b) RSTC). Furthermore, the applicant must have "already been granted protection in the third country or has had an opportunity, at the border or within the territory of the third country, to make contact with that country's authorities in order to seek their protection, before approaching the Member States in which he is applying for asylum, *or* that there is clear evidence of his admissibility to a third country" (§2 (c) RSTC). Since this principle precedes the application of the Dublin Convention, it indicates that an EU member state is only responsible for examining an asylum claim if the applicant has not crossed - also if only in transit - through a third state or when no other "safe" state exists to which the person may be sent.

Finally, the *Conclusions on countries in which there is generally no risk of persecution* (or "safe countries of origin", CSCO) foresees simplified procedures for applicants who come from "countries in which there is in general terms no serious risk of persecution".[22]

Expulsions and the conclusion of readmission agreements In parallel with the adoption of the London Resolutions and Conclusions, the Ministers responsible for immigration started to enhance their cooperation on questions of expulsion; indeed, they developed new instruments geared at the facilitated return of asylum seekers to "safe third countries" or to their countries of origin. A *"Recommendation regarding Practices followed by Member States on Expulsion"* was adopted at the same meeting in London on 30.11/1.12.1992; it called for a quick, efficient, functional and economical approach to expulsion. While expulsion largely remains a domestic issue, this London Recommendation laid down two important principles. Firstly, expulsion to or through the territory of another member state has to be limited as much as possible and has to be accompanied by substantial guarantees for that state. Secondly, it recommends expulsion from EU territory to third states and recommends that these should be as informal and expeditious as possible. For this purpose, this Recommendation proposed the conclusion of readmission agreements with the third countries concerned.

The conclusion of such agreements is in fact a crucial step in the implementation of the London Resolution on safe third countries and the London Conclusions on safe countries of origin. Since states are only bound to readmit their own citizens under international law, but retain the right to deny entry to foreigners, the effective implementation of the safe third country rule made the conclusion of readmission agreements necessary. In practice, this instrument can be seen as a direct extension of the redistribution system for the handling of asylum claims between EU member states, which is at the core of the Schengen and Dublin Conventions, outside the Union to all potentially "safe" countries. The crucial difference between the Schengen and Dublin Conventions and the readmission agreements signed with non-EU countries is that the latter do not contain any obligation on the readmitting country to examine the asylum seeker's request; indeed, they do not distinguish between asylum seekers with their precarious human rights situation and illegal immigrants.[23]

The lead in this extension of the European refugee regime was once again taken up by the Schengen members with the conclusion of a first model readmission agreement with Poland in 1991. This treaty served as a model for later bilateral readmission agreements between single member states and third countries and also provided the basis for a harmonised approach in the "*Draft Council Recommendation concerning a specimen bilateral readmission agreement*" adopted on Germany's initiative in the Council of JHA on 30.11/1.12.1994. Compared with earlier readmission agreements signed between Western European states in the 1960s, which applied to asylum seekers only if their cases had already been definitely rejected in the asylum procedure, these new treaties are increasingly being used as a legal basis for the return of asylum seekers before their status has been determined on the grounds of the safe third country rule. While older agreements were not seen as being very efficient because of the high levels of proof required in order to readmit a person, these newer agreements are characterised by their aim of facilitating readmission through a downgrading of the standards of evidence required, the use of vague formulations, and through the imposition of very long time limits during which the returning state can require readmission.

Whereas cooperation with third countries regarding readmission and return of immigrants, asylum seekers and refugees initially evolved at a purely intergovernmental level, the JHA Council decided in September 2000 to give the Commission the mandate to negotiate readmission agreements with certain third countries.

In sum, these resolutions and conclusions strongly limit the access of asylum seekers to status determination procedures in the potential receiving country. The safe third country rule applies to all asylum seekers regardless of their quality as refugees; the need for protection is no longer therefore the crucial criteria, but rather the geographical itinerary of the flight. This lack of humanitarian safeguards is also manifest in the readmission agreements which, applying to both asylum seekers and illegal immigrants indiscriminately, do not consider the special situation pertaining to refugees. From the point of view of international interdependence, these rules are clearly un-cooperative since they release the individual state from its obligations under the Geneva Convention by shifting these obligations onto another state. The fact that this responsibility can be shifted - even to countries outside the EU who have not participated in the negotiation of the safe third country rule - is the clearest indicator of such protectionist behaviour.

Apart from these substantive considerations, the form of these measures clearly underlines the primacy of state sovereignty as well. Not only are they explicitly not legally binding, but they are also informal. In fact, the Maastricht Treaty did not even provide for the adoption of instruments such as "resolutions" or "conclusions", but only for "joint actions" and "joint positions" or conventions. Thus, the ministers involved opted for informal instruments whose non-binding character was supported by their abundant use of exceptions and open formulations.

The deadlock: limping implementation and harmonisation
As mentioned above, the distinctive feature in the working programme presented by the Immigration Ministers in Maastricht was their acknowledgement of the need to harmonise substantive standards of asylum law, not only as a precondition for the proper functioning of the responsibility system of the Dublin Convention, but also as an aim in itself. In contrast to the restrictive measures against "bogus" applications contained in the London Resolutions and Conclusions, however, the harmonisation of fundamental principles of asylum law proved to be extremely cumbersome. It soon became clear that the member states were not really interested in engaging in deeper cooperation and that they were reluctant in accepting any possible constraints on their national sovereignty. As was confirmed in several interviews, the interest of states in further cooperation had faded away. This growing disinterest should not be surprising though given that the main purpose of this cooperation, common restrictions on the intake of asylum seekers, was largely achieved through the reforms of domestic asylum laws implementing the restrictive elements of the Schengen Convention and the London Resolutions and Conclusions in countries with major refugee in-takes, most prominently Germany (see Chapter Four).

After the adoption of the London agreements, cooperation slowed down significantly. Not only did it not produce any significant results before the mid-1990s, but the implementation of the Schengen Agreement and the domestic ratification of the Dublin Convention also came to a stand-still.

The limping implementation of the Schengen and Dublin Conventions By the time that the Maastricht Treaty entered into force, the free movement of persons was still a controversial issue. Even among the Schengen countries, border controls were still in place. Their removal did not begin until the Schengen Agreement finally entered into force five years after its signature on 26.3.1995. By then, all member states - with the exception of the United Kingdom and Ireland[24] - had joined the initiative. This delay in the implementation was mainly justified because of problems related to the functioning of the Schengen Information System (SIS), that is the computerised database for the maintenance of "public order and security" (Art. 93 SC). Another crucial reason was the high level of requirements for efficient external border controls, requirements which continued to delay the implementation of the Schengen Agreement in Italy (until 1.10.1997) and Austria (until 1.1.1998). A similar delay occurred with the Dublin Convention, also signed in 1990, where the ratification process took seven years. The Convention entered into force after the last member state ratified it on 1.9.1997 and replaced the parallel asylum provisions of the Schengen Agreement.

Nevertheless, even after entering into force, the application of the Schengen and Dublin rules remains contradictory and far from consistent. Not only are states reluctant to open their borders and proliferate identity checks within their territories - on the street, in trains or on highways - but they often refuse to take up their responsibilities under the system of redistribution for the handling of asylum claims. The responsibility rule of the Dublin Convention turned out to be very difficult to apply in practice. Firstly, it is often not possible to provide sufficient evidence for the fact that an asylum seeker has previously passed through another member state. Secondly, member states are reluctant to admit additional asylum seekers and hence often try to circumvent readmission requests based on this responsibility rule. The result are protracted and uncertain asylum procedures, in which the asylum seekers are often shuffled from one state to another or that they are kept in detention without being able to find a state willing to examine their claim.[25]

These problems with the implementation of the Dublin Convention have led the European Commission to reconsider the Convention's provisions and to propose its comprehensive overhaul (Commission 2000c). In its staff working paper of March 2000, the Commission states that "few if any Member States appear to regard the Dublin Convention as an unqualified success". Calling for more substantial cooperation, the Commission points out that "if a mechanism for allocating responsibility for asylum applicants is to operate effectively, it must be accompanied by common standards in procedural and substantive areas of asylum law" (Commission 2000c, §20, see also §§ 23 and 51). Accordingly, the transformation of the Dublin Convention into EC law foreseen under the provisions of the Amsterdam Treaty might be accompanied by an amendment of both the criteria for determining the state responsible for the examination of an asylum application and of the mechanisms of this cooperation.

Notwithstanding the Commission's sceptical evaluation of the Convention's effectiveness, the JHA Council has tried to enhance its implementation through the establishment of the Executive Committee on the implementation of the Dublin Convention, charged with the promotion and supervision of Convention, and the invigoration of the EURODAC project, the computerised database for the registration of asylum seekers in the EU.

The EURODAC Convention The EURODAC project was launched in 1991 with the aim to find additional computerised means for facilitating the implementation of the Dublin Convention. After eight years of negotiations, agreement on the contents of the draft Convention for the comparison of fingerprints of applicants for asylum (EURODAC) was reached end of 1998. The regulation provides for the collection of data relating to people apprehended in connection with the irregular crossing of an external border and the identification of their fingerprints. These negotiations demonstrated once more the existence of significant differences between the traditional transit countries of the South and the traditional asylum countries of the North in this cooperation. Fearing to be negatively affected by the planned Convention, the former tried to oppose the extension of the fingerprints system to include apart from asylum applicants also illegal immigrants. In its final version, this data base extends to applicants for asylum, people apprehended in connection with irregular crossing of an external border, and people found illegally present within the territory of a member state. A corresponding proposal for a Council Regulation was submitted by the European Commission in May 1999. An amended version of this proposal was formally adopted in by the JHA Council in November 2000.

"Minimum guarantees" and the harmonisation of asylum procedures One of the most important provisions of the 1991 Maastricht working programme was recognition of the fact that the functioning of the responsibility rule of the Schengen and Dublin Conventions would require the approximation of some procedural aspects of status determination. It was, however, only because of persistent pressure from the UNHCR and other humanitarian agencies that the Ministers finally agreed on *a Resolution on minimum guarantees to be accorded to asylum seekers* in June 1995. These guarantees cover the rights of asylum seekers during the examination, appeal and revision procedure of their application, as well as manifestly unfounded asylum requests at the border and the rights of

unaccompanied minors and women (see Guild/Nielsen 1996; Boeles/Terlouw 1997).

According to reactions from the UNHCR, the NGOs and scholars, these guarantees reflect the lowest common denominator among the member states. The critique centres around two points. The first point concerns the non-binding legal character of the Resolution of 20.6.1995 which implies that, even if it does contain certain safeguards, it does not ensure their observation. The second critique is more substantive and maintains that the Resolution undermines its own principles by allowing exceptions in cases where these principles were most needed. This particularly concerns the exceptions provided on the suspensive effect of appeals and the lack of procedural safeguards for manifestly unfounded and safe third country cases, as well as the application of readmission agreements (see Boeles/Terlouw 1997: 472). This second point is of particular importance given that the above mentioned resolution does not contain any procedural safeguards that would ensure that the returned asylum seekers have access to a (fair and equitable) asylum procedure in the third country concerned or that they are protected from refoulement (ECRE/Amnesty International 1995; UNHCR 1995).

Recognising the shortcomings of this cooperation under the third pillar, the European Commission is currently preparing a Community legal instrument on asylum procedures on the basis of the new provisions of the Amsterdam Treaty. Instead of proposing a complete harmonisation of asylum procedures, however, the Commission preferred to maximise the chances for adoption of such a Community instrument by proposing only a minimum level of procedural guarantees which are close to the 1995 Council Resolution and leaving a measure of flexibility for their administrative implementation (Commission 1999a). In addition to this more limited directive on minimum standards, which is due for adoption or rejection by the Council in April 2001, the Commission has presented a more comprehensive proposal on a common asylum procedure and a uniform status for those who are granted asylum valid throughout the Union Commission (Commission 2000b).

Harmonisation of the refugee definition The second substantive claim of the Maastricht programme was the harmonisation of status determination criteria so as to adopt a common refugee definition in all member states. This claim followed recognition of the fact that significant differences existed among the member states, differences which inhibited the application of the single responsibility rule, since some asylum seekers would be recognised as refugees in one country, while in another they would be rejected (Carlier et al. 1997; Arboleda/Hoy 1993).

Cooperation in these matters thus started at an early stage, immediately after the signature of the Dublin Convention in fact with the distribution of a questionnaire to the member states in July 1990. This questionnaire intended to provide insights on the commonalities and differences regarding interpretations of the definition of the Geneva Convention (printed in Spijkerbour 1993: Annex I). Although this survey was already completed by 1991 (Plender 1995: 155), the adoption of a common interpretation only became truly topical in the summer of 1994, when it was put at the top of the German Presidency's programme. Given that this issue touches the very foundations of refugee law, negotiations turned out to be very tenacious and difficult. After two additional years of discussions, the ministers concerned finally agreed on a joint position.[26] The resulting document, which sets up common guidelines for the establishment of evidence required in granting refugee status, defines the term "persecution" within the meaning of Article 1A Geneva Convention, enumerates the various grounds of persecution, and exposes the conditions the cessation of refugee status, is again generally seen to reflect the lowest common denominator between the member states. The main criticism against this Joint Position is that it is in clear opposition to the main causes of refugee flows today, because it limits the application of refugee protection to persons who are persecuted by the state or with its tolerance or complicity; it thereby excludes all those refugees fleeing from civil war and generalised violence, the people who represent the vast majority of contemporary refugee flows. Thus, the Joint Position not only illustrates the refusal to adapt the definition of a refugee to these changed circumstances, but it also departs from the liberal recognition practice which is often followed by several individual member states (Bank 1999; ECRE 1995; UNHCR 1995b).[27]

Actions taken with regard to refugees from the former Yugoslavia
At the same time that the Ministers finally agreed on a restrictive interpretation of Article 1A Geneva Convention, basically precluding civil war refugees from refugee status, member states developed innovative protection mechanisms with regard to refugees from the former Yugoslavia which take these persons out of the traditional asylum systems based on the Geneva Convention. The main innovation is the introduction of the notion of temporary protection, which in practice slightly formalises the existing procedure of tolerating these persons on a "de facto" basis and underlines the transient character of this protection until the situation in their home country calms down (Dacyl 1995; Thorburn 1995; Van Selm-Thorburn 1998; and Van Selm 2000). The aim of this new instrument is to deal quickly and effectively with sudden and massive arrivals in need of

protection, while not over-burdening existing asylum procedures. In short, the main differences between temporary protection and traditional asylum provisions are the absence of a right on the part of the refugee to have his or her case considered, the absence of an independent institution in charge of examining the asylum claim and of legal remedies against negative decisions, and, finally, the provisional nature of the residence permit together with the discretionary power of the executive to end the protection status as soon as this is deemed to be appropriate.

European action in this field was very much inspired by German, and later also by Austrian, concerns to reach some sort of burden-sharing arrangement on this matter, given that they accepted the biggest amount by far of Balkan refugees in Europe.[28] These concerns were in fact at the heart of the German Presidencies between July and December 1994 and again between January and June 1999. They found support from the UNHCR and the Council of Europe, which took the position that "persons fleeing from the former Yugoslavia who are in need of international protection should be able to receive it on a temporary basis". However, these organisations also warned that temporary protection should not be used as a means to preclude genuine refugees who would fall under the scope of the 1951 Geneva Convention from full refugee status (quoted in Van Selm-Thorburn 1998: 37).

The first EU measures taken with regard to the Yugoslav crisis were the "Conclusion on People displaced by the conflict in the former Yugoslavia" of 30.11.1992 and a "Resolution on certain guidelines as regards the admission of particularly vulnerable groups of persons from the former Yugoslavia" of 1.6.1993. While these texts did not require major changes in member states practices, the ongoing discussions on a system of burden-sharing led to a first result in June 1995 with the "Resolution on burden-sharing with regard to the admission and residence on a temporary basis of displaced persons". This latter Resolution aimed at establishing a new system of redistribution inside the EU, by taking into account prior contributions made by member states in the prevention or resolution of a crisis, the humanitarian aid provided, and by any other factors which affect their capacity for reception. It was however not implemented in the member states. A similar Commission initiative in March 1997 was withdrawn in absence of any progress; it was subsequently divided in two texts, one on temporary protection of displaced persons without any reference to burden-sharing and the other on "solidarity" and burden-sharing. A new initiative was made when Germany took up the Council Presidency in January 1999. Recognising the continued hostility of several member states to the idea of burden-sharing, namely France, the United Kingdom, Spain and, to a lesser extent, Portugal, the German presidency elaborated another proposal with flexible arrangements based on voluntary participation with financial compensation. Like earlier initiatives, this proposal had to be shelved. As a result of this deadlock, the EU failed to agree on a coherent approach to the Kosovo refugee crisis in spring 1999. This incoherence was not only reflected in the uneven distribution of refugees from the former Yugoslavia in the member states, but also in the strong divergence of admission policies, status regulations, and return policies after the expiry of temporary protection (van Selm 2000).

In analysing these processes, it is important to note that temporary protection is only one subsidiary instrument in the approach developed with regard to the crisis in the former Yugoslavia. The principal focus of activity has not been inside the EU territory but, in the ex-Yugoslav territory itself, where the burden of refugee relief remained mainly in the hands of the UNHCR and NGOs. Here, two strategies were developed which precede the flight out of the country. The first is the "internalisation" of the problem, that is the keeping of civil war victims within their area of origin in so-called "safe havens" which are more or less protected by the international community (Landgren 1995). Where internalisation is not possible, a second strategy of "containment" applies, that is the attempt to regionalise the protection of refugees within the broader area of their country of origin (Thorburn 1995 and 1996, van Selm-Thorburn 1998).

This approach was clearly demonstrated in the case of Kosovo-Albanians in spring 1999. The refugees fleeing "ethnic cleansing" by Serbian forces were primarily kept within their region of origin; in improvised and overburdened camps established near the Yugoslav border in Macedonia, Albania, and Montenegro.[29] Governments of the European Union favoured aiding the refugees as close to Kosovo as possible in order to facilitate their early return, rather than accepting them for resettlement.[30] Calls by the European Commission and some member states for each EU nation to accept a quota or share of the refugees were opposed by The United Kingdom, France and Italy. By the end of June 1999, only some 75,000 Kosovars were taken outside the region, including 13,500 to Germany; 7,500 to Turkey; 6,000 to Norway; 5,800 to Italy; 5,200 to Canada; 5,000 to the US; and 4,700 each to France and the Netherlands. The treatment of these persons in the various countries differed significantly. Most EU member states granted renewable temporary residence permits of three months. While in some countries, such as France, this scheme did not preclude Kosovo Albanians from applying for full refugee status, access to formal asylum procedures was excluded in other countries, such as Germany (Van Selm 2000). These differences are even more significant if one considers that the majority of Kosovo Albanians who fled deportation by the forces of the Yugoslav government fulfil the persecution criteria of the 1951 Geneva Convention.[31] Thus, while the concept of temporary protection was originally developed as an answer to massive refugee flows generated by situations of generalised violence, which did not conform the narrow interpretation of the Geneva Convention, the Kosovo crisis documents its extension to categories of refugees which fall within the scope of the traditional refugee regime. Herewith, temporary protection tends to develop into an additional means of circumventing humanitarian obligations under the Post-World War II refugee regime.

This tendency has prompted the European Commission to adopt a new proposal for a directive on temporary protection in the event of mass influx of displaced persons on 24 May 2000 (Commission 2000a). This directive aims at the introduction of minimum standards for granting temporary protection and seeks to enhance both uniformity and solidarity among the member states. In order to compensate for unbalanced intakes of refugees, the directive provides for solidarity mechanisms through a Community financial instrument, the European Refugee Fund proposed by the Commission in December 1999, and solidarity in the physical reception of displaced persons, on the basis of double voluntary action by the receiving member states and the displaced persons. The draft directive underlines that the operation of the Geneva Convention shall remain intact, and limits the duration of temporary protection to a maximum of two years.

The creation of a European fund for refugees
The aim to ensure a balance of effort between member states in receiving refugees and displaced persons and bearing the consequences of such intake is not limited to the field of temporary protection, but has motivated intergovernmental cooperation in asylum and refugee matters since its beginnings in the 1980s (see above and Chapter Four). Recognising the interest of the main refugee receiving countries in attaining a more equal distribution of asylum seekers in the EU, the European Commission has proposed the establishment of a European Refugee Fund with the purpose to support and encourage the efforts made by member states in receiving refugees and displaced persons and bearing the consequences of so doing (Commission 1999b). This proposal was finally adopted by the JHA Council on 28 September 2000 (Council Decision 2000/596/EC). The Fund, which will operate for five years from January 2000 to December 2004, supports member states' actions for the reception, integration and voluntary repatriation of refugees and displaced persons, including actions aimed at improving the implementation of national refugee policies. The Fund also makes separate provisions for emergency measures for one or more member states in the event of a sudden mass influx of refugees or displaced persons. Given reservations by some member states on this point,

a statement was attached to the Decision to the effect that the Council would endeavour to come to a decision, in the framework of the Directive on temporary protection, on other measures promoting the balance of effort between member states. From 2000 to 2004, each member state will receive an annual allocation from the Fund (from 500,000 euros in 2000 to 100,000 euros in 2004). The remainder of available resources will be distributed between member states proportionally to the number of recorded people assisted over the three previous years (65%) and the number of third country nationals or stateless persons as refugees or benefiting from a form of international protection granted by a member state (35% of the volume). The proportion of co-financing supplied by the Fund is 50%, but this may be increased to 75% in the member states covered by the Cohesion Fund. While the Refugee Fund may be regarded as a positive incentive encouraging member states' commitment to refugee protection, its importance stands and falls with its financial volume. If one looks at the extent of financial costs associated with the reception, integration and repatriation of refugees and displaced persons in the member states, the Fund's current financial reference amount of 216 million euro for the five years period appears to be little more than a drop in the ocean, and the prospects for a future extension of this financial volume are very dim. Against this background, the importance of the European Refugee Fund lies less in its capacity to encourage the efforts made by member states in receiving refugees and displaced persons than in its symbolic value.

The supranational voice and the strive for a comprehensive approach
As mentioned above, member states' determination to protect their national sovereignty over asylum and immigration matters prevented the European Commission from actively engaging in these policy fields. While the Commission decided to leave these areas to intergovernmental cooperation and not to interfere with these processes, the European Parliament soon took a very critical stance towards the "undemocratic" and restrictive character of intergovernmental cooperation and advocated a more liberal, and generous attitude towards asylum seekers and refugees. This approach has been maintained through subsequent parliamentary resolutions and reports (EP 1992, 1993, 1995b).

In the wake of the Maastricht Treaty, the Commission resumed its role as a policy initiator and issued a Communication "on the right of asylum" (Commission 1991). This document took as its starting point the increased "political and social importance of the right of asylum in the Community and in Member States" and the "moves ... to lay the groundwork for political union" (§1). Its impact on the contents of the cooperation process did not really increase however after the adoption of the Maastricht Treaty.

Recognising the determination of the member states to maintain full sovereignty over these matters, the Commission renounced any plans to foster a possible transfer of asylum policies to the first pillar as foreseen in the so-called *"passerelle"* of Article K.9 EU. A European Commission Report on the possibility of applying Article K.9 to asylum policies issued at the end of 1993 concluded that the time was not yet ripe for such a transfer of competency (Commission 1993).

Despite this lack of formal influence, the Commission nevertheless made several proposals, the most important of which was a Communication on immigration and asylum policies from 1994 which laid down a comprehensive approach in these fields (Commission 1994). With this document, the Commission moved very close to the liberal or humanitarian frame of the European Parliament. The approach proposed in the 1994 Communication embedded short-term policies regarding the admission of asylum seekers within a long-term cooperation process with the countries of origin in order to fight against the causes of forced migration and to promote better integration of legally resident aliens in the member states (ibid: 5, 12). The starting point was the observation that an increasingly restrictive and anti-foreigner perception in public opinion and politics had developed, but that these views were often based more on "impressions" rather than "facts" (ibid:4, §11). Nevertheless, acknowledging the increased importance of these issues and the inadequacy of unilateral national measures (ibid: foreword 5), the Commission called for a "new and deepened debate on the question"; indeed, it strove for a "global approach" which combined "realism and solidarity" in an "integrated and coherent" manner (ibid). Accordingly, the document emphasised the need to observe the fundamental principles of the Geneva Convention (ibid: 24 § 82). With regard to the output from intergovernmental cooperation, the Commission underlined the need both to harmonise substantive refugee law and to agree on certain procedural guarantees in applying the Dublin Convention and the London Resolution in order to respect the norm of non-refoulement and the rule of law (§§ 83-88). In addition, it called for the harmonisation of social reception policies (§ 89). Finally, the Commission also raised the question of de facto refugees and called for a harmonised and formalised policy towards these persons by stressing the need for solidarity among the member states (§§91-100).

Given the priorities set by transgovernmental cooperation under the third pillar, the Commission's 1994 Communication has never been formally adopted by the Council. Neither have the provisions of the 1991 work programme been fully implemented, which foresaw in addition to the implementation of the Schengen and Dublin Conventions also the harmonisation of procedural and substantive standards of refugee law (Fortesque 1995; Myers 1995).

With the Amsterdam Treaty, the Commission's right to issue initiatives in the fields of asylum and immigration has been strengthened (see below). At present, it is however very difficult to predict how far the Commission will succeed in promoting a truly supranational European asylum system. Recent proposals confirm on the one hand the Commission's traditionally sceptical attitude towards the restrictive approach of the Schengen and Dublin Conventions (Commission 2000b, 2000c). On the other hand, the limited reach of the proposed Directive on minimum standards for the examination of asylum claims witnesses the continuity of a more reactive attitude, cautious of the member states' reluctance towards deeper harmonisation and high standards of refugee protection.

Whereas the scope for Community action relating to the admission of asylum seekers and refugees in the EU continues to be limited, supranational action may be more successful in the external dimension of refugee policies concerning the relations with countries of origin and transit. First indications of this are the activities of the *High Level Working Group on Asylum and Migration* (HLWGAI) and the efforts to integrate Justice and Home Affairs concerns in the foreign policy activities of the Union. The HLWAI was set up at the General Affairs Council on 7-8 December 1998 "to establish a common, integrated, cross-pillar approach targeted at the situation in the most important countries of origin of asylum seekers and migrants". The group consists of high level officials from each EU member state and the Commission and has targeted six countries: Afghanistan, Albania and the neighbouring regions (i.e. Kosovo), Iraq, Morocco, Somalia and Sri Lanka. The action plans developed for these countries have been announced as "the first attempt by the European Union to define a comprehensive and coherent approach targeted at the situation in a number of important countries of origin or transit of asylum seekers" (European Union HLWGAI 1999, Annex: § 10). The plans, which were adopted at the first summit of the European Council on Justice and Home Affairs in Tampere in October 1999, contain a variety of measures in the field of diplomacy, trade relations, humanitarian assistance, development cooperation, as well as border control mechanisms, readmission agreements, information campaigns and exit monitoring in the countries of origin and support for host countries in the conflict region. In a working document published on 24 November 1999, the European Parliament has criticised this mixture of restrictive immigration control measures and instruments tackling the causes of migration as being inconsistent and putting the emphasis on readmission agreements and securing protection away from the EU's borders in the conflict region (Scholdan 2000). Together with the Council and the Member States, the Commission will play an active role in the implementation of these plans. Although the Commission's competencies in the fields of foreign and security cooperation are limited, its extensive powers in the field of trade policy may develop a strong potential in the fight against the causes of forced migration and in the cooperation with the countries and regions of origin. The possibility of linking trade cooperation with migration control policies is certainly part of the reasons why the JHA Council decided to give the Commission the authority to conclude readmission agreements with third countries (see above). Apart from the activities of the HLWGAI, where the Council continues to play the dominant part, an increasing involvement of the Commission in external asylum and migration policies is already salient in its economic relations with the ACP and Mediterranean countries and the countries of South Eastern Europe.

The question, whether the reforms of the institutional framework of asylum and immigration policies in the Amsterdam Treaty will increase the opportunities for the supranational actors to shape the course of political action, is discussed in the next section.

The Amsterdam Treaty: a Comprehensive Reform?

While the inclusion of asylum and immigration matters in the Maastricht Treaty was a reaction to growing public and political awareness in the member states of the importance of these issues and a growing dissatisfaction with the practice of intergovernmental cooperation, the revision of the third pillar in the Amsterdam Treaty of 1997 (AT) was primarily aimed at remedying the ongoing difficulties arising from the specific institutional configuration of that cooperation. By 1995, the critique of the third pillar had nearly become consensual (O'Keeffe 1995 and 1996; Plender 1995). The Commission (1995), the European Parliament (1995b) and the Council (1995) all issued critical reports which converged significantly with regard to their criticisms of how intergovernmental cooperation was functioning. In particular, the reports concluded that extremely limited used had been made of the new instruments provided for in Article K.3 EU (1992 version) and that the cumbersome cooperation structure - consisting of five levels requiring unanimous decisions as well as overlaps in the three pillar architecture - urgently needed reforming. These debates were at the core of the Intergovernmental Conference (IGC) in 1996 and 1997, finally leading to the adoption of the Amsterdam Treaty in June 1997. Apart from establishing the guidelines for a future (Eastern) enlargement, these debates dealt extensively with Justice and Home Affairs, and led to important changes in the institutional framework for cooperation in asylum and immigration matters. It seems that the Amsterdam Treaty finally paid due attention to the great importance that was being attributed to asylum and immigration matters in the European public by transferring these issues, from the not very prominent third, to the centre of the first pillar. At the same time, however, these important steps towards "political union" still carry the mark of more than fifteen years of intensive transgovernmentalism which not only impede the room of action for supranational actors, but also continue to shape the cognitive perceptions and normative expectations toward a common European asylum policy.

Institutional Reforms

The institutional changes in the fields of asylum and immigration belong to the most prominent reforms of the Amsterdam Treaty. These two issues were moved from the third to the first pillar and the Schengen *acquis* was incorporated into the EU framework. Asylum and immigration are included in a new Title in the EC Treaty called "Visas, Asylum, Immigration and other policies related to the Free Movement of Persons" (Title IV EC). As a general rule, the main organisational changes only occur after a "transitional period" of five years following the entry into force of the revised Treaty on 1.5.1999. During this period, crucial intergovernmental elements are being maintained. The main institutional changes and the continuity of intergovernmental elements are presented below.

The new flexibility and "closer cooperation"
One of the most important innovations of the Amsterdam Treaty is the strengthening of forms of flexible integration and especially the possibility of opt-outs introduced in this policy field. Three member states no longer participate under the new Title, namely the the United Kingdom, Ireland and Denmark. Protocol 4 EU relating to the the United Kingdom and Ireland and Protocol 5 EU relating to Denmark enable these states to choose between participating and remaining outside with respect to every measure undertaken through this Title. In particular, these states have been freed from the need to vote under any of the procedures and from any binding character regarding the measures taken, as well as from the operational costs involved. The Protocol on the application of certain aspects of Article 7a EC, in addition, allows the the United Kingdom to maintain its border controls. Similar provisions regulate the relationship of these countries with the Schengen *acquis* (Article 4 Schengen Protocol).

Denmark, which is a Schengen member, retains the right to implement those follow-up decisions regarding the Schengen *acquis* which meet its national interest. However, in Denmark such decisions will not acquire the quality of European law but will be implemented as international accords, such falling outside the scope of ECJ jurisdiction.

For the rest of the participating parties, the transfer of asylum and immigration matters to the first pillar meant a streaming up of the internal differentiation of cooperation. Much of the debate in the IGC in fact centred around the cumbersome five-level structure and the conflicts that took place between the K.4 Committee, COREPER, and the steering and working groups. By transferring asylum and immigration matters to the first pillar, the usual three-level structure of the EC system will apply. No changes have however been adopted with regard to the professional composition of the Council and working group meetings. The lead remains in the hands of the interior ministries which even increased their influence through the attachment of staff from interior and justice ministries to the permanent representations of the member states. This measure was aimed to mitigate the rivalry which had developed under Maastricht's third pillar between the COREPER, gathering the permanent representatives of the member states, and high officials from the interior and justice ministries meeting in the so-called K.4 committee, now renamed the Article 36 Committee according to the pertinent article in the Amsterdam Treaty. The leading role of the national interior ministries at the European level has gone along with a weakening of other ministries dealing with asylum and immigration matters in the member states, notably the foreign and social ministries (Guiraudon 2000). This dominance of national interior ministries has greatly contributed to the framing of the asylum question as an issue of internal security rather than human rights in the EU context.

Old and new goals

Despite strong criticism of the restrictive focus of the third pillar actors thus-far, the agenda contained in the Amsterdam Treaty clearly stands alongside the tradition of the Maastricht programme. The pertinent Article 63 EC contains a detailed list of measures to be adopted including a relatively precise time frame of five years. This list basically iterates those areas which have constituted the focus of cooperation since the early 1990s. It enumerates measures regarded as necessary for the implementation of the Dublin Convention - including minimum standards for asylum procedures and a common interpretation of the refugee definition - and the concept of temporary protection. The scope of these measures is also reflected in the "Action Plan of the Council and the Commission on how best to implement the provisions of the Treaty of Amsterdam on an area of freedom, security and justice" endorsed by the European Council at its summit in Vienna on 11./12.12.1998. This action plan bears a strong resemblance with the report issued by the Ministers responsible for immigration in the wake of the Maastricht Treaty. Cooperation under that treaty has however shown how difficult it was to realise these provisions.

An innovation of the Amsterdam Treaty is the emphasis that it puts on the genuine foreign policy dimension of refugee policies which is now being stressed in several declarations attached to the Treaty. This particularly concerns the role of foreign policy considerations in visa policies,[32] recognition of the right of member states to conclude agreements with third countries regarding economic migration and family reunion,[33] and more generally the right of member states to take into consideration foreign policy concerns with regard to asylum and immigration when either the "maintenance of law and order" or the "safeguarding of internal security" is threatened.[34] These provisions provide a link to the Union's CFSP. Considering that important aspects of asylum and immigration policy will remain subject to cooperation in the intergovernmental third pillar (especially policy cooperation against trafficking in migrants), these policy fields are now regulated by all three pillars of the Union. Of course, significant challenges to coordination among the various directorates of the Commission, the Committees of the European Parliament, and the working groups of the Council will be posed by these changes. One first response to this challenge was the setting up of the High Level Working Group on Asylum and Migration (HLWGAI) in early 1999, whose task is to establish a common, integrated, cross-pillar approach targeted at the main countries of origin and transit of asylum seekers and immigrations (see above).

The community method prejudiced
Within the Commission, the institutional weight of asylum and immigration issues was upgraded through the establishment of a new Directorate General on Justice and Home Affairs under the lead of JHA Commissioner António Vitorino. This new directorate is however very small and relies strongly on external expertise both from non-governmental and governmental actors. With regard to the competences attributed to the supranational actors, major changes will only occur after 2004, that is after the transitional period of five years after the entry into force of the Amsterdam Treaty. However, the only definite change will be the sole right of initiative for the Commission, no decision was taken considering the possible move from unanimous to qualified majority voting in the Council. In the literature, the Commission's right to issue initiatives is often seen as implying the control over the negotiation agenda and as facilitating the realisation of the common interest (Gehring 1994: 230). Nevertheless, in

the event of unanimous voting in the Council, the Commission will anticipate the position of the most reluctant government (Garret/Tsebelis 1996), thus perpetuating harmonisation on the lowest common denominator. The European Summit in Nice in December 2000 confirmed the ongoing reluctance of most member states' governments to introduce qualified majority voting in the field of refugee and asylum policies.

The trend towards a more restrictive attitude of Commission proposals can already be observed, when one compares the recent proposals concerning the harmonisation of asylum procedures (Commission 1999a) with the ambitious visions of its 1994 Communication (Commission 1994). The new procedures of the Amsterdam Treaty may thus well mean the conversion of hitherto non-binding restrictive instruments into binding ones, thus enhancing the normative weakness of a common European asylum system. With regard to the European Parliament, the consultation procedure applies, that is without having the power to alter or stop a Council decision. The right to be heard is the weakest form of participation which can be attributed to the Parliament under the EC Treaty. More effective democratic control may however result for national parliaments from the protocol on the role of national parliaments in the European Union adopted in Amsterdam. This protocol contains measures for the increased information of national parliaments and accords the Conference of European Affairs Committees of the Parliaments of the European Union (COSAC) the right to examine proposals and initiatives in the area of Title IV EC and to seek related information from the EU institutions.

A significant innovation is the introduction of ECJ competence to give preliminary and interpretative rulings[35] in asylum and immigration matters (Art. 68 EC). This competence will empower the ECJ to assure uniform interpretation of binding legislative measures taken under Title IV EC. However, this provision contains three significant reserves which might pose a challenge to the ECJ's activity in this area. Firstly, the traditional procedure for preliminary rulings under Article 234 EC (old Art. 177 EC) is modified in such a way that only national courts, whose judgement will not be open to further challenges in the respective legal systems, may request such a ruling. This may limit the ECJ's traditional role in clarifying and consolidating the *acquis* (here of Title IV EC) through the practice of preliminary rulings. Secondly, the ECJ will not have jurisdiction over internal border control when "relating to the maintenance of law and order and the safeguarding of internal security" (Art. 68 II EC). This formulation exceeds other "ordre public" clauses in the Treaty and may, if interpreted in an extensive manner, pose significant limits on the ECJ's activity in this area. The third limitation is contained in Article 68 III EC, which excludes the retroactive impact of ECJ rulings on (previous) rulings by national courts. This limit is again an important abrogation from traditional principles of EC law. Finally, the Court will have no jurisdiction over the non-binding resolutions and conclusions adopted under the third pillar unless they are translated into binding directives.[36] Of course, these inter-organisational relations are complicated by the fact that political and legal aspects of asylum and immigration policies are now spread over all the three pillars of the Union - with their different institutional settings - and by the extensive flexibility clauses, which allow for varying degrees of participation by member states and EU institutions.

With regard to non-EU actors, there is little indication that the Amsterdam Treaty will lead to an opening up of the hitherto closed negotiations structure. Although a draft article foresaw a "duty on the Council to ensure cooperation between the administrations of the Member States and the Commission and as regards asylum policy with UNHCR" (Draft Art. E, quoted in ILPA 1997a), the final article no longer mentions the UNHCR (Art. 66 EC). Instead, cooperation with this agency is merely mentioned in a declaration to the final act which states that: "consultations shall be established with the UNHCR and other relevant international organisations on matters relating to asylum policy". The article, as it now stands, concentrates on the relationships between national administrations and European institutions.[37]

Towards greater transparency
Again, one of the main criticisms of the IGC concerned the fact that secretive modes of operation persisted and that there was a lack of transparency in the third pillar. Accordingly, one focus of the institutional reforms engendered by the Amsterdam Treaty is geared towards greater publicity and more open debate regarding European policies. With regard to asylum and immigration, major changes are expected in five years (in 2004) when the Commission will have the full right of initiative, meaning that every proposal will be published straight-away regardless of the outcome of the negotiations. Finally, a major source of rigidity remains with regard to the decision-making procedures; the most striking intergovernmental element is the preservation of unanimity voting (Art. 67 EC). In the 1996-1997 IGC, his decision has mainly been attributed to the German veto on introducing qualified majority voting expressed at the last minute by Chancellor Kohl. The main reasons for this retreat by one of the strongest proponents, at least formerly, of Communitarisation were because of the opposition emanating from some Länder and the Ministry of the interior; in contrast to the foreign ministry, which had elaborated the draft for the IGC, the interior ministry did not approve further sovereignty transfers in this area. The underlying reason was the fear of being outvoted

by other member states which follow different ambitions in the fields of asylum and immigration, in particular the former transit countries of the South and the Scandinavian countries. The repeated failure to introduce qualified majority voting at the European Summit in Nice in December 2000 confirms the enduring fears of sovereignty losses in this area, regardless of changing government coalitions in the member states.

The "Republicanisation" of the Securitarian Frame

In ideational terms, the most important innovation of the Amsterdam Treaty is its new emphasis on citizenship and on the relationship between the Union and the people. In the final draft of the AT, a new title on "Fundamental Rights and Non-Discrimination" was introduced at the front of the treaty which, underlining its adherence to the ECHR, laid down the fundamental principles of the Union. These principles where then implemented in the Common Provisions of the Treaty on the European Union and comprise "liberty, democracy, respect for human rights and fundamental freedoms, and the rule of law" (Art. 6 EU). In particular, the Treaty introduces the possibility of sanctions against any member state who is seen as violating one of these principles (Art. 7 II EU), while empowering the Council to take measures regarding non-discrimination (Art. 13 EC), the equality of men and women (Art. 3 II EC), and data protection (Art. 286 EC).

While reflecting on the origins of these innovations, two main developments seem to have been decisive. The first has a longer tradition and consists of a general critique on the normative legacy of the mainly economically oriented European Union. This critique intensified after the adoption of the Maastricht Treaty and was fuelled by domestic ratification debates in several member states;[38] indeed, it occupied a central stage at the IGC. In contrast, a second decisive factor has external sources and emanates from the prospect of an Eastern enlargement of the Union. Unlike earlier enlargements, this one has, from the very beginning, been marked by an unprecedented emphasis on political considerations and the conceptualisation of democracy, human rights, and the rule of law as political conditions for membership. In this light, it is conceivable to imagine that the formal introduction of these principles into the EU framework was geared at backing up the political legitimacy of these requirements with regard to the Central and Eastern European candidate countries. This interpretation is supported by Article 49 EU, which provides that every European state that respects these principles may become a member of the Union. This normative turn in the EU's fundamental principles has gained new prominence with the *Charter of*

Fundamental Rights which was adopted at the European Summit in Nice in December 2000. Two articles of the Charter relate to refugees. Article 18 on the right to asylum confirms the international asylum right and reads:

> "The right to asylum shall be guaranteed with due respect for the rules of the Geneva Convention of 28 July 1951 and the Protocol of 31 January 1967 relating to the status of refugees and in accordance with the Treaty establishing the European Communty."

Article 19 relates to protection in the event of removal, expulsion or extradition and contains the following provisions:

> "1. Collective expulsions are prohibited.
> 2. No one may be removed, or expelled or extradited to a State where there is a serious risk that he or she would be subjected to the death penalty, torture or other inhuman or degrading treatment or punishment."

Herewith, the Charter of Fundamental Rights confirms the status quo of international refugee law, namely the right of states to grant asylum and the norm of *non-refoulement* (see Chapter Two). Up to now, the Charter has only a declamatory character, the Nice European Council decided to consider the question of it's force at a later date.

Although not legally binding, the Charter nevertheless symbolises the attachment of the originally predominantly economic European integration project to certain political values and fundamental norms. The question, how far this "republicanisation" of the EU is also reflected in the provisions on asylum policy in the Amsterdam Treaty is discussed in the following paragraphs.

Freedom of movement and compensatory measures
Although Article 61 EC presents the common asylum and immigration provisions as measures geared at the gradual establishment of an "area of freedom, security and justice", the heading of Title IV EC clearly situates them in the measures relating to the free movement of persons. Accordingly, and in continuation of the first generation cooperation, this new title shall realise freedom of movement through the adoption of "appropriate measures with respect to external border controls, immigration, asylum and the prevention and combating of crime" (Art. 2 EU). This focus on freedom of movement, rather than "justice" or "security", clearly limits the scope of cooperation under this title. This is also reflected in the fact that in contrast to the establishment of a common, comprehensive asylum and immigration policy, this Title only names

individual and thus limited "flanking measures" (Art. 61a EC) necessary for free movement. The detailed enumeration of these necessary measures in the field of refugee policy (63 EC) contains few innovations and has strong resemblance with the 1991 Maastricht Programme. This also holds for the Action Plan for the implementation of the Amsterdam provisions adopted end of 1998. Meanwhile, the Treaty is very ambiguous in what concerns the final abolition of checks at the internal borders, and free movement, originally foreseen for 1993, is suspended for at least five years after the coming into force of the new Treaty - that is 2004. In the words of Jörg Monar, "the Schengen group has succeeded in implanting its relatively limited objective of ensuring free movement as the main rationale of action in ... areas such as asylum and immigration policy", a rationale which may not allow for more than a rather narrow approach focusing more on admission and control than on protection, prevention and integration (Monar 2000: 12). The continuity of the securitarian frame is clearly stated in Article 64 EC, according to which "This Title (Title IV EC, S. L.) shall not affect the exercise of the responsibilities incumbent upon Member States with regard to the maintenance of law and order and the safeguarding of internal security". As mentioned previously, this exception clause exceeds other "ordre public" reservations in the Treaty and bears the danger of being interpreted in an extensive way.

The Spanish protocol and the differentiation of protection
A second provision which stipulated strong critique from human rights activists and the UNHCR consists of a protocol which was added to the Treaty on Spain's initiative. The "Protocol establishing the European Community on asylum for nationals of EU Member States" expressly denies the quality of refugee to citizens of EU member states and would thus, if strictly implemented, amount to a de facto geographical limitation of the scope of the Geneva Convention. As a consequence, potential refugees from EU member states may be deprived from their fundamental right to seek and enjoy asylum laid down in Article 14 of the Universal Declaration of Human Rights. The underlying assumption is that the EU already constitutes a common area of security and justice. However, its political background documents once more the influence of realist considerations; the underlying motivation of the Spanish government was to abolish the possibility for ETA and Basque separatists to find recognition as refugees in other member states, as has been the case in Belgium (which in fact opted out from this protocol).

Another change relating to the conception of refugees in the Amsterdam Treaty is the introduction of a distinction between asylum seekers, in the sense of the 1951 Geneva Convention (Art. 63 I EC), and other "refugees and displaced persons" (Art. 63 II EC) who do not fall under the scope of this Convention. Herewith, the Treaty draws a consequence from the differentiation of protection regimes and underlines the strategy of temporary protection. The provisions on temporary protection are however very vague and do not exceed the scope of earlier (unsuccessful) initiatives taken by the Commission. While acknowledging the existence of refugees who are not subsumed under the criteria of Art. 1A GC, the introduction of this provision may reinforce the trend towards the establishment of a secondary temporary protection regime which favours state prerogatives and restricts the rights of the individual refugee.

The lack of solidarity
Earlier failures to establish a system of burden-sharing find their expression in the vague formulations in this regard in Articles 63 II b and 64 II EC. In the first provision, which concerns temporary protection, the Council agrees to promote a "balance of effort between Member States in receiving and bearing the consequences of receiving refugees and displaced persons" (Art. 63 II b EC). The second relevant provision has a more defensive stance and applies in the advent of an "emergency situation characterised by a sudden inflow of nationals from a third country" to one or more Member States. In this situation, the Council "may, acting on qualified majority on a proposal from the Commission, adopt provisional measures ... for the benefit of the Member State concerned" (Art. 64 II EC). It is remarkable that, in such an "emergency situation", the speedier procedure of qualified majority voting applies here even if the general rule is that of unanimity.

In more general terms, the more realist approach to international interdependence is reflected in the extensive use of flexibility clauses, which amounts to a cooperation "à la carte" for those countries which decided to opt out of Title IV EC. Furthermore, the negotiations preceding the Amsterdam Treaty highlighted another important cleavage between the participating governments. The decision against the introduction of qualified majority voting expressed the fear of a main refugee receiving country - Germany, which has historically played a leading role in the integration of asylum and immigration matters - of being outvoted by the traditional transit countries of the South and the new Scandinavian members. Finally, several provisions of the revised Treaty also highlight a lack of solidarity of the current member states vis-à-vis future members. Firstly, applicant countries will not be allowed to negotiate flexibility clauses with regard to Title IV EC but are bound to have adopted the complete *acquis* reached in this area at the time of joining the Union. This means for Malta and Cyprus, for example, in contrast to the the United

Kingdom and Ireland, that they will not be allowed to maintain border checks on the grounds that they are islands. Secondly, this *acquis* includes the totality of legally binding and non-binding decisions adopted in this area so-far, this includes also the hitherto unpublished decisions by the Schengen Executive Committee and thus exceeds level of implementation existing in the member states (Art. 8 Schengen Protocol). This may constitute a significant hurdle for the Central and Eastern European applicant countries; they must, within a short period of time, develop and implement policies which EU member states have taken years to shape and, in some cases, are still having problems with them.

The continuity of securitisation

Notwithstanding the stronger emphasis put on common humanitarian values in the general wording of the Amsterdam Treaty, the provisions of Title IV EC stand in the continuity of the securitarian approach towards asylum seekers and refugees established in previous intergovernmental negotiations. This continuity is expressed in the trilogy of an "area of freedom, security and justice" which is primarily geared at the intensification of the ties between the Union and its citizens. The perception of refugees and asylum seekers as a threat appears at in different instances in the treaty. It is reflected in the reference to potential "emergency situations" and "sudden inflows" of refugees (Art. 64 II EC) for which a special, simplified and accelerated mode of action applies which bypasses the slightly more "democratic" normal procedure that requires consultation with the European Parliament and the consent of the various national parliaments to the adoption of pertinent measures. While the removal of asylum and immigration matters from the third to the first pillar indicates their difference to other matters of police cooperation remaining in the former, the security continuum established through "first generation" cooperation is not fully broken. Article 61 a EC includes - apart from measures regarding external borders controls, asylum and immigration - also "measures to prevent and combat crime" as necessary steps prior to the introduction of free movement. Furthermore, important and contemporarily prioritarian areas of cooperation in asylum and immigration matters will remain in the third pillar, thereby underlining their securitarian quality. These provisions mainly concern the fight against trafficking in human beings, which represents a growing concern subsumed under the category of organised crime. In this context, it is important however to note that the increasing level of this kind of trafficking is at least partly directly related to increasingly restrictive entry and visa policies and to the tightening of border controls that is being promoted in EU cooperation.[39] A further indication of the importance of securitarian concerns is the recognition that a foreign affairs dimension to these policies exists; indeed, in several declarations, the member states explicitly retain the right to consider their foreign policy interests when exercising asylum and immigration policies. These provisions open the window for an emphasis not only of the internal, but also of the external and international security dimension of refugee policy. Finally also the inclusion of the Schengen *acquis* as such reflect an adherence to the securitarian prism. In fact, a declaration was added to the Treaty which states that this transfer "should provide at least the same level of protection and security as under the ... provisions of the Schengen Convention".[40]

Conclusion

Almost fifteen years after the beginning of intergovernmental cooperation in asylum and immigration matters, the establishment of a common European asylum system has become a priority of European Union politics. Invoked by the EU Heads of State and Government in their meeting in Tampere in October 1999, this aim contrasts with the priorities set by intensive transgovernmental cooperation between JHA officials and challenges both the institutional and ideational legacies of the common asylum *acquis*.

Basically, this analysis revealed two dynamics behind the Communitarisation of refugee policies. The first is linked to the dynamics of European integration. In this respect, the confirmation of the prospect of the free movement of persons in the Single European Act launched a new wave of activism, where the question of abolishing internal borders spilled over into issues related to the immigration of third country nationals and refugees. The second dynamic behind these processes rests with the member states and concerns bureaucratic politics and political developments within these countries. On the one hand, the promotion of cooperation in these matters must be seen as a counter-reaction by bureaucratic actors to the forthcoming Europeanisation of their domain. Traditionally in charge of ensuring control over the crossing of national borders and the safeguarding of internal security as core elements of national sovereignty, the alliance of interior ministries was a means to secure control over the transformation of their field of activity. In addition, this counter-reaction was eased by the fact that informal consultations between these ministries had already existed since the mid-1970s and thus had some institutional tradition. On the other hand, the fact that the measures promoted in these consultations were generally focused on questions relating to the entry of third country nationals and, in particular, asylum seekers points to a second major domestic source, namely the increasing concern of major refugee receiving countries with the rising numbers of asylum seekers on their territories.

The way in which the asylum question was subsequently framed was heavily influenced by the specific ideational dynamics of European integration and the manner in which this cooperation was organised and, linked to that, the manner in which specific actors were able to transport and integrate their own perceptions and ideas into the deliberation process. The scope of cooperation was very much shaped by the context of the single market project and in particular the superior goal of free movement. The linkage of this cooperation with the 1986 Single European Act has defined the issue of concern in a limited manner as a side aspect of, and compensation measures for the abolition of internal border controls; the driving motive was at no point the establishment of a comprehensive common European refugee policy (apart in the initiatives from the European Commission and the European Parliament). This line of reasoning is also apparent the new provisions of Title IV EC, which still relate to the freedom of movement. The second ideational dynamic consists in the lack of a normative humanitarian framework in the EC tradition, which supported a technical perspective on refugees as one cross-border phenomenon among others. In this conception, little differentiation was made with other cross-border flows related to illegal immigration; indeed, the isolation of European cooperation from the humanitarian context of the 1951 Geneva Convention, the UNHCR or the Council of Europe shifted the human rights core of the refugee concept into the background. Finally, the multi-level constituency of the European integration process itself contributed to the framing of the refugee problem in more "realist" terms. The perpetual tension between integration and state sovereignty in the process of Communitarisation was paralleled by the inherent opposition in the concept of refugee protection between universal human rights and bounded state sovereignty. In other words, the integration of asylum policies meant not only the transfer of decision-making authority, but also threatened to weaken a core element of national sovereignty, namely the capacity of the state to control the population of its territory. The coincidence of these two dilemmas reinforced statist concerns with the preservation of sovereignty and control. With regard to the asylum frame, this had three major effects. The impact of humanitarian norms was kept to a minimum; the transfer of political authority to supranational institutions was opposed; and cooperation and solidarity among the member states was strictly limited.

The emergence and the implementation of this ideational frame - rather than the more idealist frame of the European Parliament and the

European Commission - in the policy-making process was strongly linked to the institutional configuration of the policy arena. In this regard, four institutional features characterise what has been called the structures of intensive transgovernmentalism (H. Wallace 2000). Firstly, compared to earlier efforts aimed at finding a consensus in the Council of Europe, the differentiation of membership in two concentric groups - the Schengen group comprising a core of five countries and the broader Ad Hoc Group on Immigration gathering together all EU member states - contributed significantly to the expeditious determination of the agenda. It also allowed the core member states to transfer their own concerns to those less engaged member states in the Ad Hoc Group on Immigration, countries which did not possess similar domestic difficulties regarding increasing numbers of asylum seekers and where immigration had not (yet) become an issue in public and political discourse.

A second related and equally crucial element was the homogeneous professional background of the actors involved and the personal overlap between those officials represented in Schengen and those in the Ad Hoc Group on Immigration. This homogeneity and overlap not only fostered the exchange between the concentric groups, but also favoured a specific approach. Coming predominantly from the various interior ministries, these officials carried a particular perception of the refugee question which, given their professional self-definition, focused on the border-crossing quality of asylum seekers rather than on their motivation to flee, or the situation in their home countries or their humanitarian needs. Given this limited focus, the issue of refugees was subsumed under the broader phenomenon of voluntary migration. This then facilitated its linkage with other border control concerns, such as the transnational phenomena of organised crime, drug smuggling or terrorism.

These two crucial institutional characteristics were supported by the isolation of the intergovernmental groups from other national, supranational or international actors including the traditional proponents of the international refugee regime (the UNHCR, the Council of Europe, and NGOs) and the secrecy of their operations. While this exclusivity (supported by the differentiation of membership) limited the range of perceptions and opinions in the relevant deliberations and thereby simplified the agenda of a highly complex problematique, the rule of secrecy allowed this state of affairs to be maintained until the central measures were adopted implementing a particular frame on the asylum question. The fact that this frame was already implemented in the Schengen draft agreement in 1988 - that is before the opening up of the Eastern Bloc and the subsequent perception of an impending immigration crisis - underlines the crucial importance of these ideational and institutional factors vis-à-vis external developments. This conclusion is further supported by the fact that, despite these external developments, the transgovernmental frame continued to differ significantly from that of the supranational institutions throughout the period examined.

The analysis of these framing processes is crucial for understanding both the scope and the limits of further European cooperation in refugee policy. As was argued in Chapter One, policy frames - once implemented in a political process - gain the status of ideational institutions and shape both the interpretation of the underlying problems and the choice of action. It is important to note that once institutionalised in public policies, policy frames become independent from the underlying power relations and can continue to affect the course of policy-making even after the social power relations that facilitated their emergence have change.

Taken together, these considerations pose significant limits to the scope of political reforms in the field of European asylum and immigration policies under the Amsterdam Treaty. In the further evolution of the third pillar, the specific institutional and ideational features of the first generation revealed a high level of institutional rigidity and a strong resistance to change. Despite far-reaching criticisms of the intergovernmental mode of operation and the contents of cooperation, the Maastricht Treaty merely formalised the existing structures by introducing them into the Community framework. Although the Commission was granted limited powers under the third pillar, its influence remained very limited due to the continuous closure of the transgovernmental structures. The progress made under the Maastricht Treaty enforced the restricted trend launched by the Schengen and Dublin Conventions; thus, it contributed to the further strengthening of statist prerogatives in the field of refugee protection. This particularly concerns the tightening of entry conditions and visa requirements, but also concerns the conditionalisation of access to asylum procedures through the establishment of a system of negative redistribution both inside the Union - through the Schengen and Dublin Conventions - and outside - through the safe third country rule and the conclusion of readmission agreements. Although they were claimed as prioritarian in the Maastricht debates, deeper measures - such as the harmonisation of procedural standards and recognition criteria have - faced strong opposition in the intergovernmental groups and have led to very limited results. While some innovation was reached in the policies towards refugees from the former Yugoslavia, the concept of temporary protection developed contributes further to a strengthening of the state vis-à-vis the individual refugee in so-far as it tends to be applied also to persons who fall within the scope of the Geneva Convention, as shown in the case of the Kosovo crisis. In sum, the main result of Communitarisation thus-far can be seen in the adoption of limited, mainly restrictive and legally non-binding, measures restricting access to domestic asylum procedures. The main body of procedural and substantive asylum law remains unchallenged by the European provisions, the establishment of a common European asylum system, as invoked in the Tampere conclusions of the European Council, seems far away.

If one believes in the tenacity of policy frames, the prospects for a re-orientation of EU refugee policies under the Amsterdam Treaty are weak. Several properties of the Treaty tend to underscore this interpretation. With regard to institutional features, it is important to note that although the issues of asylum and immigration have been transferred to the first pillar, this has gone along with the transfer of crucial intergovernmental elements, such as the maintenance of the unanimity rule, a limitation on the powers of the Commission and the ECJ, and an even stronger weakening of the European Parliament's role. Furthermore, the supranational institutions lack the material and immaterial resources necessary for developing a proactive role in this area, as the modest equipment of the Commission's new directorate for justice and home affairs shows.

Still, even if the supranational institutions gradually succeed in extending their powers, the ideational frame established will constitute a further constraint to comprehensive reforms. Indeed, it appears that the Amsterdam Treaty confirms the securitarian asylum frame in three main respects. Firstly, the provisions regarding asylum and immigration are still subsumed under the overarching aim to introduce freedom of movement and include only particular aspects of refugee law; the Treaty mentions at no point the aim to establish a common, comprehensive European asylum and immigration policy. Secondly, cooperation occurs "à la carte"; extensive flexibility clauses allow for various forms of participation and various degrees of political and legal commitment. Thirdly, several exemption clauses emphasise the safeguarding of internal security and hence the primacy of national interests. Finally, the provision which deprives the citizens of the European Union of their right to claim asylum in another member state may be read as a limit to the geographical scope of the Geneva Convention.

This last point, however, may also be read in a different manner and might have significant consequences for the future of the European Union. Together with the newly introduced provisions on fundamental rights and non-discrimination, the abolition of the asylum right for EU citizens underlines the civic quality of the EU and strengthens significantly - at least symbolically - the ties between the EU institutions and the people. This has mainly been achieved through the affirmation of certain fundamental rights and the introduction of control mechanisms ensuring their implementation. In this logic, the abolition of the asylum right inside the Union becomes more understandable; it may be read as a symbol of the accomplishment of an approximate republican state-building process at the European level, since - ideally - republics, which are characterised by the respect for human rights and the rule of law, do not produce refugees. Still, the legitimacy of this reading is debatable, if one considers that the existence of states is inherently linked to the possibility of persecution and that, far from providing a guarantee for the respect of human rights and the absence of persecution, the Union is not equivalent to the republican model of the state.

It is with this point that the symbolic quality of the Amsterdam Treaty is strongest. The deepening of inclusionary fundamental freedoms is a basic pillar in state formation and, as was noted in Chapter One, is inherently linked to the insoluble tension between the particularist principle of sovereignty - by which a state inter alia delimits its people - and the universalism of human rights - which apply to every human being regardless of his or her nationality. Since communitarian closure inside runs alongside exclusion of the outside, the new Title on immigration and asylum can now be interpreted as a necessary step in the deepening of the "Citizens' Europe".

The effects of this Communitarisation of asylum and immigration issues on the Europeanisation of domestic refugee policies is analysed in the following chapters with reference to the cases of Germany and France. The question of how far Europeanisation, by altering the institutional and ideational context of domestic discourses, leads to a convergence of asylum policies and thereby to a modification of historical traditions guiding this policy field is of central interest.

Notes

[1] CAHAR (78) 7 final, quoted in Uibopuu (1983: 72).

[2] CAHAR (81), quoted in Uibopuu (1983: 73).

[3] With the opening up of the Eastern Bloc and the membership of Central/Eastern European countries, the Council of Europe and CAHAR have again been gaining more importance in pan-European refugee questions and may in fact be regarded as a third, broader circle of cooperation in these matters; see Lavenex (1999).

[4] Articles 48-51 of the EC-Treaty provide for the free movement for workers within the Union. These persons possess the right to look for and accept offers of employment in a member state other than their own and, upon taking up gainful activity, to acquire the right to reside in that member state. Articles 52-58 relate to freedom of establishment for self-employed persons, and Articles 59-66 to the freedom to provide services.

[5] European Court of Justice, Judgement of the Court in Joint Cases 281, 283 to 285 and 287/85 (Germany, France, Netherlands, Denmark and the United Kingdom v. Commission) on Application for the annulment of Commission Decision 85/381/EEC of 8.7.1985 setting up a prior communication and consultation procedure on migration policies in relation to non-member countries of 9.7.1987.

[6] The meaning of the acronym "Trevi" is contested; some scholars maintain that it is an abbreviation for the words "Terrorism, Radicalism, Extremism, Violence, International", while others associate it with the Fountain of Trevi in Rome, the city in which the first meeting of the group was held (see Cruz 1993: 18).

[7] In 1971, the "Groupe Pompidou" was created by France, Germany, Italy, the Benelux, and The United Kingdom - before being later joined by Turkey (1980), Greece (1981), Norway (1983), Spain (1984), Portugal and Switzerland (1985), Finland (1987), Austria and Malta (1988) - with the aim of exchanging information and coordinating innovations in the fight against the trafficking of drugs and later also against terrorism. Other groups dealing with terrorism included the "Club of Vienna", created in 1979, which regrouped the interior ministries of Austria, Switzerland, Italy, Germany, and France together; the "Quantico Group", also created in 1979, by US, Canada, Australia, Great-Britain, Sweden, Germany and France, and the "Bern Club", regrouping representatives of the security services of the US, The United Kingdom, Denmark, the Benelux, Switzerland, Italy, France, and Germany (see Bigo 1992 and 1996).

[8] Between 1977 and 1985, the group met only six times (1977 in London, 1978 in Bonn, 1979 in Dublin, 1981 in London, 1983 in Bonn, and 1985 in Rome; see Bigo 1992: 49).

[9] In 1985, three sub-groups to "Trevi" were established: Trevi I pursued greater cooperation on terrorism; Trevi II dealt with police techniques and measures for the maintenance of public order; and Trevi III concentrated on criminality and drugs. In December 1988, a fourth sub-group was created to deal with the effects of the freedom of movement on internal security (Bigo 1992: 53). It is interesting to note that, in the mid-1980s, the issue of immigration entered the agendas of most of the above mentioned intergovernmental fora dealing with internal security matters.

[10] According to the ad hoc group, its tasks included (i) improving checks at the Community's external frontiers and assessing the value of internal controls in combating terrorism, drug trafficking, crime, and illegal immigration; (ii) evaluating the feasibility of harmonising member state's visa policies, and the effect such an action might have on improving external controls; (iii) examining methods for easing intra-Community travel without abetting terrorism, drug trafficking, illegal immigration, or other criminal activities; (iv) developing measures to achieve a common policy for the elimination of asylum abuse; and (v) addressing numerous operational issues, such as the exchange of information about spot-check systems and the prevention of passport abuse. See Ad Hoc Group on Immigration, Summary of conclusions of the meetings of the ministers concerned with immigration, SN 1131/91 WGI 735 of 7.2.1991.

[11] These are Articles 7, 17, and 20: Article 7 expresses the need to harmonise visa policies; Article 17 provides for the transfer in the long term of border controls to the external

borders and suggests, "if necessary", the harmonisation of relevant provisions regarding illegal immigration; and finally, Article 20 again proposes, "if necessary", the harmonisation of certain aspects of alien laws with regard to third country nationals.

[12] Article 2 Second Schengen Agreement reads in § 1: "Internal borders may be crossed at any point without any checks on persons being carried out".

[13] These articles are ordered in several chapters: Chapter 2 deals with "Crossing of external borders", Chapter 3 "Visas", Chapter 4 "Conditions governing the movement of aliens", Chapter 5 "Residence permits and reporting as a person not to be permitted entry", Chapter 6 "Measures relating to organised travel", and Chapter 7 "Responsibility for the processing of applications for asylum". The remaining Titles deal with "Definitions" (Title I), "Police and security" (Title III), the setting up of a common database called "The Schengen information system" (Title IV), "Transport and Movement of Goods" (Title V), "Protection of personal data" (Title VI), the "Executive Committee" (Title VII), and "Final Provisions" (Title VIII).

[14] Accordingly, only persons possessing valid travel documents, a valid visa, if required, and sufficient means of support both for the period of the planned visit and return to the country of origin, who are not on the list of undesirable persons and who are not considered a threat to public policy, national security or the international relations of any contracting party, may be granted entry into the territory (Article 5).

[15] This responsibility is given when the contracting party has either de jure (e.g. through the issue of an entry visa or a residence permit) or de facto (e.g. through illegal border crossing) permitted the entry of an asylum seeker onto its territory (Art. 30 SA and Art. 4-8 DC). If a close family member of the applicant has already been granted asylum in one contracting party, this country shall also be responsible for the examination of this application (Art. 35 SA and Art. 4 DC).

[16] It reads: "aliens who are reported for the purposes of being refused entry" must either (i) be seen as posing a "threat to public order or national security and safety" or (ii) have "been the subject of a deportation, removal or expulsion measure which has not been rescinded or suspended, including or accompanied by a prohibition on entry" (Art. 96 SA).

[17] The fact that this resolution refers to the Trevi and not to the Ad Hoc Group on Immigration shows how interlinked these two organisations actually were; as was previously mentioned, from 1986 onwards, the coordination of asylum and immigration matters was officially the task of the ad hoc group, which was formally separate from the Trevi structure.

[18] Named after the respective article of the EU Treaty, this committee replaced the earlier Group of Coordinators and linked it closer and more formally to the operational levels.

[19] Abbreviation for the French name "Centre d'Information de Réflexion et d'Echange en matière d'Asile".

[20] §1 (a) and § 6 RMUA. The latter paragraph lists as examples (a) when the applicant does not invoke one of the grounds of persecution included in the Geneva Convention; (b) the

application is totally lacking in substance; and (c) it manifestly lacks any credibility. § 7 adds the possibility of cases where the fear of persecution is clearly limited to a specific geographical area and where protection is available in another part of the country.

[21] §1 (a) and § 9 RMUA. The instances enumerated are: (a) when the application is based on a false identity; (b) the applicant made deliberately false representation about his claim; (c) in bad faith destroyed relevant documents; (d) the person fails to reveal the submission of an application in another country; (e) the applicant has had an earlier opportunity to submit the application; (f) the person has flagrantly failed to comply with national rules relating to asylum procedures; and (g) the applicant has submitted an application after having had his or her application previously rejected in another country.

[22] §1 CSCO. Evidence regarding the safe nature of these countries shall derive from: (a) an examination of previous numbers of claims and recognition rates; (b) the observance of human rights; (c) the existence of democratic institutions; and (d) stability of the country. The adoption of these restrictive measures was not uncontroversial. For example, some safeguards were added to the London Resolution on manifestly unfounded claims after a draft became public and triggered a wave of protest. These include the possibility of taking into account information received from the UNHCR (§7 RMUA), as well as some procedural guarantees such as the opportunity for a personal interview with a qualified official or simplified review procedures (§4 RMUA). Other important amendments were the introduction of a specific reference to the UNHCR in the Preamble and the removal of a clause stating that "those who fear violations of their human rights should if possible remain in their own countries and seek protection or redress from their own authorities or under regional human rights instruments" (Ad Hoc Group on Immigration, Draft resolution on manifestly unfounded applications for asylum, Progress report on discussions in the Asylum Sub-Group. Note by the Presidency, 1.11.1992, SN 3926/92 WGI 1195 AS 128, quoted in Joly 1996: 55). This blunt formulation was then replaced with the conviction "that their asylum policies should give no encouragement to the misuse of asylum procedures" (Preamble RMUA).

A similar development took place in regard to the London Resolution on safe host countries, where reference to the UNHCR was only introduced in the final version. The most controversial measure however was the notion of safe country of origin which is already manifest in the adoption of the term "conclusions" rather than "resolution". While the original intention was to draw up a common list of such countries, in the end the Ministers only adopted some general guidelines for interpreting the situation in the country of origin; the strong term "safe country" was dropped in favour of the complicated expression "countries in which there is generally no risk of persecution". Given the UNHCR's strong objections to the draft, the original aim to include its information in the assessment of a country was replaced by the more general provision to give it a "specific place" in this regard (§5 CSCO).

[23] This poses the question of their conformity with international law, especially with the norm of *non-refoulement* in Article 33 of the Geneva Convention which prohibits the return of refugees to countries where their life or freedom is threatened. This lack of humanitarian provisions has been heavily criticised by the European Parliament (1995a), the UNHCR and by NGOs. The role of these agreements in the Eastern enlargement of

the EU and their relationship with the principles and norms of the international refugee regime is discussed in Lavenex 1999. See also Schieffer 1997; IGC 1994.

[24] The main reason for their refusal to adhere can be seen from the differences that exist in the system of identity checks which, given that these countries are islands, traditionally occur at the border and not inside the country. A second reason of course is the also traditionally sceptical attitude towards European integration of the UK and the fact that if the UK wasn't in Schengen and Ireland was, then Ireland would have to police a border which it does not necessarily recognise constitutionally (see O'Keeffe 1994).

[25] See the evaluation of the Schengen Agreement's implementation by the German interior ministry, (Bundesministerium des Innern 1996a and 1997) and by NGOs (Peers 1998).

[26] Joint Position on the harmonised application of the definition of the term "refugee" in Article 1 of the Geneva Convention of 28.7.1951 relating to the status of refugees, of 4.3.1996.

[27] The fact that several member states also used to apply the refugee definition of Article 1A GC to civil war refugees - e.g. from ex-Yugoslavia - is recognised by the European Commission (Commission 1994: 27 § 93).

[28] According to the UNHCR, Germany hosted around 400,000 refugees from the former Yugoslavia in 1994; mean-while, for example, Italy took only 40,000 and Greece and Portugal around 100 each; see Thorburn 1995: 462.

[29] A peace agreement was reached in June, 1999, 72 days after NATO began to bomb Yugoslavia to prevent Serbians from forcing ethnic Albanians from Kosovo. By the time the bombing stopped, some 860,000 of the pre-war 1.8 million ethnic Albanian Kosovars had become refugees, including 443,000 in Albania; 248,000 in Macedonia; 69,000 in Montenegro; and 22,000 in Bosnia. NATO troops took the lead in establishing shelters and providing food, and then turned the operation of the refugee camps over to UNHCR and other relief agencies.

[30] According to Emma Bonino of Italy, acting humanitarian affairs commissioner of the European Union: "The further away people are from home, the more difficult it is for them to go back", quoted in Migration News 6 (8).

[31] See the recommendations of the UNHCR concerning the reception of Kosovo refugees, for example in Le Monde of 26.5.1999.

[32] Declaration to the Final Act on Article 62 II (b) EC.

[33] Declaration to the Final Act on Article 63 EC.

[34] Declaration on the responsibilities of Member States under Article 64 I EC.

[35] Preliminary rulings refer to the old Art. 177 TEC (new Art. 234 TEC), under which national courts may submit cases to the ECJ in order to clarify the validity of Council acts with regard to primary European law. Interpretative rulings can be also requested by the Council, the Commission or a member state regarding questions concerning primary and secondary law in this area. This provision can be compared with Art. 228 § 6 EC Treaty,

which relates to opinions by the ECJ on the compatibility of an international treaty with Community law (see Bank 1999).

[36] More indirect influence from the ECJ in these matters might derive from its new competences with regard to human rights, as laid down in the ECHR. In particular, this could concern the rights of refugees regarding extradition, deportation and expulsion (Art. 3 and 8 ECHR), family reunification (Art. 8 ECHR), and the detention of asylum seekers (Art. 5 ECHR); see Bank (1999).

[37] This article now reads: "The Council ... shall take measures to ensure cooperation between the relevant departments of the administrations of the Member States in the areas covered by this Title, as well as between those departments and the Commission" (Art. 66 EC).

[38] Also see the Maastricht trials by the French Conseil Constitutionnel and the Bundesverfassungsgericht in 1993; one of the initial focuses of these debates centred around the Social Charter and the social rights of workers.

[39] This point is also made by Koslowsky (1998: 20). It can thus be said that increasingly restrictive policies contribute to the illegalisation of asylum seekers who, in the absence of legal means to reach a member state, are forced to rely on such "criminal" and costly organisations. On this point, see the various contributions in the Quarterly Bulletin of IOM (the International Organisation for Migration) entitled "Trafficking Migrants".

[40] Declaration 15 EU Treaty on the preservation of the level of security provided by the Schengen acquis.

4 The Europeanisation of Refugee Policies in Germany and France

"Eine Ergänzung des Grundgesetzes muß ... weiteren Verhandlungen auf der EG-Ebene vorausgehen, und sie muß auch dem Inkrafttreten des Schengener Übereinkommen vorausgehen." (Rudolf Seiters, German Minister of the Interior, in the Bundestag on 30.4.1992)

"La France ne veut plus être un pays d'immigration." (Charles Pasqua, French Minister of the Interior, in Le Monde of 2.6.1993)

A simultaneous observation of European and domestic developments shows that, since the mid-1980s, refugee policies in Germany and France were no longer determined by domestic considerations alone. They became increasingly intermeshed within a framework of international cooperation at the European level that has led to the gradual Communitarisation of asylum and immigration matters in the EU. For a long time both purely intergovernmental and with little influence of supranational actors, this cooperation led to far-reaching agreements and conventions with regard to the entry and stay of third country nationals on the common EU territory and the processing of asylum claims.

The alternation of dynamic intergovernmental cooperation leading to the Schengen and Dublin Conventions and the 1992 London Resolution and reluctant Communitarisation under the Maastricht and Amsterdam Treaties is reflected in the ambivalent impact of Europeanisation on domestic asylum regimes in Germany and France. Although the emergence of a multi-level polity initially remained screened from public and policy discourse in the two countries, it facilitated the implementation of restrictive policies culminating in the amendment of the constitutional asylum rights in 1993. On the one hand, the development of a multi-level polity strengthened the role of particular governmental actors to the detriment of the opponents of restrictive reforms at the domestic level. On the other, the definition of asylum and immigration as common European matters altered the ideational context of the refugee question in policy discourses. By framing asylum policies as a problem of negative redistribution and as a threat to internal security, Europeanisation resonated with existing fears in the two societies. Together, the European asylum frame and the restrictive trend existing in the two countries marginalised the impact of domestic and international human rights norms and supported the adoption of protectionist policies in the name of European integration. Paradoxically, rather than enhancing international cooperation and solidarity, European integration strengthened the element of sovereignty in refugee policy and subordinated the asylum right to a multi-layered concept of national and European security.

Notwithstanding their highly symbolic nature, the French and German constitutional reforms are the expression of a significant change in national asylum policies which points at a growing convergence towards a common European approach. However, an examination of the transgovernmental cooperation process in Chapter Three has shown that the member states only engaged on a superficial coordination of their national policies which was focused on the issue of internal and external border controls and aimed at a relieving and accelerating domestic asylum procedures. This indicates the possible continuity of specific national traditions and practices in this field. After an examination of the institutional and ideational impact of Europeanisation in the processes leading to the incisive constitutional reforms in section one, the second and third sections analyse the reach and convergence of domestic asylum regimes with regard to the implementation of the European asylum *acquis* and the further evolution of asylum policies.

This longitudinal perspective allows a more precise assessment of the interaction between domestic structures and discourses, Europeanisation and policy change, in the conclusion to this chapter. It is shown that although both countries returned to their traditional domestic priorities with regard to asylum and immigration, the asylum frame established under the influence of Europeanisation continues to shape their asylum policies, irrespective of changing political majorities. In Germany, the asylum policy of the now ruling SPD/Greens coalition stands clearly in the continuity of the 1993 reforms. Notwithstanding its greater institutional leeway for reform, also the new French government did not abolish the Pasqua law and its policy stands in the tradition of its conservative predecessors. In sum, these results confirm the theoretical hypothesis that once institutionalised in public policies, policy frames become independent from the underlying power relations and continue to affect the course of policy making even after the social power relations that facilitated their emergence have changed. The importance of these findings for future European cooperation under the Amsterdam Treaty is reflected upon in the Conclusion of this book.

Policy Discourses and Europeanisation

In order to highlight the ways in which Europeanisation impacted on the perception and definition of the asylum issue in Germany and France, this first section retraces the political discourses leading to the incisive reforms of the constitutional asylum rights in 1993 which, in both countries, were legitimated with the need of implementing the EU *acquis* and, more precisely, the Schengen Convention. The following analyses start with an examination of the institutional impact of transgovernmental cooperation on the distribution of power and authority in the domestic constituencies and, in a second step, retrace the ideational impact of European integration on the factual and normative justification of the asylum reforms in parliamentary debates.

The German Case: Release from the Legacy of the Past

The discourse on limiting the asylum right has had a relatively long recent history in Germany. As was indicated in Chapter Two, the politicisation of the asylum question had already begun by the 1970s with the enhanced pressure for procedural reforms; this was gradually extended to the call for a reform of the constitutional asylum right of Article 16 GG in the second half of the 1980s. This politicisation came about as the result of conflicts between the federal government - which, until 1982, was governed by a social-liberal coalition - and the majority of conservative governments in the *Länder*; the southern *Länder* of Baden-Württemberg (CDU) and Bavaria (CSU) took a particularly confrontational position. This federal conflict was coupled with a partisan cleavage which existed between the conservative CDU/CSU on the one, and the social-democrats (SPD) and liberals (FDP) on the other hand. With that, the asylum question developed into a major electoral target in the 1980s. Whereas calls for changes to the asylum procedure largely became consensual across the political spectrum, the issue of a constitutional amendment was initially limited to the CSU and, most prominently, the then acting minister of the interior - Zimmermann (CSU) - and only a handful of individual CDU members. By the end of the 1980s, the increasing numbers of asylum seekers, the success of right-wing political parties, and the argument favouring the adaptation of the German asylum right to that of other European states all contributed to a proliferation in the call for constitutional reform from within the ruling CDU/CSU. Its coalition partner - the FDP - and the opposition SPD continued in contrast to be strongly opposed to any changes of Article 16 GG. Given that reforms of the constitution in Germany require the approval of two thirds of the votes both in the Bundestag and the Bundesrat, an amendment to this article posed a major challenge: that is, to persuade the minorities in both chambers of the necessity and reasonableness of this reform. In 1989, such a change appeared to be out of reach. Notwithstanding significant increases in the number of asylum seekers in the early 1990s - as well as other changes linked to exogenous factors such as the opening up of the Eastern Bloc and the outbreak of war in the former Yugoslavia or the endogenous problems linked to German unification - it is shown that European cooperation played a crucial role in the realisation of this 1993 constitutional reform. In the course of policy discourse, the gradual redefinition of asylum reform from a purely domestic problem into a requirement of European integration can be observed in parallel with the gradual erosion of FDP/SPD opposition to this constitutional reform. This Europeanisation of the asylum frame was the consequence of two factors: firstly, the advocacy activities of alternating ministers of the interior, whose position was strengthened due to their involvement at the European level; and, secondly, the resonance of the European asylum frame with the domestic discourse, thus leading to a re-definition of the asylum "problem" at home.

The Europeanisation of the discourse arena
With the evolution of European cooperation in asylum and immigration matters, the domestic discourse arena - understood as the institutional framework of deliberation and policy-making - gradually became enmeshed in a multi-level polity that not only created a new level of intergovernmental negotiation, but also altered the position of traditional actors domestically. The strong horizontal and vertical fragmentation of power and competences in the German "semi-sovereign state" (Katzenstein 1987) constituted important institutional barriers to the reform of the constitution. The strong role of the *Länder* is reflected in the fact that a constitutional amendment, such as Article 16 GG, requires the approval of two thirds of the votes in both parliamentary chambers, Bundestag and Bundesrat. Secondly, given that the *Länder* control the administration and the implementation of policies, the federal government often seeks their agreement before actually proposing new legislative acts. This vertical fragmentation is paralleled by the horizontal division of competences and tasks. The leading governmental role in Germany is played by the chancellor, whose outstanding competences have led scholars to speak of a

Kanzlerdemokratie, that is a "chancellor-democracy" in contrast to a parliamentarian or presidential one. However, the structural weakness of the federal cabinet, the strength of sectoral autonomy, and the practice of coalition governments limit the powers of the chancellor. Thirdly, the reform capacity of the German government is constrained by the autonomous and independent Federal Constitutional Court (*Bundesverfassungsgericht*) which, acting as the "guardian" of the constitution, is empowered to review (on appeal) any alleged violations, including legislative acts. Notwithstanding the existing pressure for a change of the asylum law in the early 1990s, European transgovernmental cooperation helped overcoming these veto points by strengthening the position of the proponents of incisive reforms and by providing the normative legitimation for these reforms. Acting as a hinge between the European and the domestic arena, the alternating interior ministers were able to link their own agenda with the moves towards an abolition of internal border controls in the EC.

In Germany, the first Schengen Agreement was prepared by the Federal Chancellery (*Bundeskanzleramt*), in cooperation with the foreign ministry; there it remained, until after the completion of Schengen II, as the responsibility of the former. However, in the course of the intergovernmental negotiations leading up to the second agreement, a gradual shift of influence could be observed away from the Federal Chancellery towards the federal ministry of the interior; the latter formally took over the lead in 1995. The strong influence of this ministry was already present in the first phase of intergovernmental negotiations between 1985 and 1988, during which most of the contents of Schengen II were drafted. This development was partly due to the professional background of the various people in charge of the Schengen negotiations within the Chancellor's Office through this period; they were representatives of the Federal Criminal Office. Furthermore, the interior ministry itself became more and more involved not only at the working group level, but also at the coordinator's level of the Central Group. According to an interview with ministerial representatives, the fact that this position was occupied by the director of the police department within the ministry, as well as the important degree of representation of that this department had at the working group level, acted in favour of a "certain preponderance" of police matters in the Schengen negotiations. As already mentioned in Chapter Three, the homogeneous composition of actors in the Schengen Group, their common professional background, and the limited number of participating member states all favoured the creation of a consensus which allowed the Schengen group to act as a "motor" for European integration in justice and home affairs, as well as presenting them with the opportunity to issue the "blueprints" for parallel cooperation among all member states in the Ad Hoc Group on Immigration.

The enhanced role of the interior ministry ran alongside a shift of emphasis within the Schengen project away from the idea of freedom of movement to an emphasis on control and internal security; this did not fail to cause some tensions to arise between the ministry and the Federal Chancellery. In particular, Chancellor Helmut Kohl was afraid that his project of anticipating the removal of internal borders would be delayed. In the words of an interior ministry representative, the actions of the Federal Chancellery and the interior ministry were guided by different motives: the ideal of freedom of movement and European integration in the case of the former and the maintenance of internal security in the latter's case. The most visible expressions of these differences during the negotiations process were made readily apparent at the Luxemburg Summit in 1991. Chancellor Kohl managed to stupefy both his European counterparts and his domestic negotiators with his proposal to put full Community competence in the fields of asylum and immigration into the framework of the Maastricht Treaty. This proposal not only ran counter to the interests of France and the the United Kingdom in keeping cooperation in these fields intergovernmental, but also antagonised his minister of the interior who, concerned with the preservation of national sovereignty over these sensitive matters, strongly favoured the continuation of existing intergovernmental forms of cooperation. The opposite situation occurred in 1997, in the context of the Amsterdam Treaty, when Chancellor Kohl, contrary to his earlier assertions, then supported the interests of the interior ministry and the *Länder* by opposing the introduction of qualified majority voting in the Council.

The stability of the CDU/CSU and FDP government over the period at hand allowed the German negotiators to pursue clear policy-objectives at the European level and to translate domestic goals into European agreements. This was also true for some of the *Länder*, in particular Bavaria through the then acting minister of the interior, Friedrich Zimmermann, from the Bavarian regional party, the CSU. These actors succeeded in linking the reform of the asylum right with the project for the free movement of persons in the EC right from the beginning. This is documented in a report by the Standing Conference of interior ministries of the *Länder* from 1984; this stated that the abolition of internal border controls made the elaboration of "compensatory measures" for the safeguarding of internal security necessary, including measures in the field of asylum policies.

This important role played by the executive and, in particular, the ministers of the interior found its reflection in the legislative process leading to the constitutional revision in 1993. Although the question of asylum seekers had been on the German political agenda since the late 1970s, the development of European cooperation on this matter and its contents were not communicated to the Bundestag and Bundesrat before the finalisation of the draft Second Schengen Agreement in 1989. Still, the full contents of the Schengen and Dublin Conventions, their importance with regard to immigration and asylum, as well as the progress of cooperation in the framework of the Maastricht Treaty and the 1992 London Resolutions, did not become salient until the ratification debates for the Schengen Agreement took place in 1992.

Whereas the debates among the parliamentary groups and the parties were separated from the intergovernmental discourse for some time, contacts were established at a bilateral and horizontal level among deputies of the German Bundestag and members of the French Senate. These contacts took place in the context of a French Senate initiative to increase transparency and the flow of information on the Schengen Agreement to the domestic legislature in 1991. According to a report on these bilateral consultations from December 1991, some conservative German deputies explicitly expressed the wish that France might exert pressure on Germany in order to make it restrict its constitutional asylum law (Sénat 1991).

The Europeanisation of the asylum frame
This section addresses the question of how far the evolution of cooperation at the European level and the adoption of common "European" asylum policies impacted on the factual and normative development of the asylum discourse in Germany. As has already been argued, the thematisation of asylum seekers and the quest for a reform of the asylum right had already emerged in the mid-1970s and became increasingly politicised at the end of the 1980s. Across political parties, an increasing support for a comprehensive re-organisation of the asylum procedure could be observed. An amendment to the constitutional asylum right, however, as the CSU and a growing segment of the CDU were calling for, seemed out of reach. It conflicted with the strong normative value that Article 16 GG had, as it symbolised the dissociation and the moral consciousness of the "new" Federal Republic vis-à-vis the horrors of national socialism (see Chapter Two). This call encountered strong opposition not only from the SPD, but also from the coalition partner - the FDP - and parts of the CDU. Notwithstanding the dramatic multiplication of refugee and immigration flows in the early 1990s, and the outbreak of xenophobic attacks against asylum seekers and foreigners in various parts of Germany, [1] the argument of a "European need" to adapt German asylum policy to the perceived lower standards of other member states and to build a common European

approach offered the normative basis on which a compromise between the proponents and the original opponents of a constitutional reform was reached. This was due to the fact that, throughout the controversies, the wish to establish a common European asylum policy was shared across the political spectrum. The critical issue behind this apparent consensus, however, was the question of whether a revision of the constitution was a necessary pre-requisite for European cooperation and harmonisation, as sustained by influential members of the CDU/CSU, or - only if strictly necessary - an eventual consequence of a future comprehensive harmonisation, as was being maintained by the SPD and FDP.

The argument that European integration and, in particular, the Single Market project would make an amendment to Article 16 GG unavoidable had already emerged in the mid-1980s and was again being put forward by the same actors who, for domestic reasons, were calling for a revision of the constitution. The most fervent proponents of this line of argument were the respective ministers of the interior: first Friedrich Zimmermann (CSU), then from April 1989 onwards Wolfgang Schäuble (CDU), and from November 1991 Rudolf Seiters (CDU). These controversies reached their peak in the context of Schengen's ratification in early 1992 and evolved in parallel with the reform of the asylum procedure law, designed to relieve pressure on the asylum system. Whereas the SPD and FDP saw this reform as a means of avoiding a constitutional amendment, the CDU/CSU upheld their calls for a reform of Article 16 GG. In fact, a preliminary consensus on the European "need" to amend this article had already been reached before the new asylum procedure law could enter into force in June 1992.

While the CDU's position concerning the consequences of European harmonisation for the individual asylum right was not yet fully clear at the end of 1991,[2] it became more assertive after Chancellor Kohl's attempt to enshrine a common European asylum policy in the Maastricht Treaty failed. From that moment forward, the CDU/CSU went on to argue that, even in the absence of such a common policy, the ratification and implementation of the Schengen Agreement had already made a reform of Article 16 GG inevitable. This change in argument significantly weakened the opposition of the FDP and SPD. This was particularly true for the FPD which in 1987 had already agreed to adapt the individual asylum right to common European standards if this was required by a common European asylum policy. Its first reaction to this new CDU/CSU argument in early 1992 was to deny vehemently that the intergovernmental agreements presupposed constitutional reform. In particular, justice minister Klaus Kinkel (FDP) accused his coalition partner of violating the coalition agreement which provided that comprehensive European harmonisation should precede any constitutional change (SZ 8.1.1992 and FAZ of

8.1.1992). This position began to change once the CDU/CSU and in particular Schäuble, the former interior minister and acting chairman of the CDU/CSU parliamentary group, threatened to block ratifying the Schengen Agreement if the FDP and SPD did not agree to an amendment of Article 16 GG (Schäuble in FAZ of 18.4.1992). This politically highly sensitive threat gained additional momentum through Schäuble's successful proposition to link the debate on ratifying the Schengen Agreement with a CDU/CSU motion for a revision of Article 16 GG (BTDrs 12/2453 of 23.4.1992).

The debate on the ratification of the Schengen Agreement and the motion of the CDU/CSU, which took place on 30.4.1992, is crucial in understanding the ideational impact of Europeanisation on the domestic asylum discourse (BT PlPr 12/89). It also marks the beginning of the movement towards persuading the SPD and FDP of the need for a constitutional amendment. On the one hand, traditional domestic "problems" - such as the abuse of asylum procedures, civil war refugees, social and economic strains - were thrust into the background. On the other, the question of an amendment to Article 16 GG was redefined into a debate on the commitment to European integration and support for a common European asylum policy. This shift consisted of a superimposition of the domestic asylum "problem" at the factual level with a hypothetical situation in the European single market. At the normative level, it signified the subordination of the moral value of Article 16 GG to the overarching norm of European unity. In his introductory speech, interior minister Seiters adopted a very similar line of argument to the one developed at the European level and presented the issue of concern as a "challenge" resulting from an "area without internal borders" in Europe (ibid.: 7297 ff.). Invoking the threats for "internal peace" in Germany and the Union posed by international organised crime, illegal immigration, drugs trafficking, and the "ever swelling stream of refugees and asylum seekers", Seiters called for the creation of a "European security union" and, as part of that process, a common European asylum policy. This would presuppose an amendment to Article 16 GG. This amendment was presented not only as a requirement, but also as a precondition for the ratification of Schengen and for further European harmonisation. Without this amendment, Germany would be the "loser" of European cooperation, the *"Reserveasylland"*, which, because of its liberal asylum law, would be compelled to admit all otherwise rejected asylum seekers. At the end of his speech, Seiters strongly emphasised the normative importance of this decision which, in the case of a failure, would mean a serious hindrance in the process of European integration as a whole and that would impede the realisation of the ideals held by "Adenauer, de Gaulle, Schuman ... [and] de Gasperi".

The same line of argument was also used by Schäuble, chairman of the CDU/CSU parliamentary group and ex-interior minister, who added the point that, at the European level, the goal was a "just distribution of refugees in Europe" (ibid.: 7315).

Reacting to this argument, which not only warned of a possible impediment to European integration, but also presented the implementation of Schengen as a solution to the asylum "problem" at home, the positions of the FDP and SPD began to waver. This was particularly true in the case of the FPD, whose spokesman thanked the CDU/CSU for their initiative and assured them of his parliamentary group's "positive participation" (ibid.: 7320f.). On 16.6.1992, this change was confirmed by the FDP's Executive Board which stated that their party agreed with a constitutional amendment even in the absence of a comprehensive European asylum policy.[3] In contrast, the SPD maintained that they would consider an eventual constitutional amendment only after the adoption of a comprehensive, that is material and procedural, harmonisation of asylum policies in the EU (SZ of 14.5.1992). However, the chairman of the SPD parliamentary group, Klose, was already hinting at the possible participation of his group in a "European solution to the asylum problem" (ibid.: 7300 ff.) - leaving the question open whether this would be possible prior or only after a comprehensive harmonisation (ibid.: 7319).[4]

This trend found its confirmation in the aftermath of the Schengen ratification debate. At the regional level, an agreement between the CDU and SPD in Baden-Württemberg was quickly found in the context of negotiations concerning the building of a grand coalition in early May 1992. At the federal level, this change was expressed in an internal document written by Wartenberg, the internal affairs spokesman of the SPD parliamentary group, in which he appealed to his party in late may 1992 to consider a constitutional reform before there was comprehensive European harmonisation (SPD 1992). This initiative was taken over by the party leadership later that summer. In the so-called "Petersberg Resolution", the party leadership under Engholm decided to support a constitutional amendment which would implement the European asylum "*acquis*" on the condition that a special status was created for civil war refugees and that the means at the disposal of the BAFl were augmented (SZ of 2.8.1992).

This decision provoked a large wave of protests within the SPD which upheld the SPD's traditional values. Although these concerns continued to shape the SPD's position in the parliamentary debates which followed,[5] a decision in favour of a constitutional amendment had already been taken. This was confirmed at an extraordinary SPD party rally in November 1992 (SZ of 18.11.1992). This new position of the SPD formed the basis for the final "asylum-compromise" (*Asylkompromiß*) between the CDU/CSU, the

SPD and the FDP on 6.12.1992, which was translated into a draft bill in January 1993 (BT Drs 12/4152) and adopted by 521 votes to 132 on 26.5.1993.[6]

The French Case: Symbolic Politics or Turnabout?

France's revision of its constitutional asylum right in 1993 differed in two important respects from that of Germany: the immigration discourse had a broader scope and the institutional conditions made a constitutional reform easier. In contrast to Germany, where the aim of restricting the constitutional asylum right had already emerged in the mid-1980s and where it quickly occupied a position of primary concern in the political foreigner discourse, this call emerged unexpectedly in France in 1993 and was nearly exclusively justified by the need to implement the Schengen Agreement. As was indicated in Chapter Two, at the beginning of the 1990s, as well as throughout the 1980s, the major concern in the French political discourse was not refugees, but rather illegal immigration and questions of integration, multiculturalism and citizenship. These questions were directly linked to the national self-understanding and the colonial past. This wide scope of the immigration discourse was fuelled by the traditionally strong ideological cleavage between the Left, with its commitment to internationalism and solidarity, and the Right, which traditionally focuses on the "national" interest (see Weil 1995a: 216). These identities of the traditional political parties came increasingly under pressure with the growth of the extremist National Front (FN),[7] which developed into the "ideological reference point" of the established political parties (Mény 1996: 111). This went hand in hand with a "move to the right" by the RPR and the disorientation of the Centre (ibid; Schain 1996). Frequent changes in the governing majorities between 1980 and 1993 were accompanied by unrelenting partisan debates over the issue of immigration, as the Right tried to attract its full right-wing electoral potential and the Left trying to mobilise French citizens of foreign origin, the *boeurs*. Despite these debates, the electoral programmes of the RPR and PS increasingly converged in the 1980s, combining a strong emphasis on the repression of illegal immigration with a – in the case of the PS stronger – promotion of integration among immigrants already resident in the country. The issue of asylum seekers was, however, not at the top of the political agenda (see Chapter Two).

   Secondly, France's highly centralised "statist" political structure made the adoption of fundamental reforms easier than was the case in Germany's interlocked polity. Basically, the constitutional amendment of 1993 depended on attaining the consent of both the Prime Minister and the

President. This condition was however complicated through the presence of a political "cohabitation" between a conservative government, under the premiership of Balladur, and the socialist President Mitterrand. In particular the latter's commitment to the protection of human rights and France's understanding of itself as a country of immigration and "terre d'asile" rendered such a reform difficult. Thus, restricting the highly symbolic constitutional asylum right and implementing restrictive European policies posed two major challenges in France: firstly, it required a modification of the original foreigner discourse, implying the construction of an asylum "problem"; and, secondly, the political leadership had to be persuaded.

The following sub-sections analyse the impact of European integration on the French asylum discourse in the period between the ratification of Schengen in June 1991 and the revision of the Constitution in December 1993. This time period can be divided in two phases: a first phase between 1991 and early 1993 under the socialist government and a second phase after the coming into power of an RPR/UDF coalition in March 1993 culminating in the constitutional debate. The second phase was launched by interior minister Charles Pasqua calling to "reduce immigration to zero" (interview with LM of 2.6.1993) through a comprehensive reform of the French immigration system subsequently known as the "Pasqua laws". These proposed changes included a reform of the nationality code, a law on identity checks, and a new aliens bill that placed heavy restrictions on entry and access to asylum procedures, restricted the social rights of immigrants, and enhanced expulsion measures.[8] As with Germany's reform, this legislation fully implemented the provisions of the Schengen Agreement that Pasqua had actively negotiated during a previous stint as minister of the interior between 1986 and 1988, as well as the London Resolutions. The implementation of these agreements launched a heated and polemical debate on the status of the constitutional asylum right which culminated in a reform of the French Constitution being passed in November 1993.

The Europeanisation of the discourse arena
Similar to the German experience, the progression of intergovernmental cooperation at the European level induced a transformation of the original settings of political deliberation and decision-making in the French polity and strengthened the position of the main advocator of incisive reforms, interior minister Charles Pasqua.

The regulation of constitutional reforms in France gives the political leadership an extraordinarily powerful role as it basically requires agreement between the Prime Minister and the President (Luchaire 1994: 26). According to Article 89-3 of the Constitution, the President takes the initiative for a constitutional revision on a proposition from the Prime

Minister ("*projet*"). This initiative must be approved by the two chambers of parliament and then validated either via a referendum or by the Congress uniting deputies and senators. Another procedure, which has thus far never been applied in France, allows for the possibility of a parliamentary initiative favouring constitutional revision ("*proposition*") which must be approved by referendum (Art. 89-2). Although less powerful than the German Constitutional Court, the French Constitutional Council also played and important role in the reform of the asylum right. This is due to its active interpretation of the Constitution, particularly the Preamble containing the individual liberties, freedoms, and "great principles" of the Republic (Classen 1993). It thus evolved into the executive's "watch dog" and acts as a "guarantor of ... common values" (Mény 1996: 134).[9] In the 1990s, the Constitutional Council significantly clarified the status of the constitutional asylum right in its rulings on the Schengen Agreement and the reform proposals of interior minister Pasqua.

In 1993, two conditions facilitated the passing of a restrictive asylum reform in France: the weak position of the socialist opposition and of Socialist President Mitterrand and the strengthening of the minister of the interior due to Europeanisation. Mitterrand's position was constrained by his personal involvement in the Schengen process, legislative majorities alternating and because of *cohabitation* with a conservative government in the two crucial phases of "Europeanisation"; this happened during the first phase of intergovernmental negotiations between 1986 and 1988 (Prime Minister Chirac), and again in the implementation phase of these negotiations from 1993 to 1995 (Prime Minister Balladur). In both of these periods, the socialist President was constrained in his ability to shape the course of the policy discourse by the necessity to respect the elected majority. This situation was made even more difficult in the second *cohabitation*, during which his political party, the PS, represented only 19.2% of the National Assembly.

Although Mitterrand was responsible for launching the Schengen project, his influence weakened steadily with his lack of involvement in the negotiations leading to Schengen II in 1990. These negotiations, which made the introduction of free movement increasingly contingent on so-called compensatory measures for the safeguarding of internal security, were no longer in his sphere of influence. Instead, they were dominated by the cooperation which existed mainly between representatives of the various interior ministries. In the French ministry of the interior, the leading division was the DLPAJ, the "*Direction des libertés publiques et des affaires juridiques du ministère de l'Intérieur*". The lead of the interior ministry had been facilitated by a 1986 reform of the newly elected RPR government which, upon abolishing the ministry of Immigration created by the previous socialist government, increased its autonomy both at the national and the intergovernmental levels. This favoured the "hard-liner" Charles Pasqua (RPR) in particular; he occupied this ministry in the two crucial phases of intergovernmental negotiations: during the two years leading up to the draft Schengen II Agreement between 1986 and 1988 and during the domestic implementation phase between 1993 and 1995.

This dominant role of the interior ministries in processes at the European level had important repercussions on the domestic polity. Not only did it weaken the role of the President, but it also weakened the positions of other ministries competent in asylum and immigration matters. This was particularly the case for the social ministry, which was nearly completely excluded from the negotiations process. This also holds true for the ministries of foreign and European affairs, which basically operated in the "shadow" of the ministryof the interior (Keraudren 1994: 129). As in Germany, the first Schengen Agreement of 1985 had mainly been prepared by the foreign affairs ministry (see Masson 1991: 106). However, it subsequently lost its imput at the working group level and dealt primarily with diplomatic contacts and coordination without having any real impact on the contents of cooperation. This devaluation of its functions did not fail to create tensions domestically (Bigo 1996: 120; Keraudren 1994: 129; Sénat 1993). These were documented in the Council of ministers when Pasqua presented his draft bill on 2.6.1993. On this occasion, the ministries of justice, foreign and social affairs expressed criticism and introduced several amendments to the bill (MNS 6/1993).

These tensions were also salient at the European level with efforts to introduce a supplementary political level through the creation of the Coordinators' Group in 1989, which aimed at restricting the dominance of the working groups (see Chapter Three). However, the professional background of the officials placed in these newly created positions again reflected the dominant role of the interior ministry. Officially attached to the ministryof foreign affairs, the French representative in the Coordinators' Group was a prefect from the interior ministry, Hubert Blanc. A renewed attempt to find a more balanced distribution of EU competences at the domestic level was made in the context of the Maastricht Treaty establishing the K.4 Committee. The domestic coordination of ministries was taken over by a mission attached to the Prime Minister's office, the General Secretariat of the Inter-ministries Committee for European Economic Cooperation (SCGI), which has the task of coordinating activities and arbitrating at any conflicts that develop among the ministries at the national level. This mission did not weaken the role of the interior ministry. Rather, its position was strengthened since it was again chaired by a prefect - Maccioni - who was also the French representative in the K.4 Committee and the Schengen central group at the European level.

Finally, the position of the interior ministry was strengthened through the lack of communication and information of the Parliament about the development and contents of transgovermental cooperation. The Schengen Agreement of 1990 was only presented to the parliament in June 1991, when the Minster of European Affairs, Elisabeth Guigou, anxious to contain the newly unified Germany, urged its ratification (Sénat 1993). The lack of available information led one senator to assume that there were not five deputies who could locate Schengen on a map of Europe in 1991 (Senator Masson quoted in MNS 6/1991). Given the urgency with which the ratification took place, the deputies did not realise the link that existed between domestic reforms and the European Agreements until it was officially established by interior minister Pasqua in late 1993 (see below). As a result, no debates on the contents of the intergovernmental negotiations took place between 1985 and 1991. Taken by surprise regarding this request to ratify Schengen through an urgency procedure in 1991, the Senate decided to set up a control commission charged with verification of the implementation and functioning of the agreement. The subsequent reports prepared by this commission contributed greatly to the information about the contents and proceedings of the Schengen Agreement (Sénat 1993, 1994). Nevertheless, interior minister Pasqua succeeded in presenting his asylum reforms as a necessary step in the implementation of this agreement, culminating in the reform of the constitutional asylum right in 1993.

The Europeanisation of the asylum frame
As indicated in Chapter Two, the French foreigner discourse in the 1980s and early 1990s differed from the German one in that it was less concerned with asylum seekers in the first place and that it concentrated on the more general questions of ongoing illegal and legal immigration, family reunification, integration, citizenship and multiculturalism. At that time, the adaptations needed in the field of asylum policy were perceived as being minimal. Given the success of the procedural reforms in 1989 and the decreasing numbers of refugees, neither the discourse of the ruling PS nor of the majority of those in the opposition RPR and UDF indicated any intention to introduce major changes to French asylum policies. This interpretation finds support in the debates surrounding Schengen's implementation in the summer of 1991 and the subsequent debates on the first application law, modifying the bill on the entry and stay of foreigners, which introduced carrier sanctions and legalised the administrative practice in transit zones. These debates focused primarily on the divide between

pro-Europeanists and Euro-pessimists. While the socialists saw Schengen's implementation as a contribution to the "European construction, to which the government is profoundly committed",[10] the conservative RPR and the communist PC, although from different perspectives, feared an "abandon of sovereignty" in an "*Europe passoire*".[11]

The concerns with sovereignty and border controls in the Schengen debates of the early 1990s related to the problems of drug trafficking and illegal immigration; the category of "bogus" asylum seekers was only very rarely explicitly subsumed under this category.[12] On the contrary, the main arguments on asylum seekers centred on the issue of how to avoid negative effects arising from the proposed regulations (carrier sanctions and transit zones) on the asylum right and access to asylum procedures in France. Across the political spectrum, strong concerns were expressed on the safeguarding of the generous asylum right as a core republican value.[13] This concern is not only reflected in Prime Minister Edith Cresson's consultation of the Constitutional Council on the conformity of the proposed bill with the constitutional asylum right, which was supported by the socialist deputies and senators. It is also reflected in an initiative issued by a group of RPR and UDF deputies after the ratification of Schengen, when they submitted the ratification law to the Constitutional Council with a request to establish its constitutional conformity. Basing their arguments on earlier rulings of the Council on European agreements, the group argued that Schengen undermined national sovereignty in the following regards: it violated the functioning of the institutions of the Fifth Republic and threatened the continuity of the life of the nation, the warrantee of fundamental liberties, and the exercise of refugee protection. With regard to the latter the deputies claimed that the provisions did not contain enough guarantees regarding the criteria for determining which state was responsible for examining a request and that it was not sure that all asylum applications would be examined effectively (Oellers Frahm/Zimmermann 1996: 258). This initiative, which expressed conservative concerns with the loss of sovereignty, was accompanied by the creation of a control commission in the Senate. This commission was charged with supervising the implementation of the Schengen Agreement in order to prevent any negative effects, particularly with regard to immigration and drugs, and with the increase of democratic control over the intergovernmental agreement (Sénat 1991).

The Constitutional Council's ruling, released on 25.7.1991, established that the Schengen Agreement was in conformity with the French Constitution. All points presented by the deputies were rejected. With regard to asylum, the Council added a material aspect to the originally purely procedural question put down by the deputies: namely, the conformity of Schengen with the constitutional asylum right. Referring to the redistributive rule of Article 29 SA, according to which only one country shall be responsible for examining an asylum claim, the Council argued that the rejection of an asylum seeker without an examination of his or her claim was in accordance with the constitutional asylum right of §4 Preamble. The Council explicitly referred to the exception clause in Article 29 IV SA, which preserves the right for every contracting party to examine a claim even if it is not responsible under the provisions of the Agreement.[14]

The link between Schengen and the reform of the asylum right only entered the policy discourse with the debates on the "Pasqua laws" in 1993. These controversies started with the confidential advice issued by the Council of State on the draft bill on the entry and stay of foreigners. This advice recommended limiting the proposed extension of the competences of the police and the interior ministry in the pre-screening of asylum claims (LM of 27.5.1993). A few days later, the Consultative Commission on Human Rights published a very critical report in which it confirmed several concerns which had been previously expressed by human rights associations (LM of 27.5.1993 and LM of 3.6.1993). Condemning the "spirit" of the proposed reforms, the Commission stated that they represented "a serious retrogression in the protection of fundamental human rights" and that they "compromised the exercise of the asylum right, in contradiction of Article 14 of the Universal Declaration of Human Rights, by subjecting it to the discretionary judgement of the administrative authority" (Commission Consultative 1994: 379). On the same day, the Union of Magistrates (USM) issued a communication in which it regretted not having been consulted on the proposed measures. It declared that it opposed "any uncontrolled transfer of competences to the advantage of the administration or the police" because "it is the judicial authority which, according to the Constitution, guarantees individual liberties" (quoted in LM of 6-7.6.1993).

In the parliamentary debates, the controversies on the asylum right reached their peak after the ruling of the Constitutional Council, which, in the longest decision that it has ever rendered, censured 8 of the 51 articles in the draft bill.[15] Iterating its position in the 1991 ruling on the conformity of the Schengen Agreement, the court recognised the existence of a fundamental right to asylum based on §4 of the Preamble to the Constitution - guaranteeing every asylum seeker access to an asylum procedure in France - that would prohibit their direct expulsion on the basis of the responsibility rule in the European agreements or the safe third country notion.

Reacting to this ruling, interior minister Pasqua immediately called for a constitutional reform. In justifying this call, Pasqua adopted the same line of reasoning which had characterised the German asylum reform just a few months before; he claimed that, with this ruling, "the Schengen Convention becomes inapplicable. One cannot abolish border controls without this compensatory measure" (Pasqua quoted in LM of 17.6.1993). Referring to the high numbers of asylum seekers in Germany, he depicted the risk of a considerable augmentation in asylum claims in France threatening "French preoccupations in the field of security" (ibid.). From that moment on, reforms of the asylum right were presented as the application of the Schengen Agreement and, by that, were increaslingly separated from the factual situation of asylum seekers in France.

The debates on the constitutional revision document the adoption of this line of reasoning by most members of the ruling coalition. Without a constitutional amendment, France would be hindered in participating in the system of redistribution for the handling of asylum claims and would have to examine the claims of "all otherwise rejected asylum seekers".[16] These debates shifted away from the strictly domestic "problems" to a potential situation in the European territory and reframed the role of France from that of being an example in Europe to that of a victim of integration.[17] In contrast to the debates in 1991, when the PS emphasised that the French asylum right and republican tradition should be a "model for the European construction"[18] and that despite the problem of large scale migrations, "one has to maintain this formidable capacity of France to be a "lighthouse" for those who believe in freedom and our values",[19] European integration was now seen as compelling a limitation of the liberal tradition. In this scenario, one of the most frequent justifications for reform was made with reference to the German situation and the potential risk emanating from the "more than 500,000 asylum seekers" in that country, who, after reform of the German constitutional asylum right, threatened to enter France.[20] These references to a hypothetical number of asylum seekers in Europe and to the German reforms document the perception of the situation of interdependence as being one of negative redistribution, a situation in which the "burden" of asylum seekers would necessarily be shifted to those states with more generous regulations; thereby, it legitimised a restrictive harmonisation of asylum laws.

In this re-configuration of the territorial entity, the main concern of the French debate remained the safeguarding of state sovereignty. While the traditional resentments of the RPR towards the Schengen Agreement were appeased by an emerging consensus on the need to adopt a common European approach to the asylum "problem", the concern with state sovereignty was redirected against the Constitutional Council for its "interference" in political affairs.[21] These concerns where also dominant in the Congressional debates on the constitutional revision. Immediately after affirming that "European cooperation represents the only realist way"[22] to cope with the pressure of immigration, Prime Minister Balladur engaged in a serious critique of the Constitutional Council's unilateral extension of its jurisdictional scope to include the general principles of the Preamble which were "sometimes more philosophical and political than juridical, sometimes contradictory and, in addition, conceived at very different epochs than ours" (ibid.). Towards the end of 1993, the asylum reform became increasingly part of a larger debate over the institutions of the Republic which did not limit itself to the powers of the Constitutional Council, but extended it to debate the competences of the President and the Council of State. With regard to the President, this concerned the question as to whether constitutional revision through a referendum according to Article 89-2 Constitution would require his consent, as Mitterrand maintained, or not (LM of 5-6.9.1993).

In an attempt to decouple the question of an amendment to the constitutional asylum right away from the polemics of the foreigner discourse, Prime Minister Balladur and President Mitterrand sought to present the issue from a formal and unemotional point of view. Their decision to refer the question on the need for a constitutional revision to the highest administrative court, the Council of State, demonstrates their wish to give an "objective" appearance to the debate and to detach it from political considerations. After the court had confirmed the need to revise the French Constitution in order to participate fully in Schengen, both the political leaders[23] and the participants in the parliamentary debates underlined the technical character and limited reach of the reform. This argument in fact represented the compromise reached between critics of the constitutional reform inside the ruling UDF/RPR political parties, the President, and the government. This consisted in preserving France's traditional identity as a "terre d'asile", while opening the way for European cooperation based on mutual trust in a community of values and the existence of identical commitments in the "sphère européenne".[24] In the end, the provisions of the Pasqua law which had been censured by the Constitutional Council, were adopted without any great controversy on 26.11.1993, only five days after Congress adopted the Constitutional revision.

The Implementation of European Provisions

In France and Germany, two countries which "granted a nearly identically formulated fundamental right of asylum" (Oellers-Frahm/Zimmermann 1996: 249), the implementation of the EU "*acquis*" in asylum matters, in particular the 1990 Schengen/Dublin Agreements and 1992 London Resolutions, yielded a radical transformation of the post-World War II refugee regimes; this found its most symbolic expression in the constitutional revisions. This transformation concerns a crucial aspect of the refugee regimes, namely the provisions related to entry into the territory and access to asylum provisions. The European texts do not, however, affect material asylum law; the normal recognition procedure and the criteria for recognising an asylum seeker as a refugee remain within the full competence of the individual member states.

The changes introduced to domestic asylum policies can be divided into two categories: firstly, policies limiting access to the territory and the asylum procedures; and, secondly, "simplified procedures" for certain categories of asylum seekers.

Access to the Asylum Regimes

The Schengen/Dublin Agreements and London Resolutions contain three instruments inhibiting the access of asylum seekers to asylum regimes in the member states: visa-policies, carrier sanctions, and non-admission to the asylum procedure on the basis of the Schengen/Dublin system and the "safe third country rule".

Visa policies
The Schengen Agreement stipulates that third country nationals who want to enter the common territory must be in possession of valid travel documents, a visa where applicable, as well as sufficient means of subsistence which also covers return travel to the place from which they have come. Furthermore, the Schengen states have agreed to harmonise their visa policies (Art. 20 SA) and have established a list of 133 states whose citizens need a visa to enter a Schengen state. With Schengen's introduction into the EU Treaty, the JHA Council translated this list into a regulation, based on Article 100c EC (adopted on 12.3.1999). This list includes all of the countries from which the majority of asylum seekers originate. In addition, the EU member states retain the right to require visas from countries other than those on the common list. While this harmonisation and the introduction of a common visa can be a good thing

for tourists, since it opens access to all of the member states, it is of course a constraint for asylum-seekers, since the state which issues the visa is the only state responsible for examining that particular case; in the case of a state denying the issue of a visa, the applicant will not have access to another member state either.

While *de jure*, the absence of a valid visa does not exclude access to an asylum procedure as such,[25] it can be reason for the application of a simplified procedure under the heading of "manifestly unfounded" claims (see below) which then limits the rights of the applicant. In addition, visa requirements inhibit the flight and freedom of movement of the persons concerned on their way to a country of refuge. Given the overarching motive of reducing the entry of third-country nationals, the Schengen Executive Committee follows a restrictive policy and embassies are instructed to limit the numbers of visas issued. The decision to grant or deny a visa is a discretionary administrative act; it is not requested to explain its decision and no legal remedies are possible. As a consequence, the application of visa requirements becomes one of the first obstacle in the search for protection and, thus, the embassies of the member states have been conferred with a sort of pre-screening function, in which the granting or denial of a visa can determine at an early stage the chances that an asylum seeker has in finding protection (Hathaway 1993: 723).

In *Germany*, the imposition of visa requirements on major refugee producing countries had already begun in 1980 as a means of reducing the attractiveness of Germany as an asylum country. The list of countries with a visa obligation was steadily enlarged and today accounts for all of the countries on the common list (MNS 7/1998). In *France*, the application of visa requirements towards refugee producing countries began in 1986 with the unilateral suspension of bilateral agreements on the free movement of persons and the introduction of visa requirements.[26] In the 1990s, French visa policies were increasingly adapted to the Schengen list (see EP 2000).

Carrier sanctions

Apart from stipulating the conditions for crossing the external border, Schengen also provides for sanctions on carriers which enable the entry of third country nationals who do not possess the required documents, including visas (Art. 26 SA). Apart from returning the alien to his or her place of provenience, the member states have also agreed to impose fines on the airway/shipping/rail/road company which thus carries "undocumented" migrants.

In *Germany*, this obligation on carriers to check the travel and identity documents if its passengers and to return undesired aliens at their own cost was already an administrative practice by the early 1980s (Münch 1992:

84). Monetary sanctions were then introduced in 1987.[27] In *France* their introduction was linked to the implementation of the Schengen Agreement in domestic legislation and was achieved through the law of 26.2.1992. According to the new Article 20 *bis*, introduced into the ordinance of 2.11.1945 on the entry and stay of foreigners, the minister of the interior is authorised to impose a fine of 10,000 F on transport companies. Contrary to Germany and to most other EU countries, the socialist government introduced certain safeguards with respect to refugees into this article, namely the suspension of a fine if the asylum seeker is finally admitted onto the territory, if that person's claim has not been rejected as "manifestly unfounded", if the transport agency can establish that it did check the documents, or finally if these documents are not "manifestly forged" (Castagnos-Sen 1996: 86).

Non-admission
The heart of the common European asylum policy is in determining the *responsibility* of only one member state for the examination of an asylum claim (Art. 29 III SA; Art. 3 II DC). The other states agree to send an applicant back without examination of his or her claim to the country responsible under the criteria enumerated in the Schengen/Dublin Agreements. Originally limited to the EU member states, this responsibility rule was later extended to all "safe third countries" according to the 1992 London Resolution.

The implementation of these redistributive rules faced major obstacles in Germany and France because of the presence of a subjective asylum right in the national constitutions prohibiting the return of asylum seekers without their claim being examined. In both countries, this led to a limitation of the constitutional asylum right, although the necessity and appropriateness of a constitutional revision or the possibility of applying the redistributive rule via a simple legislative revision was strongly contested. In *Germany*, the redistributive rule of the Schengen/Dublin Agreements and the notion of "safe third countries" were implemented in the law amending the constitutional asylum together with the new Asylum Procedure Act of June 1993.[28] According to §18II of the new Asylum Procedure Act, asylum seekers who present themselves at the border can be denied entry and herewith access to an asylum procedure by the Federal Border Guards (*Bundesgrenzschutz*) if he or she

- comes from a safe third country (§ 26a, see below);
- comes from another safe country where he or she stayed for a specified period and may have found already protection (§27 I or II); or

- if the alien poses a threat to the general public.

As a general rule, persons to whom one of these non-admission grounds apply must be sent back immediately to a "safe third country". According to Article 16a II (3) GG in connection with §34a II Asylum Procedure Act, the courts are explicitly prohibited from granting any suspensive effect to appeals against returns to "safe third countries". An exception to the immediate return of asylum seekers at the border on safe third country grounds is established in §18 (3) of the Asylum Procedure Act; that is, in such cases, where Germany is considered responsible for examining an asylum request on the basis of international agreements (for example, the Schengen or Dublin Agreements) or where the ministry of the interior ordered entry for international or humanitarian reasons.[29]

The application of this rule and the immediate return of asylum seekers at the border to non-EU member states made the conclusion of readmission agreements with the "safe third countries" concerned necessary. This derives from the fact, that under international law, states are only obliged to take back their own citizens, but not third country nationals. Although often not mentioned explicitly in the agreements, they provide the legal basis for the rejection of asylum seekers whose application has not yet been examined on the grounds of the "safe third country" rule (see below, section 4.3).

If the applicant has succeeded in entering Germany, he or she is lodged in a retention centre and may claim political asylum before the competent status determination office, the BAFl. According to Article 16a II of the German Constitution, the BAFl can deny this person access to the asylum procedure if he or she

> "enters the country from a member state of the European Union or another third country where the application of the Convention relating to the Status of Refugees and the European Convention for the Protection of Human Rights and Fundamental Freedoms is assured."

Accordingly, safe third countries are the EU member states and other countries that fulfil the above mentioned conditions as specified by legislation requiring the consent of the Bundesrat. The "safe third country rule" also applies to cases where the applicant has been merely in transit through the third country. The duration of that person's stay is not taken into consideration; what counts is that an application for asylum should have been made at the first possible opportunity. In such cases, measures terminating the person's sojourn may be carried out irrespective of any other remedy sought by the person concerned. The "safe third country" rule is further specified in § 29a of the Asylum Procedure Act. According to current legislation, the following countries, apart from the members of the EU, have been declared as "safe": Norway, Poland, Switzerland, and the Czech Republic; that is all of the countries that have land borders with Germany. Thus, de jure, only an applicant arriving by air directly from a country of persecution may lodge an asylum application according to Article 16a GG "Politically persecuted persons shall enjoy asylum".

In *France*, the redistributive clauses of the Schengen/Dublin Agreements and the "safe third country rule" were introduced with the "Pasqua Law" (law no. 93-1417), together with the new Article 53 in the Constitution (law no. 93-1256). For the first time in France's history, the Pasqua Law introduced the provisions on the admission of asylum seekers into the general legislation concerning the entry and stay of aliens and not into the specific legislation regulating the asylum procedure with the OFPRA and the recognition of refugees.[30] The possibility of rejecting an asylum seeker prior to the examination of this claim by the competent authorities - the OFPRA, the CRR, and the courts - was introduced both in the procedure applying at the border and in that applying inside the country (see Chapter Two).

In both cases, applicants must be denied access to the asylum procedure if another state is responsible in accordance with the Schengen/Dublin Agreements. If the application is made at the border,[31] which concerns only 2-4% of all applications in France (see Brachet 1997: 12), the minister of the interior, after consultation with the minister of foreign affairs, may deny entry and thus access to the OFPRA in four cases:

- if the applicant falls under the responsibility of another member state according to the Schengen and Dublin Agreements;
- if the application is manifestly unfounded;
- if the applicant represents a threat to public order, for instance if he or she figures on the list of undesired aliens of the Schengen Information System; or
- if the applicant has passed through a third country in which he or she can effectively be readmitted.

These four grounds for rejection are not enumerated in the law but constitute the administrative practice of the border officials; basically, these officials are the DICCILEC ("Direction centrale du contrôle de l'immigration et de la lutte contre l'emploi des clandestins"), established as part of the interior ministry by Pasqua in 1994, and the DAF (Division Asile aux Frontières), which in turn depends on the Foreign ministry.[32]

During the examination period on whether one of these four exclusion grounds applies, the applicants, like other voluntary migrants, have to be detained in so-called waiting zones.[33] Decisions regarding their maintenance in waiting zones is taken by the head of the border police or a deputy. Retention centres have been established at airports, ports and, since 1994, also railway stations with international traffic. Pending admission to the territory, the asylum seekers have no access to the agency responsible for examining their case, the OFPRA. Lawyers and human rights associations face difficulties in contacting asylum seekers in waiting zones: strict authorisations for access by the UNHCR and NGOs were only introduced in 1995 and can be withdrawn at any time by the minister of the interior.[34] If the request is considered manifestly unfounded, the applicant is denied entry into the territory; legal remedies are possible through the administrative tribunal, but they have no suspensive effect. If none of the exclusion grounds apply, the asylum seeker is referred to the prefectures, where the more common asylum procedure for applications inside the country applies.

Applications inside the territory were regulated in the new Chapter VII inserted by the Pasqua Law of 1993 in the ordinance of 2.11.1942 entitled "On Asylum Seekers".[35] Up to this time, asylum seekers could immediately present their claim to the OFPRA, but this reform made access to an asylum procedure conditional on the accordance of a provisional admission permit by the prefectures, the local branch of the interior ministry. According to Article 31*bis*, provisional admission could be denied by the prefect:

- if the applicant falls under the responsibility of another member state according to the Schengen and Dublin Agreements;
- if the applicant can effectively be admitted to a third country in which he or she can effectively be protected, in particular against refoulement - this provision was altered by the 1998 reform, see below;
- if the presence of the applicant in France represents a serious threat to public order; or
- if the asylum claim is based on deliberate fraud, is abusive or is presented only in view of impeding an imminent expulsion.

The existence of the first criteria, the responsibility of another member state according to the Schengen and Dublin Agreements, excludes access to the asylum procedure and the applicant is returned to the responsible state without the possibility of calling the OFPRA. This procedure is regulated in a *circulaire* of 21.3.1995. Accordingly, the prefect first consults the list of undesirable persons in the Schengen Information System (SIS), then determines the responsible country, contacts the latter, and finally transfers the asylum seeker to that country. Legal remedies against expulsion are possible, however they have no suspensive effect and any claim would thus have to be made from outside the territory. The other three criteria do not prevent access to OFPRA, but the request will only then be examined in an accelerated procedure.

Simplified Procedures

The introduction of simplified procedures for certain categories of asylum seekers corresponds to the implementation of the formally non-binding London Resolutions of 1992. As already indicated in the previous sub-section, Germany and France differ with regard to their implementation of the safe third country rule: while in Germany the possibility of returning an asylum seeker to a "safe third country" excludes access to the asylum procedure, in France it does not lead to an automatic return if the application is lodged inside the territory, which is where the vast majority of applications are presented in France. This sub-section concerns the application of simplified procedures in "manifestly unfounded" cases and with regard to the rule of "safe countries of origin".

In *Germany*, simplified procedures have been introduced both for "manifestly unfounded" cases and for persons originating from countries considered as "safe". According to §30(3) Asylum Procedure Act, applications may be rejected as "manifestly unfounded" under a shortened and accelerated asylum procedure, if:

- essential points of an alien's claim are unsubstantiated, if the claim is contradictory or if it is based on forged or false evidence;
- an alien gives false information about his identity or nationality or refuses to provide such information in asylum proceedings; or
- an applicant for asylum flagrantly fails to comply with the obligations to cooperate in asylum proceedings, unless he or she is not answerable for this.

If the BAFl rejects an asylum application on one or several of these grounds, the applicant must leave the country within a week. He or she can apply within one week to the administrative court for provisional legal protection and, as a rule, a decision must be taken within a week. In interlocutory legal protection proceedings, the administrative court may set aside the expulsion only where there are serious doubts regarding the legality of the decision. In contrast with these simplified procedures, the "full" or traditional asylum procedure contained the full range of legal remedies foreseen in the German judicial system, including two administrative and one constitutional instance of revision.

Simplified procedures have also been introduced for applicants from "safe countries of origin". According to Article 16a III GG and §29a Asylum Procedure Act, an application made by a person from a "safe country of origin" must be refused as manifestly unfounded unless the alien can prove the assumption that, despite the general situation in the country of origin, he or she is in danger of political persecution (refutable presumption). The legislator may determine a country of origin as "safe" when, on the basis of the legal situation, the application of the law, and the general political circumstances, it seems safe to assume that neither political persecution nor inhuman or degrading punishment or treatment are practised.[36] Currently, the following countries are designated as "safe countries of origin": Bulgaria, the Czech Republic, Ghana, Hungary, Poland, Romania, Senegal, and the Slovak Republic.

A special accelerated procedure has been set up for applicants coming from "safe countries of origin" arriving at airports (§18a Asylum Procedure Act). This procedure also applies to applicants who have no valid passport. Accordingly, these persons have to be kept in a special transit area at the airport until their case is decided by the BAFl. While the asylum proceedings are in progress, the applicants are not allowed to leave the transit area to enter the national territory. In the case of rejection by the BAFl, the applicants may apply for provisional legal protection within three days. As a rule, the decision by the administrative court should be taken within fourteen days.

Similar to the "safe third country" rule, the efficient implementation of the notion of "safe countries of origin" also requires the cooperation of the countries at stake. This cooperation was ensured through a second category of readmission agreements which only apply to the nationals of the signatory parties; these shall enable their swift return to their countries of origin (see below).

In *France*, the London Resolution on manifestly unfounded asylum claims was translated into accelerated procedures for asylum seekers representing a threat to the public order and fraudulent or abusive asylum claims (points 3 and 4 of the above mentioned Art. 31*bis*). In these cases, the prefect may impose an expulsion order without delay; however, the prefect must await the decision of the OFPRA for its execution. Under these conditions, asylum seekers are usually detained in administrative retention centres and are obliged to present their application to the OFPRA "immediately" (interior ministry circular of 8.2.1994). This means that it is very difficult in practice for these candidates to gather the necessary documents, to find legal counselling, or to find an interpreter in order to prepare an orderly application. As far as the procedure within the OFPRA is concerned, these cases do not require a personal interview with the candidate and a negative decision allows for the immediate execution of the expulsion order. Appeals can be lodged with the CRR, but they have no suspensive effect and have to be made from outside the territory. This contrasts with the "full" normal procedure which contains a preliminary right to stay in the territory until the definitive decision on an application - including an examination by the OFPRA, the CRR, and in some cases the Council of State - has been taken.

Although the question of asylum seekers in provenance from so-called "safe countries of origin" in accordance with the 1992 London Conclusions is not addressed in the law, accelerated procedures have been adopted by the OFPRA which effectively implement these Conclusions. If an applicant comes from a country in which no serious human rights violations are reported, the OFPRA may renounce the personal interview stage and simplify the examination of the case (Amnesty International/France Terre d'Asile 1997: 36f).

Summary: Towards Convergent Asylum Regimes?

The 1993 reforms of the asylum law in Germany and France reveal a high degree of convergence and document the implementation of the relevant provisions of the Schengen/Dublin Agreements and the London Resolutions. Both reforms formally maintain the constitutional asylum right. Article 16a I GG still reads: "Politically persecuted persons shall enjoy asylum"; this is as formulated by the founders of the Grundgesetz. In France, §4 of the Preamble was not amended and still reads: "Everyone persecuted because of his actions on behalf of liberty has the right of asylum in the territories of the Republic". However, the 1993 reforms introduced significant limitations on this right which grant the respective states extended possibilities in averting refugee flows. In short, these changes include instruments limiting access to asylum procedures, as well as simplified procedures for certain categories of asylum seekers, allowing for a quicker return of rejected asylum seekers to their countries of origin or to other third countries. The effects of these new instruments on the system of refugee protection have been three-fold: (1) asylum policies have moved closer to the field of immigration control and asylum seekers have been increasingly subsumed under instruments aimed at the fight against illegal immigration; (2) the impact of the executive and particularly the interior ministry on the asylum system has been strengthened *vis-à-vis* the traditional agencies in charge of the asylum procedure; and (3) the impact of the judiciary on the asylum procedure has been weakened.

Originally exempted from the instruments of immigration control aimed at limiting the entries of voluntary migrants, asylum seekers have increasingly been subjected to these instruments in both countries; this includes visa requirements, as well as more generally for the identity documents in the absence of which an asylum request may be considered "manifestly unfounded". The application of these instruments, which were originally conceived for voluntary migrants, has been enforced by the introduction of sanctions on carriers enabling the entry of asylum seekers who do not fulfil these requirements. Apart from these measures of pre-entry control, the redistributive system of the Schengen/Dublin Agreements and the "safe third country" rule also conceive of the question of refugee protection as an issue of border control. The Schengen Agreement, which provided the blueprint for the more limited Dublin Convention, is not focused on asylum seekers and most provisions apply to (illegal) immigrants and refugees alike. The same is true for the readmission agreements applying the "safe third country" and "safe country of origin" rules concluded by Germany, which do not explicitly discriminate between the return of asylum seekers, whose claim has not been examined on substantive grounds, and illegal immigrants (see below).

These instruments of direct rejection at the border and the increased powers of the administration before admission to the asylum procedure establish a sort of pre-screening procedure outside of the formal asylum system which significantly strengthens the role of the executive. In addition, the introduction of carrier sanctions shifts the liabilities onto the shoulders of private transport companies who are neither skilled in nor accountable for screening genuine from bogus refugees.

Finally, the introduction of simplified procedures lead to a downgrading of legal and procedural safeguards in estimating the validity of claims and limit the impact of the judiciary. If legal remedies are foreseen, they have no suspensive effect, so that counter-claims have to be made from outside the country, thus making a successful conclusion highly improbable. The weakening of the judiciary has been further helped by the formalised use of so-called "extraterritorial" waiting-zones at airports and other borders which, by definition, are excluded from the domestic legal system. The strongest manifestation of this weakening of the judiciary has been illustrated in the political processes leading to the constitutional revisions. Both the French and the German governments actively supported the establishment of a redistributive system for the handling of asylum claims, through the Schengen and Dublin Conventions and its extension to other safe third countries, although domestic constitutional constraints guaranteed every asylum seeker access to their procedures. In order to circumvent its sanctioning by the Constitutional Court, the German government preventively changed the constitution. In France, a negative ruling by the Constitutional Council was neutralised ex-post by the constitutional revision of 25.11.1993.

Beyond this convergence, the implementation of the European agreements also indicates important differences which point at the persistence of particular national traditions. The first difference concerns the wordings of the constitutional revisions. On the one hand, both texts, Article 16a GG and Article 53 of the French Constitution, are cautious to maintain the asylum right and contain parallel provisions allowing for the implementation of the European agreements. On the other, the French revision also expresses typical French concern with the safeguarding of sovereignty when it stipulates in paragraph two that France retains the right to grant asylum even if it is not responsible under those agreements (thereby iterating the exclusion clause of Art. 29 IV SA).

A second difference refers to the implementation of the "safe third country" rule, which is less stringent in France than it is in Germany. In France, the possibility of rejecting an asylum seeker on the grounds that he or she can receive protection in a "safe third country" - even if that person has been there only in transit - was contained both in the criteria for admission to the asylum procedure at the border and also on the territory. However, this rule may lead to that person's immediate return without substantive examination of their claim only if the application has been presented at the border; inside the territory, an accelerated procedure with the OFPRA applied which was amended in 1998 (see section 4.3). According to information from the NGOs and the UNHCR, no clear criteria exist for the application of this rule at the border, as it is not mentioned in any law. Until a negative ruling of the Council of State towards the end of 1996, rejections on the basis of the "safe third country" rule must have been relatively frequent in France however; for the year 1996, an interior ministry report states that 33% of all rejections at the border utilised this clause (Ministère de l'Intérieur 1996). In its decision of 18.12.1996, the Council of State put a limit on this interior ministry practice by stipulating that the application of the "safe third country" rule must only be limited to the members of Schengen (MNS 2/1997). Since then, the "safe third country" rule at the border has not been abolished, but it is now only applied in combination with other reasons for an immediate rejection at the border: for example, when a claim is assessed as being "manifestly unfounded" (Ministère 1996; EP 2000: 75). In its ruling, the court maintained that the 1992 London Resolutions were non-binding and that they had no legal effect as long as they were not transposed into national law.

Finally, a third difference concerns the application of the London Conclusions on "safe countries of origin" which, while firmly implemented in German legislation, have not been explicitly dealt with in the 1993 French reforms. However, these principles have been adopted in practice by the OFPRA, which examines such cases in accelerated procedures, and were formalised in a renewed reform in 1998 (see below, section 4.3).

In sum, it appears that the French reforms leave more leeway for an interpretation of the European *acquis* and are less closely connected with European policies. This conclusion finds support in France's broader attitude to the Schengen Agreement which, since its early ratification in 1991, has been characterised by a high degree of reluctance regarding its full implementation. This reluctance is all the more ironic considering the fact that the constitutional revision was justified and legitimated by the "need" to implement the Schengen Agreement fully.

Lastly, it remains to be said that these legislative changes concern only one aspect of asylum policies which, however, is absolutely crucial for the principles of refugee protection, particularly observation of the norm of non-refoulement: namely, access to (full) asylum procedures. The normal asylum procedures in the specialised agencies - the OFPRA and the BAFl - have not been changed, nor have the criteria for interpreting the refugee definition been harmonised, although this would be necessary for the effective functioning of the redistributive principle (see Chapter Three). This corresponds to the fact that, at the European level, apart from the achievements of the "first generation" of intergovernmental cooperation, progress under the Maastricht Treaty has been much slower and has generated only limited and legally non-binding agreements. Considering this slow-down in Communitarisation since 1993, the question which next emerges is the degree to which subsequent developments in Germany and France point to a consolidation of the 1993 reforms or whether the reinvigoration of specific national traditions in the field of asylum policy can be observed.

The Scope of Europeanisation

After the parallel "crisis" of the asylum right in 1993, policy developments in Germany and France revealed both the stability of the measures adopted with the implementation of the European agreements and, at the same time, the reinvigoration of particular domestic concerns in the policy field. While the German policy discourse on asylum seekers came to a halt after the compromise reached among the main political parties in December 1992 and its legal codification in May 1993, basically because none of the important political actors tried to change this state of affairs, asylum policies re-emerged on the political agenda in France in 1998 and underwent a limited, but in certain respects liberal, revision under the socialist government of Lionel Jospin. These differences point at variations in the implementation and stability of the European asylum frame which, in turn, raises the question of the role of specific domestic traditions in the processes of Europeanisation.

Germany: Consolidation of the European Frame

The German asylum policy after 1993 stands firmly in the tradition of the 1993 reforms and demonstrates the perseverance of the asylum frame established in the debates analysed above. The 1993 reforms signified a comprehensive reorganisation of the asylum system. In addition to the above mentioned measures implementing the European accords, they also included a law revising benefits for asylum seekers which provides that assistance should usually be granted in the form of benefits in kind and the rates have generally been reduced.[37] In addition, a new Article 32a was introduced into the Foreigners Act which lays down temporary admission arrangements for war and civil war refugees. This regulation was part of the asylum compromise of 6.12.1992 and basically responded to the SPD's call to establish a special procedure for those persons outside the one based on Article 16 GG under which they did not generally find recognition. Although formally introduced in the Foreigners Act, the new §32a soon became the new focus of political debates between the *Länder* and Federal Government. These unresolved questions which regarded in the first line the temporary protection refugees from the former Yugoslavia became the major point of controversy in the German asylum discourse after 1993, while the question of Article 16(a) GG disappeared from the political agenda. The second focus in Germany's asylum policies after 1993 has been on its Central and Eastern European neighbours and on the inclusion of these newly liberalised countries in the emerging system of European immigration control.

Temporary protection

After the significant limitations introduced into the formal asylum procedure, the German asylum discourse focused on the repatriation of civil war refugees from the former Yugoslavia falling under the category of "temporary protection". This corresponded to the fact that Germany had admitted the biggest number of refugees from this region by far in the EU; over 300,000 Bosnian refugees were granted temporary protection in this country. Again, as with the politicisation of Article 16 GG, the politicisation of war and civil war refugees evolved along federal and partisan lines and had its basis in differences between the *Länder* - which were not only charged with the implementation of protection, but also with the repatriation of these refugees - and the Federal Government.

Following the amendment of July 1993, a new Article 32a was introduced in the Foreigners Act which provides a special "temporary protection" status for war and civil war refugees outside the asylum proceedings. At the same time, this group of people, who are given a residence allowance in line with the Foreigners Act, are excluded from asylum proceedings for the duration of the residence allowance. This change, which was designed to take some of the pressure off the asylum proceedings, has however taken six years to come into effect. The reasons for this are the prescription of unanimity between the *Länder* and the federal interior ministry for the application of this norm and the omission to regulate the question of costs, leading to ongoing disputes between the Federal and *Länder* Governments over financial responsibility in these matters.

Facing these difficulties and the ongoing arrival of refugees from the former Yugoslavia, the German government followed a similar strategy to the one pursued with Article 16 GG and tried to reach an agreement at the European level on the establishment of a system of burden-sharing in the temporary protection of civil war refugees (see Chapter Three). However, considering the highly heterogeneous situation existing in the individual member states in this regard, these plans have not (yet) led very far. The recent response of the EU member states to the Kosovo refugee crisis in spring 1999 is a clear evidence of this. Already before the escalation of refugee movements following NATO attacks on the Republic of Yugoslavia beginning in March, the newly elected German government (SPD/Greens) reinvigorated the efforts of its predecessors to reach agreement burden-sharing in situations of massive and sudden influxes of asylum seekers in the EU. At an informal JHA Council meeting in Berlin in February 1999, the German presidency put forward a corresponding paper which proposed voluntary burden-sharing with the possibility of financial compensation in such situations. At the same time, the paper - which was refused by several other member states - criticised the standards proposed by the European Commission as being too generous and contrary to the idea of an early return of temporary refugees. Indeed, SPD interior minister Otto Schily underlined that temporary protection should be considered as the last option, priority being given to securing safe havens close to the crisis area (Migration News Sheet 3/1999). Accordingly, when, in the following months, nearly one million Kosovo Albanians were forced to flee their country, the German government strictly limited its intake of refugees to a quota of 13,000 persons and maintained that it was not prepared to carry (once again) the burden of Yugoslav refugee flows in Europe (van Selm 2000). This limited number of persons made it finally possible to find consensus between the *Länder* and the federal government on granting temporary protection according to Article 32a Foreigners Act, for the first time since the adoption of this Article in 1993.

Measures taken with regard to Central and Eastern Europe
After the 1993 reforms, the second emphasis of German refugee policies has consisted in the implementation of the newly adopted instruments, particularly vis-à-vis its Central and Eastern European neighbours (CEECs). With the opening up of the "Iron Curtain", these countries were immediately perceived as a potential major source of illegal immigrants and (bogus) asylum seekers, as well as a major transit region for refugee flows coming from further East or South to Western Europe. In an effort to avoid these perceived threats, the focus of German asylum policies shifted towards the tightening up of its Eastern border, and the intensification of its relations with its Eastern neighbours in the common fight against undesired migration flows. This concerned in particular the conclusion of readmission agreements with the newly determined "safe third countries" and "safe countries of origin" and the support of multilateral efforts to export high standards of border control technology to Central and Eastern Europe (Lavenex 1999).

The implementation of the "safe country" rules As mentioned in Chapter Three, the implementation of the "safe third country" and "safe country of origin" rules required the conclusion of intergovernmental readmission agreements with the "safe" countries concerned. These agreements officially pursue three purposes: the fight against illegal immigration, the realisation of burden-sharing by more countries, and, by having a preventive influence on potential immigrants, facilitating the conditions for a gradual reduction in or abolition of the control on the internal borders of the countries bound by the agreements (Budapest Group 1996).

The negotiations leading to the conclusion of such readmission agreements can be traced back to a coordinated initiative in the Schengen framework in 1991 with the signature of a multilateral and "model" readmission agreement between the Schengen states and Poland. This agreement, which applies not only to citizens of the contracting parties, but also to nationals of third countries, including asylum seekers who passed through the Polish territory, corresponds widely to the redistributive mechanism of the Schengen and Dublin Conventions (Czaplinski 1994).[38]

At the bilateral level, the German government started negotiations with the "safe third countries" already in parallel with the domestic debates on reforming Article 16 GG. A first readmission agreement was signed with Poland on 7.5.1993 and a second with the Czech Republic on 9.11.1994. Similar to the "safe third country" rule, the successful application of the "safe countries of origin" rule also presupposed the consent of these countries in cooperating in the repatriation of their citizens. This cooperation was ensured on the basis of a second kind of readmission agreement which, contrary to the first, is limited to the mutual obligation to take back one's own country nationals. The German government has concluded such agreements with Romania (24.9.1994) and Bulgaria (9.9.1994).

Since these agreements are logically to the detriment of these CEECs, which have become important transit countries for asylum seekers and voluntary migrants heading to the West, they have been accompanied by the lifting of visa requirements between the contracting parties and the provision of material aid. In accordance with their main target, that is the reinforcement of Eastern borders against illegal immigration, these bilateral processes also include intensive transfers of border control technology and equipment, the training of border officials, and changes in criminal law (for instance, against trafficking of persons and the forging of documents). Within this framework, 120 million DM have been transferred to Poland, which has borders with Germany, Belarus and the Ukraine, and 60 million DM to the Czech Republic. According to a member of the German interior ministry, these funds are intended to "diminish the financial burden resulting from the amendment of the German asylum law and the readmission agreement(s)", to enhance border protection and to establish infrastructure for coping with asylum seekers and refugees (Schieffer 1997: 194). These bilateral efforts at tightening immigration and border control standards in Central and Eastern Europe are embedded in a broader multilateral framework of intergovernmental consultations, in which Germany plays the leading role. With the clarification of the EU *acquis* in justice and home affairs, these cooperation processes now occupy a central role in the eastward enlargement of the Union (Lavenex 1999).

The effects of these processes on the CEECs are considerable. Facing the requirement of enforcing their borders and of establishing basic standards of refugee protection, these countries are left with the task of balancing German and, more generally, Western European demands for internal security with the values of human rights and refugee protection.

This task is complicated by the fact that in contrast to their Western neighbours, these countries do not share the liberal and humanitarian tradition of the post-World War II period and did not participate in the international refugee regime before. Whereas all CEECs have made significant efforts to conform their justice and home affairs policies to the EU *acquis*, the difficulty of meeting high standards of immigration control with refugee protection was reflected in a ruling of the German Federal Constitutional Court in 1996, which laid down some conditions for the application of the "safe third country" rule.

The Federal Constitutional Court's 1996 ruling
As was mentioned above, the implementation of the 1993 reforms remained uncontroversial among the main political parties.[39] Although many legal experts criticised the constitutional amendments with regard to their form and contents (see Ulmer 1995: 26ff), the new Article 16a GG was ruled to be in conformity with the constitution by the Federal Constitutional Court on 14.5.1996.[40] This ruling brought to an "end" a series of appeals taken before the Federal Administrative and Federal Constitutional Court concerning, in particular, the "safe third country rule". With regard to this rule, the court confirmed that this provision is fully compatible with the constitution and that the presumption of safety need not be individually rebuttable. In reference to the topic of this thesis, the most interesting point in this ruling is the presentation and justification of the 1993 reform as a basis for a comprehensive European refugee policy aimed at the establishment of a system of burden-sharing among the participating states.[41] This exposition of motives reappears at various prominent places in the text and is presented as the overarching purpose of the "safe third country" rule. This line of argument indicates that the Federal Constitutional Court has adopted the Europeanised asylum frame of the 1993 reforms and now considers the German asylum right to be a part of a common European system of responsibility allocation. This is justified with the assertion that all European states, having signed the Geneva Refugee Convention and the European Convention on Human Rights, share common values and a "broad common legal conviction" (ibid.). In this context, the Court explicitly asserts that every alien entering Germany by land is excluded from the right to refer to Article 16a GG, since all countries bordering Germany are pre-determined as being "safe". Therefore, it is not necessary to establish through which country the alien has entered, the only criteria is that he or she could have found protection there.[42] To underpin this reasoning, the Court introduced a new legal notion, that is of the "normative establishment of certainty" (*"Normative Vergewisserung"*). According to this notion, the legislator establishes by

law the certainty that the third country is "safe" for refugees in the sense that the norm of non-refoulement of Article 33 GC and Article 3 ECHR (see Chapter Two) is respected.[43]

Finally, an important argument of the Court with regard to the broader dynamics of international "cooperation" in the redistribution of asylum seekers is the conclusion that a third country cannot be considered safe if it returns asylum seekers to "fourth" countries where no formal procedure or protection against refoulement exists. While maintaining that Germany is not bound to ensure that the asylum seeker effectively has access to an asylum procedure in the third country, this conclusion implies that it must take into consideration the practice of this country with regard to the "safe third country" rule and avoid applying it in situations which might lead to the chain-deportation of the asylum seeker to a place where that refugee is no longer safe from refoulement.

While the ruling on "safe countries of origin" fully confirmed the constitutionality of this notion and the organisation of the simplified procedure,[44] some very limited amendments were required in relation to the airport procedure.[45] While the Court confirmed that the retention of asylum seekers in "transit zones" at an airport during the accelerated procedure neither constituted detention nor a limit on freedom (the argument being that the individuals were free at any time to leave for the country from which they came or for any other country), it nevertheless ordered that a mechanism be established to provide asylum seekers in the airport procedure with legal counsel; it also recognised that the 3-day deadline for lodging and submitting grounds for an appeal against the first instance decision may be too short and thus allowed for a 4-day extension (for critical judicial reviews on these rulings see Marx/Lumpp 1996; Frowein/Zimmermann 1996; Maaßen/de Wyl 1996, 1997; Tomuschat 1996). In sum, the rulings of the Federal Constitutional Court put an end to the debates on the asylum right, which had in any case moved on, and confirmed the core of the reforms, that is the redistributive system of the Schengen and Dublin Conventions and the "safe third country rule", as the basic plan for a pan-European multilateral system of burden-sharing in the field of refugee protection.

France: A Resurgence of the Republican Tradition?

The two and a half years of conservative government after the Pasqua law was passed document the efforts to introduce further restrictions on the entry of aliens and its determination to enhance the expulsion possibilities of those migrants without authorisation to stay. In sharp contrast to the arguments of the interior minister and the French Government supporting the about-turn in 1993, the state was cautious to safeguard its sovereignty and continued to delay Schengen's full implementation. The limits of Europeanisation were very clearly expressed by interior minister Pasqua in the Senate in May 1994 when he claimed that a further integration of asylum and immigration matters, as was being supported by the European Parliament and the Commission, was not acceptable. Communitarisation would not correspond to the text and the spirit of the Schengen Agreement and it was "capital" that the member states preserved their sovereignty in these matters (Pasqua in the Senate on 3.5.1994).

Beyond this ambivalent attitude towards Europeanisation, an important development in this period was a growing mobilisation and expansion of protests against this radical turn in French immigration policy; in fact, this prepared the ground for the reorientation of the socialist government elected in the spring of 1997.

Further restrictions and growing public protest

The implementation of the Pasqua law began in January 1994 with the creation of a new "immigration police" charged with combating illegal immigration and illegal labour (*"Direction du controle de l'immigration et de la lutte contre l'emploi clandestin"*). One month later, he introduced exit visas for the citizens of thirteen countries for reasons of "national security" which were not further defined.[46] At the same time, the application of the new law gave way to the swift and unbureaucratic expulsion of irregular migrants, including asylum seekers rejected on the basis that their claims were felt to be "manifestly unfounded". In turn, this provoked strong protests not only from human rights associations, but also from the courts and judges' unions. After several lower courts had turned down expulsion measures ordered by the interior ministry, Pasqua criticised the judges for "creating a jurisdiction contrary to the law" (Pasqua in Le Figaro of 18.4.1994) and engaged in a heated debate with the minister of Justice, Méhaignerie, who maintained that the independence of the judges was a "pillar of democracy" (Méhaingerie in LM of 26.4.1994). Meanwhile, Pasqua announced that expulsion orders had increased by 66.4% in 1994 and that the effective deportations had gone up by 30% (MNS 1/1995).

During 1995, the protests against restrictive immigration and asylum policies magnified. For instance, the National Consultative Commission on Human Rights, a consultative body attached to the Prime Minister's Office, sharply condemned the 1993 immigration bills and their implementation. This protest was supported by the departure of three very active members from that Committee; it was joined by a manifestation of civil servants employed in those services dealing with foreigners, including the ministries of social and foreign affairs, police departments, and the OFPRA (MNS

4/1995). Meanwhile, expulsions continued to face opposition from the courts, including the European Court of Human Rights (MNS 4/1995).

The Debré law The new RPR/UDF government which came into power in May 1995 under Prime Minister Juppé, President Chirac and the new minister of the interior Debré, adhered to this policy line and introduced further restrictions to the Pasqua law on the entry and stay of foreigners. The entry into force of the Schengen Agreement was further delayed and, despite protests from Belgium and Germany, interior minister Debré reintroduced all checks at the French border in July 1995, invoking the threat posed to public order and national security following a wave of terrorist attacks (MNS 8/1995). The intention of tightening the immigration bill was first uttered at the end of 1995 (LM of 7.1.1995) and it re-entered the policy discourse in March 1996. Backed by the very strict claims of a report issued by a National Assembly commission published one month later (Assemblée Nationale 1996), Debré proposed several far-reaching restrictions aimed, as he proposed, at facilitating the application of the Pasqua laws. These concerned *inter alia* the certificates of accommodation required to enter France, the obligation on hosts to inform the mayor of the departure of the alien concerned, as well as long-term residency permits, expulsions, access to medical care and school for clandestine migrants and, with regard to asylum seekers, the formal introduction of a list of "safe countries of origin" simplifying the procedure before the OFPRA (LM of 7.3.1996). With these proposals, the protests targeted against the restrictive turn in immigration policies gained a new dimension. The Consultative Committee on Human Rights accused the project of containing "inopportune and dangerous" provisions and of intensifying the inappropriate amalgam between asylum seekers and clandestine immigrants, immigrants and terrorists, as well as foreigners who resided legally in the territory with undocumented aliens; they said that this would lead to dangerous confusions and give rise to racist prejudices and xenophobia.[47] Faced with this opposition and the strengthening protests of the "sans papiers" movement, Prime Minister Juppé first decided to shelve the Debré proposals, but then renewed part of them in October 1996. This new initiative no longer contained specific provisions regarding asylum seekers, but focused on combating illegal immigration, inter alia via the prolongation of administrative detention measures, through the widening of the control capacities of mayors and prefects, including an obligation on persons hosting aliens to report the departure of their guests to the mayor.

The magnification of public protest Debré's proposal to oblige hosts to report the departure of their foreign guests was at the centre of a negative opinion issued by the Council of State; the latter condemned the provision for infringing on the individual liberties and private lives of the hosts (LM of 18.12.1996). From that moment on, the polemics on immigration reached a new peak and the mobilisation of protest developed an unprecedented scope. Not only were conservative mayors split over the issue of the certificates of accommodation, but senators were too (LM of 5.2.1997). In the meantime, a new social movement emerged, the "movement of the artists" - well-known personalities from the cinema, writers, scholars, lawyers, doctors, journalists, et cetera - who soon began to dominate the public discourse. Although it began as a protest against the Debré proposals, the movement soon evolved into a protest against the growing influence of the Front National as well, both in political and ideological terms, and against the silence of the Left (see Perotti 1997).

During this period, the socialist opposition initially distanced itself from this wave of protest. Although the PS had voted against the Pasqua laws in 1993, they had by this time accepted their contents and their leader, Lionel Jospin, announced in 1996 that his party did not intend to introduce new changes to the immigration bills (LM of 20.4.1996). According to several observers of the immigration discourse, the PS and particularly Jospin had concluded a sort of tacit agreement with the ruling coalition and President Chirac on the occasion of the 1995 presidential elections, through the terms of which both sides agreed not to let the polemics on immigration re-emerge (Perotti 1997). This position changed in the light of the intensity of the social movements in early 1998. Jospin urged Prime Minister Juppé to withdraw the reform project (LM of 18.2.1997) and the PS forcefully countered this legislative proposal in parliament. In this period, the traditional discourse on nationality, Republican values and the role of immigration in society resurged, culminating in heated debates on the identity of France and the values of the Left. The question of asylum seekers, however, was no longer at the centre of all this attention and was hardly even mentioned. In the final version adopted in parliament, the Debré law was slightly softened and the obligation on hosts to "denounce" their guests was removed.

Jospin and the 1998 reforms
This reorientation of the French immigration discourse received new impetus after the unexpected dissolution of the National Assembly by President Jacques Chirac on 21.4.1997 and the following election campaigns. Sustained by the manifestation of pro-immigrant public opinion against the Debré law, the socialists, who initially distanced themselves from these social movements, put a promise regarding the abrogation of the Pasqua and Debré laws onto the top of their agenda. This priority was

upheld after their outstanding victory in the 1997 legislative elections and was forcefully expressed in Prime Minister Jospin's declaration on the general principles of his government before the National Assembly on 19.6.1997. At this occasion, Jospin proposed the conclusion of a "new Republican pact" with the French people, as well as a moral reorientation founded on (i) "a return to the sources" of the Republic; and (ii) "the modernisation of ... democracy" (Jospin 1997). In his call for a revaluation of republicanism, the comprehensive reform of immigration policies was mentioned right at the beginning of his speech after a short passage on the education system. Focusing first on the nationality code, Jospin underlined that the principle of *ius soli* was "consubstantiel" to the French nation and, turning then to the question of immigration, he called for the definition of a strict and just policy which, taking account of the economic, social and human reality of this phenomenon, combined the interests of the nation with respect for human rights and the rule of law. He announced a comprehensive revision of the legislation already in place; this would be conducted by an interministerial mission under the lead of Patrick Weil, a former ministerial official in the 1981 PS government and a recognised expert on French immigration policy.

The mission: combining realism with humanitarianism This interministerial mission presented its two reports on nationality and immigration at the end of July 1997. With regard to nationality, the report called for the re-establishment of *ius soli* in a highly symbolical manner, although this principle had never been abolished in France. In contrast to the 1993 Méhaingerie law, also referred to as one of the Pasqua laws (see above), this proposal called for the abrogation of the requirement for a voluntary French citizenship application for second generation immigrants and reintroduced its automatic granting at the age of 18. Whereas this reform proposal, taken over by minister of Justice Elisabeth Guigou in her draft bill, did not provoke major controversies across the political spectrum - it was criticised for being at best more symbolic than substantial in nature - the reform of the immigration bill gave rise to intensive debates within the ruling coalition. Contrary to the promises made during the electoral campaign, the report did not call for an abrogation of the Pasqua and Debré laws but, taking the existing laws as a point of departure, called for the recognition of common interests between the Right and the Left and a de-dramatisation of the immigration discourse.

The Chevènement law The reform proposals listed in the report were largely subsumed by the law presented by interior minister Jean-Pierre Chevènement from the political party "Movement Démocratique des

Citoyens" in October 1997. In general terms, this law expressed the overall aim of finding an "equilibrium" and "consensus" among the main political parties on immigration policy. While the initial reaction of the opposition to this draft law was quite moderate, the preservation of a strict stance on immigration provoked heavy protests from the Greens and Communists in particular who called for the total suppression of the Pasqua and Debré laws and threatened to split the governing coalition. This protest was supported by a very negative recommendation on the project by the Consultative Committee on Human Rights which had not been taken into account by the French Government. In the parliamentary debates on the immigration bill in December 1997, the protests of parts of the Left was paralleled by increased opposition from the Right. Anxious to find a consensus and to de-dramatise the debates, the government decided to prolong the legislative procedure in the National Assembly; in the end, it lasted more than 100 hours.[48] Despite its rejection by the Senate - which is dominated by the opposition - the bill was adopted by the National Assembly on 8.4.1998. Calls by members of the RPR and UDF against the bill, submitted to the Constitutional Council one day later, were rejected on most points in May 1998.[49]

Despite this strong polemisation in the policy discourse, the debates on reforming the asylum law were relatively calm were not so controversial. Rather, the focus of the foreigner discourse returned to traditional French concerns with illegal immigration and family reunification that was linked to its colonial past. This is astonishing considering that, in contrast to the limited nature of most of the other amendments the provisions on asylum were said to introduce some major innovations into the existing laws. In the parliamentary debates, these changes were presented with reference to the traditional principles and norms governing the French refugee regime, such as the "vocation de la France à l'universalité" and the "idéal républicain".[50] This reaffirmation of French values was not contested much by the opposition, which, although invoking the risk of abusive asylum claims,[51] also maintained the "sacred" character of the asylum right.[52] Was this perhaps because the Chevènement law, contrary to this humanitarian rhetoric, did not change much to the earlier restrictions on the asylum right?

A limited reform With the Chevènement law, the provisions relating to asylum seekers, specifically for applications which are made inside the country, were removed from the ordinance of 2.11.1945 on the entry and stay of foreigners, and were introduced into the specific asylum law creating the OFPRA of 1952. This measure was meant to underline the specificity and rights of asylum seekers in contrast to voluntary immigrants, thus re-affirming France's Republican tradition. In addition, two other changes were adopted. Firstly, the constitutional asylum right of §4 Preamble was revalued by introducing a new category of asylum seekers who could be recognised by the OFPRA on the grounds of their "action in favour of liberty" (Art. 2 Asylum Law of 8.4.1998). This measure was particularly directed at clarifying the situation of many Algerian asylum seekers who, fearing persecution from non-state actors - in particular from fundamentalist Islamic groups - were previously not recognised as refugees under the definition of the 1951 Geneva Convention. The second major change was the formalisation of the hitherto only informal practice of according temporary territorial asylum to asylum seekers who, although they did not fall under the refugee definition according to the Geneva Convention, could not be returned to their country of origin because of humanitarian reasons. Thus, France introduced a formal procedure for so-called de facto refugees which accords the minister of the interior, on the initiative of the OFPRA and after consultation with the foreign ministry, the discretionary right to issue a temporary residence permit for one year to such refugees (Art. 2 Asylum Law). Finally, the new law abrogated the application of the "safe third country" rule to asylum claims presented inside the territory and replaced it by adopting simplified procedures in the case of asylum seekers whose country of origin has been qualified as "safe" under Article 1C5 of the 1951 Geneva Convention (Art. 10 II Asylum Law). Apart from these changes, the Pasqua law of 1993 was not revised and indeed, the regulations regarding applications at the border were not affected.

Do these renewed revisions of the asylum law in France represent a departure from the restrictive turn five years earlier? In fact, these reforms underline the importance of the constitutional asylum right by establishing a new basis for providing asylum in accordance with the refugee definition in §4 Preamble and have thereby widened the scope of persons able to obtain refugee status. However, the range of persons fitting the description of "persecuted on grounds of his or her action in favour of liberty" is very limited, as it is geared at providing a basis for the protection of Algerian dissidents and does not include today's main causes of refugee flows, namely civil war and generalised violence. According to minister of the interior Chevènement, constitutional asylum can only apply to a small number of "hommes et femmes d'élite" (Chevènement in the National Assembly on 15-16.12.1997). Accordingly, the application or interpretation of this new norm by the OFPRA and the courts also points to a more restrictive reading.[53]

Secondly, the importance of limiting the "safe third country" rule is also moderate given that France is surrounded by EU or Schengen member states; thus, asylum seekers entering the country by land could - de jure - always be returned to one of those countries.

Finally, with the codification of "territorial asylum" to be granted on a temporary basis by the interior ministry, France has formalised the already existing practice of temporary protection in France and confirmed it as a discretionary right of the state. In the words of interior minister Chevènement, temporary protection shall be compatible with the "political, diplomatic, economic, cultural and strategic" interests of the state (ibid., see also Amnesty International 1999). The decision about temporary protection is taken by the interior ministry, it is discretionary and needs no explanation regarding motives.[54] In addition, this new provision is implemented in a restrictive manner and shall be limited to "threats or risks resulting from persons or group other than the public authorities of that country".[55] Herewith, it excludes very important nationalities fearing generalised violence in their home country; be it in Congo, Sri Lanka, or, as recently shown, Kosovo. In fact, France has admitted only a small number of Kosovo Albanians following NATO air-strikes in spring 1999,[56] and their status has been regulated rather in an ad hoc and informal manner than on the basis of existing laws and regulations (see Lavenex 2000). Herewith, France has clearly expressed its reluctance to a deeper Europeanisation of its refugee policy.

Conclusion

The implementation of the Schengen and Dublin Conventions and the 1992 London Resolutions marked a radical change in the domestic asylum policies of Germany and France. The implementation of these European agreements occurred in the form of highly symbolic revisions of their constitutional asylum rights which in turn introduced serious impediments on the access of asylum seekers to asylum procedures; it also downgraded legal and administrative standards in the processing of "manifestly unfounded" asylum claims. In both countries, the development of European integration strengthened the domestic position of the promoters of restrictive reforms to the detriment of the opposition and provided the normative legitimation, upon which consensus could be reached. In both countries, the coming into power of the Left in 1997 and 1998 respectively - which was originally opposed to the conservative reforms of 1993 - did not challenge the restrictive *acquis* established under the preceding governments.

When reflecting about the impact of Europeanisation, the two case studies indicated the intervening role of differing domestic structures with regard to the modalities of constitutional reform and the scope of institutional actors that needed to be persuaded of the necessity and legitimacy of the reforms. In the fragmented and federal German polity, the constitutional amendment required the consent of a variety of domestic actors; in particular, it needed support from the coalition partner FDP and the FDP ministers in the ministries of foreign affairs and justice, the majority of the opposition (the SPD), the *Länder*, and, last but not least, the federal constitutional court. Adopting a two-level perspective, it was shown that in the presence of strong differences between the promoters of this reform in the CDU/CSU and the actors mentioned above, domestic consensus was significantly facilitated by the institutional characteristics of intergovernmental negotiations at the European level and their repercussions on the domestic polity. The case study in Section 4.1 demonstrated that Europeanisation led to a concentration of competences in the national executive and particularly in the ministry of the interior, the latter acting as a hinge between the European and the domestic polity. Coupled with the scarcity of inter-organisational relations linking the European with the domestic arena and the secretive mode of operation at the European level, the interior ministry not only took the lead in representing German positions at the European level but also in the importation of European accords in the domestic discourse. As a consequence of this strengthened position, the respective interior ministers succeeded in gradually redefining their originally domestic calls for a restriction of the constitutional asylum right into a precondition and requirement of European integration. In this framing process, they assured the support of both the coalition partner FDP and the SPD at the federal and *Länder* levels. The involvement of these multiple and heterogeneous actors in the reform process and the need for their consensus in amending the constitution implied a broad discourse arena and thus a far-reaching persuasion process in favour of the reforms. While this persuasion of course depended on the success of the corresponding ideational framing process (see below), the institutional breadth of the discourse arena explains the organisational scope of the policy frame and thus the range of political actors which it comprises. This, in turn, indicates why political controversies on Article 16a GG faded away after the constitutional revision and also explains the unquestioned maintenance of the status quo by the new SPD/Greens coalition government after their coming into power in the autumn of 1998.

In ideational terms, the success of the European asylum frame in Germany was due to the strong resonance of its securitarian orientation with the domestic polemics on the asylum right and the strong normative appeal of European integration across German political parties. The focus on "bogus" asylum seekers resonated well within the context and vision of increased numbers of "economic" refugees in the long-lasting domestic asylum discourse and the concern with rising numbers of asylum seekers ever since the 1980s. Secondly, the perception of Germany as the "Reserveasylland" of Europe, which had already been advocated since the mid-1980s, supported the calls for a downward harmonisation which went along with lower European standards. This also sustained the calls for a redistribution of asylum seekers in Europe and the adoption of new instruments for the direct rejection of asylum seekers at the border. The decisive legitimatory argument, however, was the packaging of the restrictive reforms as the requirements of European agreements; of course, this resonated fully with the strong traditional support for European integration in Germany. This packaging thus provided a normative compensation for restrictions on domestic humanitarian principles and norms, as the judgement of the federal constitutional court of 1996 reflects.

In France, Europeanisation led to a similar concentration of competences within the ministry of the interior which was to the detriment of other ministries involved in asylum and immigration questions, as well as the President, the legislature, and the courts. This concentration of competences was intensified by the lack of communication between the actors involved at the European level and their domestic counterparts; as a consequence, there was a dearth of information coming to the French Parliament on the proceeding and the contents of intergovernmental negotiations. Similar to the German case, these institutional conditions allowed the interior minister to present his own reform proposals as the requirements of European integration which were aimed at implementing the Schengen Agreement. By framing these reforms as European requirements, he eventually assured the consent of President Mitterrand to a modification of the constitutional asylum right. This discursive strategy required a major transformation of the traditional foreigner discourse, focusing much more on questions of illegal immigration, integration and citizenship. This transformation was reached through reference to a potential "flood" of asylum seekers coming to France in a border-free Europe. With this potential threat to national sovereignty, asylum seekers were introduced into the traditional foreigner discourse in France, thus giving up the special status of refugees as symbols of French commitment to human rights and republicanism. As a consequence, refugees became part of the securitarian discourse which centres on civic and ethnic fears with the maintenance of sovereignty and the survival of the nation (see Chapter Two). Whereas this strong focus on sovereignty and national identity resonated well with the traditional discourse of the Right, the presentation of restrictive reforms as requirements of Schengen appealed to the Socialist's commitment to European integration.

However, in comparative perspective, Pasqua's reform proposals encountered a smaller number of veto-points in order to be adopted than was the case in Germany. As a result of the strong position of the political leadership in France, the constitutional reform required a narrower scope of political consensus which consisted mainly in agreement between President Mitterrand of the PS under a *cohabitation* with the RPR/UDF government. In legislative debates, reforms could be passed without the consent of the opposition, including the Socialist Party which voted against the "Pasqua law". Contrasting these findings with the German case, it is possible to conclude that in institutional terms, the incisive reforms of 1993 required the persuasion of a narrower group of actors in France, which in fact mainly consisted of the executive leadership.

According to institutionalist reasoning, this condition could have had two effects on the stability of the 1993 changes. Firstly, since the persuasion process did not include the majority of the opposition, the PS could introduce new changes to the asylum law which were no longer linked to Europeanisation after returning to power in 1997. Secondly, this reorientation was facilitated again by the high degree of autonomy that the executive leadership in France has; this allows for a high degree of unilateral action with a relatively small number of veto-points. Finally, also the lower pace of Communitarisation at the European level after 1993 and the weaker commitment of the new interior minister Chevènement to European cooperation in these matters would point at the possibility of new, comprehensive reforms to be conducted. However, the longitudinal analysis of French refugee policies after 1993 has shown that this about-turn did not occur. Notwithstanding the negative vote in 1993, the PS gave up its opposition to the new asylum laws in the years which followed. In contrast to their humanitarian rhetoric, the recent reforms under Prime Minister Jospin did not release the restrictive *acquis* introduced by the previous conservative government. At the same time, these changes confirmed the limited reach of Europeanisation which, limited to the question of access to domestic asylum procedures, was mainly used as a means to impose limitations on domestic liberal traditions. Beyond the question of access, however, national refugee policies in Germany and France returned to their traditional priorities, limiting the scope for further harmonisation and solidarity.

Notes

[1] The xenophobic attacks started when riots broke out against foreigners and asylum seekers in Hoyerswerda (September 1991), before proliferating in Hünxe (October 1991), Greifswald (November 1991), Mannheim (May 1992), Rostock (August 1992), and other places; see Blanke (1993); Prantl (1993). For an analysis of the media's role in the escalation of xenophobia, see Brosius/Esser (1995).

[2] See the answer given by Parliamentary State Secretary (*Parlamentarischer Staatssekretär*) Horst Waffenschmidt (CDU) to a question from his parliamentary group regarding the necessity and form of an adaptation to the constitutional asylum right in the European context: "It can not yet be definitely determined, which consequences will finally arise" (BTDrs 12/1607 of 15.11.1991).

[3] See FAZ and SZ of 17.6.1992. This position was not shared by all members of the FDP, however, as can be seen from the statements by Justice Minster Leutheusser-Schnarrenberger in August 1992 and Deputy Burkhard Hirsch (FDP), who continued to deny the argument that European harmonisation required a constitutional amendment (BT PlPr 12/89 of 30.4.1992: 7335). Nonetheless, acceptance of a constitutional reform was later translated into a "10-points-programme" by the FDP parliamentary group on 4.9.1992 (his also included the call for an immigration law) and was confirmed at the party rally in Bremen on 2/3.10.1992 (FDP 1992).

[4] Klose's new consensus orientation was confirmed one year later in the parliamentary debates on the adoption of Article 16aGG, when he recalled that it had been "a long way since that debate of April 1992, when we already seemed close to one another" (BT PlPr 12/160 of 26.5.1993: 13510).

[5] For example, see the chairman of the SPD Parliamentary group during the debate in the Bundestag on a CDU/CSU initiative regarding a constitutional reform, in which he reminded his listeners of the particular "German guilt" and the importance of the asylum norm for his party (debate of 15.10.1992, BT PlPr 12/112: 9576f). In the final debate leading up to the adoption of the constitutional amendment he emphasised the "historical and political-moral" foundations of the German asylum right (debate of 26.5.1993, BT PlPr 12/160: 13509).

[6] See BT PlPr 12/160 of 26.5.1993; the CDU/CSU voted unanimously in favour, the SPD 132 in favour of and 101 against the reform, in the FDP it was 73 to 6 while the Greens and PDS voted unanimously against.

[7] The FN became a central actor in the French political landscape with its success at the municipal elections in 1983 and the European elections in 1984 (11%). In the elections to the National Assembly, the party increased its votes from 9.9 % and 9.8% in 1986 and 1988 respectively to 12.6% in 1994 (Mény 1996: 105). In the presidential elections of 1988, Le Pen attracted 14.4% of the vote (see Schain 1996: 176).

[8] Law no. 93-933 of 22.7.1993; Law no. 93-992 of 10.8.1993; Law no. 93-1417 of 30.12.1993.

[9] In contrast to the German Constitutional Court, the Constitutional Council can only review laws with regard to their constitutionality prior to their proclamation (Art. 61 of the Constitution); once in force, only an Act of Parliament can enact an amendment or abrogation (Classen 1993: 229; Oellers-Frahm/Zimmermann 1996: 253).

[10] Jean-Pierre Sueur (PS), secrétaire d' Etat, in the debate of the National Assembly of 19.12.1991: 8274. Similarly also Minister of European Affairs Guigou before the Senate on 27.6.1991: 2189.

[11] Pierre Mazeaud (RPR) in the debate of the National Assembly of 19.12.1991: 8271 and Gilbert Millet (PC) ibid: 8277. The metaphor of "Europe passoire", Europe as a sieve, expresses the fear of porous borders in Europe.

[12] In the debate of 19.12.1991 in the National Assembly on the introduction of carrier sanctions and transit zones the issue of bogus asylum seekers is mentioned only once and at the end of the debate (by Gérard Gouze, PS: 8271) and nowhere in the Schengen ratification debate in the Senate of 27.6.1991.

[13] Minister of European Affairs Elisabeth Guigou during the Schengen ratification debate in the Senate 27.6.1991: 2187, Michel Pezet (PS), in the debate of the National Assembly of 19.12.1991 : 8258; and on the same occasion Jean-Jacques Hyest (UDF): 8268 and 8269, Gilbert Millet (PC): 8267 and Francis Delattre (UDF): 8264.

[14] Ruling of the Conseil Constitutionnel 91-294 DC of 25.7.1991: §31; see also LM 27.7.1991. This was the first time that a court explicitly recognised the constitutional value of this paragraph in the Preamble, although its content had always been implicitly upheld in the liberal practice according to which every asylum seeker had access to an asylum procedure and the right to stay on the territory for its duration (see Chapter Two).

[15] Decision of 12/13.8.1993 no. 93 - 325 DC.

[16] Interior Minister Charles Pasqua in the National Assembly on 27.10.1993: 5030; see also Minister of Justice Pierre Méhaignerie in the National Assembly on 27.10.1993: 4959 and in the Senate on 16.11.1993: 4255.

[17] Jean-Pierre Philibert (RPR), Rapporteur, in the National Assembly on 27.10.1993: 4956; Minister of Justice Pierre Méhaignerie: 4958 and in the Senate on 16.11.1993: 4257; Interior Minister Charles Pasqua (RPR): 4286.

[18] François Loncle (PS) in the debate in the National Assembly on 19.12.1991: 8260.

[19] Michel Pezet (PS) in the debate in the National Assembly on 19.12.1991: 8259.

[20] In the National Assembly on 27.10.1993: Minister of Justice Pierre Méhaignerie (UDF): 4960; Minister of European Affairs Alain Lamassoure (UDF): 5010; Interior Minister Charles Pasqua (RPR): 5030.

[21] Jean-Pierre Philibert (RPR), Rapporteur, in the National Assembly on 27.10.1993: 4953-4.

[22] Prime Minister Eduard Balladur in the Congress on 19.11.1993; see also LM of 20.11.1993.

[23] See President Mitterrand in an interview with Le Monde, LM of 27.10.1993 in which he emphasises that "la révision constitutionnelle ne touche en rien la situation des demandeurs d'asile qui s'addressent directement à la France"; and Eduard Balladur in his speech before the Congress on 19.11.1993 and in LM of 31.8.1993 and 3.9.1993.

[24] Minister of Justice Pierre Méhaignerie (UDF) in the Senate, 16.11.1993: 4256 and in the National Assembly, 27.10.1993: 4255. See also LM of 27.11.1993.

[25] This derives from Article 31 Geneva Convention which prohibits the imposition of legal sanctions on the illegal entry and stay of persons who have arrived directly from places where their lives or freedoms have been threatened.

[26] *De jure*, the absence of a visa does not impede access to an asylum procedure when the applicant is already in the country; this is confirmed in the rulings of the Constitutional Council (no. 79-109 DC of 9.1.1970 and no. 86-216 DC of 3.9.1986), the Council of State (ruling of 27.9.1985) and in Article 31 *bis* of the ordinance of 2.11.1945.

[27] §4 of the law amending the asylum procedure and aliens' law of 6.1.1987, BGBl. I: 89.

[28] Gesetz zur Änderung des Grundgesetzes (GG) of 28.6.1993, BGBl I: 10002; and Gesetz zur Änderung asylverfahrens-, ausländer- und staatsangehörigkeitsrechtlicher Vorschriften of 30.6.1993, BGBl I: 1062.

[29] The application of this paragraph to applicants coming from another country which is party to the Schengen Agreement was modified by a ruling of the Federal Constitutional Court in 1996; see below.

[30] In 1998, these provisions were taken out of the general ordinance on the entry and stay of foreigners and introduced in the law of 1952 on the OFPRA; see below.

[31] Applications at the borderare regulated by the Decree of 27.5.1982, which introduced Art. 35 *quater* in the Ordinance of 2.11.1945.

[32] The four grounds for exclusion are enumerated Ministère de l'Intérieur 1996; on the entry procedure at the border and waiting zones, see Amnesty International/ France Terre d'Asile 1997; Anafé 1997 and 1998; Brachet 1997: 11 and Julien-Laferrière 1996: 41.

[33] Law of 6.7.1992 legalising the already existing practice of waiting zones. On the retention practice and the risk of violations to individual liberties in French waiting zones, see the case Amuur against France decided by the European Court of Human Rights on 26.6.1996, case no. 17/1995/523/609.

[34] Decree of 2.5.1995 no. 95-507 regarding the access of the UNHCR and NGOs to asylum seekers in waiting zones. The NGOs authorised to enter the waiting zones were fixed by an interior ministry "arreté" of 7.12.1995.

[35] With the 1998 reform, these provisions were introduced into the 1952 law on the OFPRA; see below.

[36] The criteria used in this determination are the recognition rates for asylum applicants in previous years, the general political situation, an observance of human rights, the readiness of the state of origin to allow independent international human rights organisations access to its territory, and the stability of the country.

[37] Asylbewerberleistungsgesetz adopted on 30.6.1993 and in force since 1.11.1993. This law was tightened in 1996 (see MNS 7/96) and again a second time, although in more limited respects, in the summer of 1998 in the face of federal elections, see MNS 7/98 and 8/98. According to Amnesty International (1995), this new regulation seriously challenges the successful conduction of an asylum procedure, since many asylum seekers can no longer pay the costs of lawyers and eventual translations (ibid: 36).

[38] The agreement with Poland has been used as a model for later bilateral readmission agreements between single member states and third countries; it has also provided the basis for a harmonised approach in the Draft Recommendation concerning a specimen bilateral readmission agreement between an EU member state and a third country, adopted on Germany's initiative by the JHA Council on 30.11/1.12.1993.

[39] Even the Greens, who, as long as they were in the opposition, protested against the - according to them - "erosion of the basic asylum right" ("Aushöhlung des Asylgrundrechts", see the biannual information brochure produced by the office of MEP Claudia Roth, Bündnis 90/Die Grünen) did no longer question the state of affairs after seizing power in autumn 1998.

[40] The court's decision consisted on a ruling on "safe third countries": 2 BvR 1938/93 and 2 BvR 2315/93 of 14.5.1996; one on "safe countries of origin": 2 BvR 1507/93 and 2 BvR 1508/93 of 14.5.1996; and one on the airport procedure: 2 BvR 1516/93 of 14.5.1996.

[41] "Mit der Reform des Asylrechts hat der verfassungsändernde Gesetzgeber eine Grundlage geschaffen, um durch die gegenseitige Anderkennung von Asylentscheidungen eine europäische Gesamtregelung der Schutzgewährung für Flüchtlinge mit dem Ziel einer Lastenverteilung zwischen den an einem solchen System beteiligten Staaten zu erreichen" (BVerGE 2 BvR 1938/93 and 2 BvR 2315/93 of 14.5.1996: §1).

[42] This interpretation was later confirmed in a Federal Administrative Court (BVerwG) ruling which denied the right to claim asylum of a group of Kurds who were locked up in a lorry during their entire journey to Germany and could therefore not affirm through which country they had transited. The Court pointed out that all neighbouring states were safe third countries and that if a foreigner excluded himself from the possibility of finding protection there, that person was responsible for not being able to lay claim to the right of asylum. The BVerwG also pointed out that the "safe third country" rule should be seen as part of an overall European regulation which contributes to an equitable sharing out of the (asylum) burden in Europe; see BVerwGE of 2.9.1997.

[43] Only very rare situations would justify a suspension of this certainty and an exception to the application of the "safe third country rule" in particular such as, when the German government has not yet reacted to changes in the third country concerned.

[44] 2 BvR 1507/93 and 2 BvR 1508/93 of 14.5.1996.

45 2 BvR 1516/93 of 14.5.1996.

46 See LM and Libération of 15.2.1994. This instrument of exit control had already been introduced during Pasqua's first period as minister of the interior in 1986; however, this circular been turned down by the Council of State as being in breach of the fundamental right to free movement.

47 See Recommendation of the Consultative Commission on Human Rights, published on 3.6.1996; and LM of 6.6.1996

48 The debates in the National Assembly took place on 4-5. 12.1997 and 9-17.12.1997; see LM of 18.12.1997.

49 Constitutional Council, Decision no. 98-399 DC of 5.5.1998. The calls from RPR/UDF members contested three areas: visa policies, sanctions against humanitarian associations, and, with regard to asylum seekers, the right of the UNHCR representative to participate in the CRR on decisions regarding the granting of constitutional asylum; see below. On this, also see Julien-Laferrière 1998.

50 Interior Minister Chevènement in the National Assembly on 15-16.12.1997.

51 For example, Robert Pandraud (RPR) in the National Assembly on 15-16.12.1997.

52 For example, Richard Cazenave (RPR) in the National Assembly on 15-16.12.1997.

53 According to an article in LM of 9.4.1999, only two persons have benefited from this constitutional asylum right since its introduction in 1998.

54 According to the law professor François Julien-Laferrière, this exception from the need to motivate negative decisions derogates from the general principle of administrative law laid down in the law of 11.7.1979 according to which individual negative administrative decisions, in particular those which restrain the exercise of public liberties or, more generally, represent a police measure, must be motivated.

55 See interior ministry circular of 25.6.1998 on the implementation of this law, quoted in Amnesty International 1999.

56 By August 1999, 6,339 Kosovo Albanians had reached France, information from the UNHCR office in Paris.

Conclusion

This book has shown that the Europeanisation of refugee policies is characterised by a competition between two conflicting policy frames: the frame of human rights on the one hand and that of internal security on the other. This competition can be read as a replication of the fundamental tension between universal human rights and particularistic state sovereignty, inherent in the modern state system, in the process of Europeanisation. Rather than transcending this tension, the construction of the European Union has tended to intensify it by linking national fears of losing control over immigration with the fears of waiving sovereignty to supranational actors. The comparison of France and Germany, two major players in the integration process with a strong tradition of refugee policy, has shown that Europeanisation has gone along with a convergent limitation of access to domestic procedures, notwithstanding important differences in the numbers of asylum seekers and their degree of politicisation in the two countries. These developments are not only an indication of a transformation of traditional post-World War II refugee regimes in Europe, they are also an expression of the broader dynamics of inclusion and exclusion in the process of European integration, and point at the opportunities and challenges involved in the transformation of the European Community from an economic actor to a political Union.

In asylum and immigration policy, this transformation from an economic logic of cooperation to genuine political aspirations has gone along with the establishment of new forms of deliberation and policy-making, which differ from the traditional structure of Europeanisation based on the Community method. The sensitivity of these issues, their linkage to specific national histories and identities, their high degree of politicisation in the member states, and also the lack of consensus on the fundamental principles of a contemporary refugee policy have all contributed to a strong reluctance on the part of the governments of member states towards the empowerment of supranational actors. Instead, a structure of intensive transgovernmentalism has taken shape, which strengthens the impact of bureaucratic networks of justice and home affairs officials both at the European level and in domestic polities. Retracing the development of this cooperation from the mid-1980s to the Amsterdam Treaty, this study identified four main characteristics of intensive transgovernmentalism: the organisation of cooperation in concentric circles operating on the basis of unanimity, with the Schengen group playing the leading role; the homogeneous and exclusive professional background of justice and home affairs officials acting in bureaucratic networks; the isolation of this cooperation from other national, supranational or international actors; and a technocratic policy style coupled with a high level of confidentiality.

These structures of cooperation, and the manner in which the asylum issue was framed in the European context, pose significant limits to the goal of a "common European asylum system" based on human rights and the 1951 Geneva Convention claimed by the EU Heads of State and Government meeting in Tampere in October 1999. Under its current constitution, the European multilevel system lacks the ideational and normative foundations necessary for the creation of a common sense of responsibility and a unified approach towards third country nationals in need of protection. These limits of Europeanisation are reflected in the dynamics supporting the emergence of asylum and refugee matters on the European agenda and in the interaction between intergovernmental cooperation and domestic developments in Germany and France. The salience of co-operation in these matters was linked to the single market project and the prospect of an abolition of controls at the internal borders. From the very beginning, cooperation has been framed as a limited side-aspect of the realisation of free movement inside the Union, the goal was not the development of a common European refugee policy. In the absence of an overarching framework of norms and values structuring the relations between European institutions and third-country nationals who are not residents of a member state, the professional concern of law and order officials with questions of policing and control gained an unchallenged priority in the process of Communitarisation. The establishment of intensive transgovernmentalism isolated European co-ordination of asylum and refugee policies from their traditional humanitarian framework in the Council of Europe or the UNHCR and led to a realist framing of the asylum problem, which prioritises internal security over human rights considerations. In this framing, the central issue of concern is not individual refugees and their rights, but freedom of movement and the question of territorial borders. From this perspective, refugees and asylum seekers are one phenomenon of cross-border movements among others, which needs to be controlled. In the light of an unequal distribution of refugee flows between traditional transit countries and major countries of destination, such as Germany, protection has been increasingly perceived as a zero-sum game, in which international interdependence and the abolition of borders lead to a negative redistribution of asylum seekers in Europe.

Coupled with pressure from the main refugee receiving countries, these factors have contributed to a securitisation of the asylum problem, which justifies a sort of regulatory competition among the member states for the most restrictive provisions. The Schengen and Dublin Conventions, as well as the measures adopted under the third pillar of the Maastricht Treaty, have led to selective harmonisation, which reflects the lowest common denominator between the traditional refugee-receiving countries. Up to the present date, the main achievements of European cooperation have been the limitation of access to domestic asylum procedures, the adoption of simplified procedures in "manifestly unfounded" asylum cases, and the uncoordinated propagation of temporary protection for war and civil war refugees. Originally limited to EU member states, this cooperation has soon transcended the Union's borders and has led to the unilateral incorporation of neighbouring countries in Central and Eastern Europe into this new system of access control. The driving forces behind this expansion were the adoption of strict policies for the crossing of the Union's external borders and the extension of the system of negative redistribution for the handling of asylum claims of the Schengen and Dublin Conventions through the "safe third country" rule. More substantive harmonisation, however, such as the criteria for determining who qualifies as a refugee or national status determination procedures, has stagnated. Moreover, as recent refugee crises in the former Yugoslavia have shown, the member states have repeatedly opposed the idea of 'burden-sharing' and temporary protection still follows very disparate and often informal national practices.

The absence of a humanitarian tradition in the EU framework and the weakness of supranational competence have supported this defensive approach by limiting the resonance of more liberal and comprehensive initiatives, expressed *inter alia* by the European Parliament and the European Commission. Its driving force, however, came from the member states; it was promoted by the structure of transgovernmental cooperation and the influence it confers to the ministers of the interior. In Germany, the European asylum frame resonated well with the long-lasting politicisation of asylum seekers, while the reference to the cooperative context of European unification and the establishment of a common European refugee policy provided the normative legitimation, upon which the departure from the idealist post-World War II consensus could be passed. The overarching European finality of Germany's asylum reforms provided the crucial normative justification for its release from the legacy of the past, that is, the guilt of national socialism, symbolised in the generous formulation of Article 16 in the German constitution. Far from being only a rhetorical tool, this European normativeness was confirmed in the ruling of the Federal

Constitutional Court of 1996, in which the 1993 reforms found their definitive approval.

In France, by contrast, the implementation of the European asylum frame required a modification of the traditional foreigner discourse and the weakening of the country's traditional republican understanding as "terre d'asile". This was achieved through the introduction of asylum seekers into the already heated foreigner discourse and their linkage with the traditional concerns regarding the safeguarding of sovereignty and French identity. In this process, domestic fears of losing control over undesired entries coincided with the Euroscepticism of the French Right, thus reinforcing the focus on realist sovereignty considerations to the detriment of republican values. In turn, the consent of the Socialist President Mitterrand to the incisive asylum reforms, then acting under political cohabitation with the conservative government, was based on his commitment to the idea of European integration and the Schengen Agreement.

In both countries, reference to the need to adapt their own asylum provisions to the European accords thus altered the cleavage structures in their respective political discourses and provided the ideational basis on which consensus concerning limitations to the humanitarian tradition could be found. By this, both countries adopted almost convergent reforms of their asylum laws in 1993, which implemented the European asylum *acquis*. In short, the main elements of these reforms have been threefold: firstly, more limited access to their territories through visa requirements and carrier sanctions; secondly, the exclusion of certain categories of asylum seekers from the asylum procedure on the basis of the Schengen and Dublin Conventions and the "safe third country" rule; and, finally, the adoption of simplified asylum procedures for "manifestly unfounded" asylum claims.

In a longitudinal perspective, however, the degree to which Europeanisation affected domestic policies was constrained by the intervening influence of domestic institutional and normative structures. With regard to institutional factors, it has been demonstrated that Europeanisation impacted more strongly on the fragmented German federal polity, where the creation of political consensus for a constitutional reform required that multiple veto points be overcome and meant that a large variety of participating actors had to be persuaded. Once achieved, this broad scope of persuasion provided a stable consensus, which continues to be the basis for political action despite changing governmental majorities. In France, by contrast, the strong autonomy of the political leadership allowed this constitutional reform to be passed without the consent of the opposition and, conversely, enabled the opposition to re-introduce changes after coming back into power in 1998. However, while this greater institutional leeway of the French executive leadership would have predicted a return to the republican tradition under the Jospin government, the analysis of French asylum policies until the summer of 1999 has shown the perseverance of the realist frame established in the 1993 reforms. Notwithstanding their humanitarian rhetoric, recent reforms of the asylum law have neither amended the restrictions imposed on the access to asylum procedures, nor their simplification in "manifestly unfounded cases" by the preceding conservative governments. Instead, the comparison of policy developments in Germany and France after 1993 has shown both the stability of the 1993 reforms implementing the European *acquis*, and the re-emergence of specific domestic concerns, which are beyond the limited reach of European cooperation. Thus, in Germany, recent political debates have centred on the question of temporary protection for refugees from the former Yugoslavia, while the implementation of the 1993 reforms has led to the unquestioned incorporation of Germany's Eastern neighbours into this new system of immigration control. In France, the focus has been on the situation of Algerian refugees, while the general foreigner discourse has returned to its traditional concerns with illegal immigration, integration and citizenship.

To sum up, these findings illustrate the interdependence of institutional and ideational factors in the process of Europeanisation. Shifts in the distribution of power across policy-making levels and arenas imply that the actors who are strengthened by this will have increased possibilities to sell their ideas and to persuade political opponents. Conversely, the advocacy-activities of these actors are always embedded in an ideational, normative context which shapes the range of framing devices available and determines their ability to persuade political opponents and hence to resonate in policy discourse. The review of current developments in European and domestic refugee policies shows that once institutionalised in public policies, frames gain the status of ideational institutions and become independent from the underlying power relations that facilitated their emergence. Indeed, the realist asylum frame implemented in the 1993 reforms continues to shape the course of policy-making in Germany and France, even after its former opponents have seized power in government.

These findings indicate both the scope and the limits of further European integration in refugee matters. Considering independent dynamics that policy frames can develop once they are institutionalised in a particular polity, one may conclude that the establishment of a truly common EU refugee policy, which pursues the goal of comprehensive harmonisation on the basis of the principles of the international refugee regime, would require a re-organisation of the institutional structures of cooperation and the implementation of a corresponding ideational framework in the EU system. On the one hand, this study has shown that without the participation of actors representing the values and orientations of the international refugee regime - such as the UNHCR or NGOs - and without the full involvement of supranational institutions, member states' executives tend to pursue a realist, protectionist approach, which weakens the humanitarian core of refugee policies and inhibits cooperation. On the other hand, the foundations of domestic refugee policies rest in liberal and humanitarian principles, which indicates that the Communitarisation of this policy field will not succeed without agreement on corresponding values at the European level and their backing in the European treaties. In the absence of such comprehensive institutional reforms, the limits of contemporary refugee policies become more and more salient. These limits are already visible inside the Union, be it in the reticent and reluctant implementation of the Schengen and Dublin Conventions, or in the inherent redistributive dynamics of these agreements. As the controversies surrounding the arrival of Kurdish and Albanian refugees in Italy since early 1998, or the difficulties in finding a system of burden-sharing for the admission of refugees from the former Yugoslavia show, this system of negative redistribution may well create tensions between the traditional refugee-receiving countries eager to limit additional intakes and the former transit-countries of Southern Europe, which are gradually being transformed into refugee-receiving countries themselves. A similar development occurs at the Union's borders with the unilateral inclusion of the associated countries of Central and Eastern Europe in Western asylum and immigration control policies, through their designation as "safe third countries". Last but not least, the ongoing tragedy in the former Yugoslavia and the difficulties facing the EU member states in offering a common, humanitarian approach to the massive refugee flows indicate the limits of the realist, securitarian frame of contemporary European refugee policies. Without a re-affirmation of the common humanitarian tradition, Europeanisation risks favouring the proliferation of protectionist policies in the name of internal security to the detriment of human rights, thereby contributing to a further destabilisation of the post-World War II refugee regimes.

Although claiming a reorientation of European refugee policies, the Amsterdam Treaty carries several legacies of this transgovernmental cooperation. Although asylum and immigration matters have been transferred from the third to the supranational first pillar, this has not gone without the maintenance of crucial intergovernmental elements such as the unanimity rule and limitations on the role of the Commission, the European Parliament and the European Court of Justice. In addition, the supranational institutions lack the resources necessary for taking up a proactive role in these fields, as the modest equipment of the Commission's new directorate shows. But even if the supranational actors were given more influence, the Treaty still lacks the substantive basis for establishing a comprehensive European refugee policy. First of all, this aim is mentioned at no point in the Treaty. Instead, asylum and immigration matters are still linked to the question of internal border controls and the substantive provisions mainly iterate the goals of the work programme adopted at Maastricht. Secondly, cooperation occurs *à la carte*; this concerns no longer only the selective implementation of the *acquis*, but also the introduction of extensive flexibility clauses allowing for various forms of participation and various degrees of political and legal commitment. Thirdly, the creation of a common policy would need to address the problem of negative redistribution among old and new refugee-receiving countries, thus raising the requirement of solidarity among current and future member states as well as neighbouring countries. Last but not least, this solidarity would have to be based on a consensual definition of the criteria determining a refugee and the exercise of protection, as well as a common commitment towards the protection of third-country nationals and their human rights. In other words, the adoption of a common European refugee policy would presuppose a high degree of political integration, involving supranational governance, enforcement mechanisms and shared causal and normative understandings. As long as these preconditions are not given, Europeanisation threatens to contribute to the further destabilisation of the system of refugee protection.

It may be that the first steps towards this political union have already been made. One possible way to transfer the idealist assets of the Western liberal tradition incorporated in the post-World War II refugee regimes onto the European level might be the de-coupling of cooperation in asylum and immigration matters from the more narrow goal of freedom of movement and its linkage with the fundamental principles of the Union, and the development of a European Charter of Fundamental Rights. Indeed, such a shift would recognise that the Europeanisation of asylum and immigration policies is innately linked to the political construction of the European community and that it plays a crucial role in the definition of who belongs to the European Union and who does not. This would also recognise the links between the deepening of the "Citizens' Europe" with the rights and duties towards third-country nationals and particularly towards those who are in need of protection. Transgressing the limited frame of internal border controls, the recognition of the broader political implications of a common European refugee policy would thus become part of a more general debate about the political nature of the EU and the ethical principles that shape its constitution.

Bibliography

Primary Sources

Ad Hoc Group on Immigration (1991), *Summary of conclusions of the meetings of the ministers concerned with immigration*, SN 1131/91 WGI 735.

Amnesty International (1995), *Zwei Jahre neues Asylrecht: Auswirkungen des geänderten Asylrechts auf den Rechtsschutz von Flüchtlingen*, Köln, Amnesty International.

Amnesty International (1999), *Une année d'application de l'asile territorial. Quelques premières observations*, Paris, 11 Mai 1999.

Amnesty International and France Terre d' Asile (1997), *Droit d'Asile en France. Etat des Lieux*, Paris, Amnesty International.

Anafé (1997), *Zones d'attente des ports, des aéroports, et des gares ferroviaires. Visite des associations habilitées*, rapport 1996-1997, Paris, Anafe.

Anafé (1998), *Guide de l'accès des etrangers au territoire français et du maintien en zone d'attente*, Paris, Anafe.

Assemblée Nationale (1996), *Rapport de la Commission d'enquête sur l'immigration clandestine et le séjour irrégulier d'étrangers en France, Rapporteurs*, Jean-Pierre Philibert et Suzanne Sauvaigo, no. 2699 of 10.4.1996.

Budapest Group (1996), *Report on the Implementation of Readmission Agreements*, BG 11/96C.

Bundesministerium des Innern (ed.) (1986), *Bericht der internministeriellen Kommission Asyl*. Teil II, Bonn, 2.7.1986.

Bundesministerium des Innern (ed.) (1987), *Bericht über den Stand der Harmonisierung des Asylrechts in Europa*, Bonn, 29.10.1987.

Bundesministerium des Innern (1991a), 'Erklärung des Bundesministers des Innern Wolfgang Schäuble', *Bulletin*, Presse- und Informationsamt der Bundesregierung Nr. 85, 9.8. 1991, Bonn.

Bundesministerium des Innern (1991b), *Statement von Bundesinnenminister Dr. Wolfgang Schäuble anläßlich der Eröffnung der Konferenz über Fragen der illegalen Zuwanderung aus und über Mittel-und Osteuropa am 30/31.10.1991 in Berlin*, Bonn, Pressereferat im Bundesministerium des Innern.

Bundesministerium des Innern (1991c), *Bericht des Bundesministers des Innern über die Ministerkonferenz über Maßnahmen zur Eindämmung illegaler Einreisen aus und über Mittel- und Osteuropa in Berlin am 30/31.10.1991, Bonn*, Pressereferat im Bundesministerium des Innern.

Bundesministerium des Innern (1994), *Asyl-Erfahrungsbericht 1993*, Doc. A3-125415/10, Bonn, Bundesministerium des Innern.

Bundesministerium des Innern (1995), *Asyl-Erfahrungsbericht 1994*, Doc. A3-125415/11, Bonn, Bundesministerium des Innern.

Bundesministerium des Innern (1996a), *Jahresbericht Schengen. Erfahrungen und Perspektiven*, Bonn, Bundesministerium des Innern.

Bundesministerium des Innern (1996b), *Das Schengener Abkommen.* Dokumentation des Bundesministeriums des Innern zum Schengener Durchführungsübereinkommen (SDÜ) anläßlich des ersten Jahrestages der Inkraftsetzung, Bonn, Presse- und Informationsamt der Bundesregierung.

Bundesministerium des Innern (1997a), *Schengen Erfahrungsbericht 1996*, Bonn, Bundesministerium des Innern.

Bundesministerium des Innern (ed.) (1997b), *Texte zur Inneren Sicherheit*, Band II., Bonn, Bundesministerium des Innern.

Bundesministerium des Innern (ed.) (1997c), *Aufzeichnungen zur Ausländerpolitik und zum Ausländerrecht in der Bundesrepublik Deutschland*, Doc. A1-937 020/15, Bonn, Bundesministerium des Innern.

CDU (1989), 'Beschlüsse des Parteitages' der CDU in Bremen, 9.9.1989.

CDU (1992), 'Beschluß des 3. Parteitages' der CDU Deuschlands zur Asylpolitik, 25.-28. Oktober 1992, Düsseldorf.

Commission Consultative des Droits de l'Homme (1994), *1993. La lutte contre le racisme et la xénophobie. Exclusion et droits de l'homme*, Paris, La documentation Française.

Commission of the European Communities (1985a), 'White Paper on the Completion of the Internal Market', *COM (85) 310 final*.

Commission of the European Communities (1985b), 'Guidelines for a Community Policy on Migration', *COM (85) 48 final*.

Commission of the European Communities (1985c), 'Decision of 8 July 1985 setting up a prior communication and consultation procedure on migration policies in relation to non-member countries', *Bulletin of the European Communities*, Supplement 9/85.

Commission of the European Communities (1988), 'Proposal for a harmonisation of asylum and immigration policies', *COM (88) 640 final*.

Commission of the European Communities (1991), 'Communication on the right of asylum', *SEC (91) 1857 final*.

Commission of the European Communities (1993), 'Report on the possibility of applying Article K.9', *SEC (93) 1687 final*.

Commission of the European Communities (1994), 'Communication on immigration and asylum policy', *COM (94) 23 final*.

Commission of the European Communities (1995), 'Intergovernmental Conference (1996)', *Commission Report for the Reflection Group*, Luxembourg, OOPEC.

Commission of the European Communities (1996), 'Report to the IGC', *Commission Opinion*, Luxembourg, OOPEC.

Commission of the European Communities (1997), 'Proposal to the Council for a Joint Action Based on Article K 3 (2) (b) of the Treaty on European Union Concerning Temporary Protection for Displaced Persons', *Com (97) 93 final*.

Commission of the European Communities (1998), 'Towards an Area of Freedom, Security and Justice', in, *Bulletin EU* 7/8-1998, COM (1998) 0459 of 14.7.1998.

Commission of the European Communities (1999a), *Towards common standards on asylum procedures*, Working document, March 1999.

Commission of the European Communities (1999b), 'Proposal for a Council Decision establishing a European Refugee Fund', *COM (1999) 0686* of 14.12.1999.

Commission of the European Communities (2000a), *Temporary Protection in the event of a mass influx of displaced persons*, IP/00/518 of 24.5.2000.

Commission of the European Communities (2000b), 'Communication on a common asylum procedure and a uniform status for those who are granted asylum valid throughout the Union', *COM (2000) 755 final* of 22.11.2000.

Commission of the European Communities (2000c), *European Commission Staff Working Paper Revisiting the Dublin Convention*, Working document, March 2000.

Coordinators' Group (1992), *Report to the Personal Representatives on the implementation of the Treaty on European Union in the fields of justice and home affairs*, CIRC 3624/2/92 of 29.4.1992.

Council of Europe (1953), Parliamentary Assembly, *Resolution 23 (1953)*.

Council of Europe (1965), Parliamentary Assembly, *Recommendation 434 (1965)*.

Council of Europe (1967), Committee of Ministers, *Resolution 67 (14)* of 29.6.1967.

Council of Europe (1976), Parliamentary Assembly, *Recommendation 878 (1976)*.

Council of Europe (1977), Committee of Ministers, *Declaration on Territorial Asylum* of 28.11.1977.

Council of Europe (1981), Committee of Ministers, *Recommendation R (81) 16* of 5.11.1981.

Council of Europe (1985), Parliamentary Assembly, *Recommendation 1016 (1985)*.

Council of Europe (1988), Parliamentary Assembly, *Recommendation 1088 (1988)*.

Council of Europe (1996), *Activités du Conseil de l'Europe dans le domaine des migrations*, Strasbourg, CDMG (96).

Council of the European Communities (1991), 'Non-Paper – Draft Treaty Articles with a View of Achieving Political Union of 12.4.1994', *Agence Europe* no. 1709/1710 of 3.5.1991.

Council of the European Communities (1992), *Explanatory note to the London Resolutions and Conclusions*, Press Release, Doc. 10518/92 (Presse 230) of 30.11.1992.

Council of the European Union (1995), *Report on the functioning of the Treaty on European Union*, Brussels, Council Secretariat.

CSU (1992), *Neuregelung des Asylrechts*. Leitantrag des Parteivorstandes, 56. Parteitag der CSU, 6./7.11.1992, Nürnberg.

Die Grünen (1986), *Erklärung der Alternativen Liste/Die Grünen zum Flüchtlingskongreß*, 26.9.1986, Bonn, Die Grünen im Bundestag.

Die Grünen (1992), *Farbe bekennen - Gegen Rassismus und Fremdenhaß - Für eine Humane Flüchtlings- und Einwanderungspolitik!*, Beschluß der 14. Ordentlichen Bundesversammlung, 15.-17.5.1992, Berlin-Hohenschönhausen.

ECRE (European Council on Refugees and Exiles) (1993), *Asylum in Europe. Review of refugee and asylum laws and procedures in selected European countries*, 2 vol., London, ECRE.

ECRE (1995), *Note on the harmonisation of the interpretation of Article 1 of the 1951 Geneva Convention*, London, ECRE.

ECRE and Amnesty International (1995), Press release on minimum guarantees for asylum procedures of 10.3.1995, London, ECRE and Amnesty International.

European Council (1992), *Presidency Conclusions*, Edinburgh 11-12.12.1992.

European Council (1999), *Presidency Conclusions*, Tampere 16.10.1999.

European Parliament (1987a), Committee on Legal Affairs and Citizens' Rights, *Report on the right of asylum*, Rapporteur, H. O. Vetter, Doc. A2-227/86/A and A2-227/86/B of 23.2.1987.

European Parliament (1987b), Committee on Legal Affairs and Citizens' Rights, *Resolution on the right of asylum*, Doc. A2-227/86 of 12.3.1987.

European Parliament (1987c), Committee on Legal Affairs and Citizens' Rights, *Resolution on the asylum policy of certain member states*, Doc. B2-512/87 of 18.6.1987.

European Parliament (1992), Resolution on the harmonisation within the European Community of asylum law and policies of 18.11.1992.

European Parliament (1993), Report on the general guidelines of a European refugee policy, A3-0402/92 of 3.12.1993.

European Parliament (1995a), Report on the draft Council Recommendation concerning a specimen bilateral readmission agreement, Rapporteur, Claudia Roth, Document A4-0194/95.

European Parliament (1995b), Report on the functioning of the Treaty on European Union with a view of the 1996 Intergovernmental Conference - implementation and development of the Union, PE 212.450/fin.

European Parliament (2000), *Asylum in the EU Member States*, Working Paper of the Directorate General for Research, Civil Liberties Series, Libe 108 EN.

European Union High Level Working Group on Asylum and Migration (1999), Final Report.

FDP. Die Liberalen (1989), *Liberale Positionen zur Aussliedler-, Asyl- und Ausländerpolitik*. Beschluss des Bundeshauptausschusses Saarbrücken vom 25.2.1989 und des Bundesvorstands vom 27.2.1988, Bonn.

FDP. Die Liberalen (1992), Liberale Forderungen an eine Ausländer- und Asylpolitik, Beschluß der F.D.P. anläßlich des Bundesparteitages am 2/3.10.1992, Bremen.

IGC (Intergovernmental Consultations on Asylum and Migration Policy in Europe) (1994), Working Paper on Readmission Agreements, Geneva.

ILPA (International Law Practitioners' Association) (1996), European Update, December.

ILPA (International Law Practitioners' Association) (1997a), European Update, March.

ILPA (International Law Practitioners' Association) (1997b), European Update, June.

Jospin, Lionel (1997), 'Discourse before the National Assembly given on 19.6.1997', *Libération* of 20.6.1997.

Ministère de l'Interieur (1996), *Zones d'attentes des ports, des aéroports et des gares ferroviaires,* Bilan synthétique de l'année 1996.

Sénat (1991), *Rapport de la Commission de contrôle crée par le Sénat pour examiner la mise en oevre de l'accord de Schengen,* 18.12.1991.

Sénat (1993), *Rapport d'Information no. 167 (1991-1992),* Rapporteur, Paul Masson.

Sénat (1994), *Rapport d'Information no. 384 (1993-1994),* Rapporteur, Paul Masson.

SPD (1989), 'Beschlüsse des Parteitages' der SPD, 20.12.1989, Berlin.

SPD (1992a), *SPD-Sofortprogramm,* Außerordentlicher Parteitag der SPD, 16-17.11.1992, Bonn.

SPD (1992b), Vorlage für die Sitzung der SPD-Bundestagsfraktion am 2. Juni 1992, betrifft, Zuwanderung/Asyl, Gert Wartenberg, Bonn, 21.5.1992.

The Ministers Responsible for Immigration (1991), *Report to the European Council meeting in Maastricht on asylum and immigration policy,* SN 4038/91 WGI 930 of 3.12.1991.

UNHCR (1995a), Update, UNHCR concerned by EU agreement on asylum procedures, Geneva, UNHCR, 10.3.1995.

UNHCR (1995b), *Note on Agents of Persecutions,* Brussels, UNHCR, March.

Secondary Sources

Acherman, Alberto and Gattiker, Mario (1995), 'Safe Third Countries, European Developments', *International Journal of Refugee Law,* 7 (1), 19-38.

Andersen, Sven S. and Eliassen, Kjell A., (eds) (1993), *Making policy in Europe. The Europeanisation of national policy-making,* London, Thousand Oaks.

Arboleda, Eduardo and Hoy, Ian (1993), 'The Convention Refugee Definition in the West, Disharmony of Interpretation and Application', *International Journal of Refugee Law,* 5 (1), 66-90.

Bade, Klaus J. (1994), *Ausländer, Aussiedler, Asyl in der Bundesrepublik Deutschland,* Bonn, Bundeszentrale für Politische Bildung.

Bank, Roland (1999), 'The Emergent EU Policy on Asylum and Refugees', *Nordic Journal of International Law,* 68, 1-29.

Barkin, Samuel J. and Cronin, Bruce (1994), 'The state and the nation, changing norms and the rules of sovereignty in international relations', *International Organization,* 48 (1), 107-130.

Barwig, Klaus and Lörcher, Klaus and Schumacher, Christoph (eds) (1989), *Asylrecht im Binnenmarkt. Die europäische Dimension des Rechts auf Asyl,* Baden-Baden, Nomos.

Barwig, Klaus et al., (1994), *Asyl nach der Änderung des Grundgesetzes. Entwicklungen in Deutschland und Europa,* Baden-Baden, Nomos.

Becker, Joachim (1993), 'Die Städte sind überfordert. Kommunale Erfahrungen mit Asylbewerbern', *Aus Politik und Zeitgeschichte* 7, 53-59.

Bieber, Roland and Monar, Joerg (eds), (1995), *Justice and Home Affairs in the European Union. The development of the Third Pillar*, Brussels, European Interuniversity Press.

Bigo, Didier (ed.) (1992), *L'Europe des polices et de la sécurité intérieure*, Brussels: Editions Complexe.

Bigo, Didier (1996), *Polices en réseaux. L'expérience européenne*, Paris, Presses de Science Po.

Blanke, Bernhard (ed.) (1993), *Zuwanderung und Asyl in der Konkurrenzgesellschaft*, Opladen, Leske und Budrich.

Boeles, Pieter and Terlouw, Ashley (1997), 'Minimum Guarantees for Asylum Procedures', *International Journal of Refugee Law*, 9 (3), 472-491.

Boer, Monica den (ed.) (1997), *The Implementation of Schengen, First the Widening, Now the Deepening*, Maastricht, European Institute of Public Administration.

Boer, Monica den and Wallace, William (2000), 'Justice and Home Affairs', H. Wallace and W. Wallace (eds), *Policy-Making in the European Union*, Oxford, Oxford University Press, 493-518.

Bolten, José (1991), 'From Schengen to Dublin, The new frontiers of refugee law', H. Mejiers et al., (eds), 8-38.

Bommes, Michael (1999), *Migration und Nationaler Wohlfahrtsstaat. Ein differenzierungs-theoretischer Entwurf*, Opladen, Westdeutscher Verlag.

Bosswick, Wolfgang (1997), 'Asylum Policy in Germany', in P. Muus, (ed.), 53-77.

Brachet, Olivier (1997), 'L'impossible organigramme de l'asile en France. Le développement de l'asile au noir', *Revue Européenne des Migrations Internationales*, 13 (1), 7-36.

Brosius, Hans-Bernd and Esser, Frank (1995), *Eskalation durch Berichterstattung? Massenmedien und fremdenfeindliche Gewalt*, Opladen, Leske und Budrich.

Brown, Chris (1992), *International Relations Theory, New Normative Approaches*, Brighton, Harvester Wheatsheaf.

Brubaker, Rogers (1992), *Citizenship and Nationhood in France and Germany*, Cambridge MA, Harvard University Press.

Buergenthal, Thomas (1997), 'The Normative and Institutional Evolution of International Human Rights', *Human Rights Quarterly*, 19 (4), 703-723.

Bull, Hedley (1995), *The Anarchical Society. A Study of Order in World Politics*, 2nd edition, London, Macmillan.

Busch, Heiner (1992), 'Kleine 'Freiheit' durch große 'Sicherheit'. Das Europa der Polizei', *Vorgänge*, 120 (6), 53-64.

Butt Philip, Alan (1994), 'European Union immigration policy, phantom, fantasy or fact?', *West European Politics* 17 (2), 168-191.

Butterwegge, Christoph and Jäger, Siegfried (eds) (1992), *Rassismus in Europa*, Köln.

Buzan, Barry (1993), 'Introduction, The Changing Security Agenda in Europe,' O. Waever et al., (eds), 1-14.

Callovi, Giuseppe (1992), 'Regulation of immigration in (1993), Pieces of the European Community Jig-Saw Puzzle', *International Migration Review*, 26 (2), 353-372.

Carlier, Jean-Yves and Vanheule, Dirk. (eds) (1997), *Europe and Refugees. A Challenge?*, The Hague, Kluwer.

Carlier, Yves et al. (eds) (1997), *Who is a Refugee? A Comparative Case Law Study*, The Hague, Kluwer.

Carr, E.H. (1946), *The Twenty Years Crisis, 1919-1939*, New York, Harper and Row.

Castagnos-Sen, Anne (1996), 'La Problématique Européenne et les Questions Soulevées par la Convention d'Application de l'Accord de Schengen', *Migrations Société*, 48 (8), 77-88.

Chock, Phyllis Pease (1995), 'Ambiguity in policy discourse, Congressional Talk about Immigration', *Policy Sciences*, 28 (2), 165-184.

Clark, Ian (1996), 'Traditions of Thought and Classical Theories of International Relations', I. Clark and I.B. Neuman, (eds) 1-19.

Clark, Ian and Neuman, Iver B., (eds) (1996), *Classical Theories of International Relations*, London, Macmillan.

Classen, Claus Dieter (1993), 'Asylrecht in Frankreich, Zur Bedeutung der verfassungs- und völkerrechtlichen Vorgaben', *Die Öffentliche Verwaltung*, 46 (6), 227-236.

Coleman, William D. (1998), 'From Protected Development to Market Liberalism, Paradigm Change in Agriculture', *Journal of European Public Policy*, 5 (4), 532-651.

Colomer, Josep M., (ed.) (1996), *Political Institutions in Europe*, London and New York, Routledge.

Cornelius, Wayne, Martin, Philip and Hollifield, James, (eds) (1994), *Controlling Immigration*, Stanford, Stanford University Press.

Costa-Lascoux, Jacqueline (1993), 'Continuité ou rupture dans la politique francaise de l'immigration, les lois de 1993', *Revue Européenne des Migrations Internationales*, 9 (3), 233-261.

Cowles, Maria G., Caporaso, James A. and Risse, Thomas (eds) (2000), *Transforming Europe, Europeanization and Domestic Change*, Ithaca, NY, Cornell University Press.

Cruz, Antonio (1993), *Schengen, ad hoc Immigration Group and other intergovernmental Bodies*, Brussels, Briefing Paper no. 12 of the Churches Committee for Migrants in Europe.

Curtin, Deirdre and Meijers, Herman (1995), 'The principle of open government in Schengen and the European Union, Democratic retrogression?', *Common Market Law Review*, 32 (2), 391-442.

Curtis, Michael, (ed.) (1997), *Western European Government and Politics*, New York, Longman.

Czaplinski, Wladislav (1994), 'Aliens and Refugee Law in Poland, Recent Developments', *International Journal of Refugee Law*, 6 (2), 636-642.

Dacyl, Janina (1995), 'Europe needs a new protection system for 'non-convention' refugees', *International Journal of Refugee Law*, 7 (4), 579-605.

Danish Refugee Council (1998), 'Safe third country policies in European countries', *http://www.drc.dk.*

Davy, Ulrike (1996), *Asyl und internationales Flüchtlingsrecht. Völkerrechtliche Bindungen staatlicher Schutzgewährung*, Wien, Verlag Österreich.

De Jong, Cornelius (1995), 'Proactive Policies with Regard to Situations of Mass Influxes', in S. Perrakis (1995) (ed.), 139-143.

Di Maggio, Paul J. and Powell, Walter W. (eds) (1991), *The new institutionalism in organizational analysis*, Chicago and London, The University of Chicago Press.

Diez, Thomas (1998), *From Ideas to Discourse. Foreign Policy Analysis between Beliefs, Norms and Texts.* Paper presented at the ECPR Session, 23-28.3.1998, Warwick.

DiMaggio, Paul (1998), 'New Institutionalism, Avenues of Collaboration', *Journal of Institutional and Theoretical Economics*, 154 (4), 696-705.

Eder, Klaus (1992), *Framing and Communicating Environmental Issues. A Discourse Analysis of Environmentalism*, Florence, European University Institute.

Eder, Klaus (1995), *The Institutionalization of Environmentalism. Ecological Discourse and the Second Transformation of the Public Sphere*, Florence, European University Institute.

Faist, Thomas (1994), 'How to define a foreigner? The symbolic politics of immigration in German partisan discourse, 1978-1992', *West European Politics*, 17 (2), 50-71.

Farine, Philippe (1993), 'Objectif, 'Immigration Zéro'', *Migrations Société*, 28-29, 9-17.

Favell, Adrian (1998), *Philosophies of Integration. Immigration and the Idea of Citizenship in France and Britain*, London, Macmillan.

Federal Ministry of the Interior, 'Recent Developments in the German Law on Asylum and Aliens', *International Journal of Refugee Law*, 6 (2), 265-270.

Fennelly, Nial (2000), 'The Area of 'Freedom, Security and Justice' and the European Court of Justice – a Personal View', *International and Comparative Law Quarterly*, 49 (1), 1-14.

Fernhout, Roel (1995), 'The Treaty on European Union. Suggestions for revision. Justice and Home Affairs, Immigration and Asylum Policy', *Paper of the T.M.C. Asser Institut* of 16.9.1995.

Foot, John (1995), 'The Logic of contradiction, migration control in Italy and France', in R. Miles and D. Thränhardt, (eds) 132-158.

Fortescue, Adrian (1995), 'Opening Statement', in S. Perrakis (ed.) (1995), 7-9.

Fortesque, Adrian (1995), 'First experiences with the Implementation of the Third Pillar Provisions', in R. Bieber and J. Monar, (eds) 19-28.

Freeman, Gary (1994), 'Can liberal states control unwanted migration?', *The Annals of the American Academy*, 534.

Frowein, Jochen and Zimmermann, Andreas (1996), 'Die Asylrechtsreform des Jahres 1993 und das Bundesverfassungsgericht', *Juristen Zeitung* 51 (15-16), 753-764.

Gamson, William A. (1988), 'Political Discourse and Collective Action', *International Social Movement Research*, 1, 219-244.

Gamson, William A. (1992), *Talking Politics*, Cambridge, Cambridge University Press.

Garrett, Geoffrey and Tsebelis, George (1996), 'An Institutional Critique of Intergovernmentalism', *International Organization*, 50 (2), 269-299.

Geddes, Andrew (2000), *Immigration and European Integration. Towards Fortress Europe?*, Manchester, Manchester University Press.

Gehring, Thomas (1994), 'Der Beitrag von Institutionen zur Förderung der internationalen Zusammenarbeit. Lehren aus der institutionellen Struktur der Europäischen Gemeinschaft', *Zeitschrift für Internationale Beziehungen* 1 (2), 211-242.

Gerber, Jean-Pierre (1984), 'Wir brauchen eine europäische Asylpolitik', H. Däpp and R. Karlen, (eds) *Asylpolitik gegen Flüchtlinge*, Basel, Lenos, 97-126.

Giesler, Volkmar and Wasser, Detlef (1993), *Das neue Asylrecht. Die neuen Gesetzestexte und internationalen Abkommen mit Erläuterungen*. Bonn, Bundesanzeiger.

Glahn, Wiltrud von (1992), *Der Kompetenzwandel internationaler Flüchtlingsorganisationen - vom Völkerbund bis zu den Vereinten Nationen*, Baden-Baden, Nomos.

Goebel-Zimmermann, Ralph (1995), 'Handlungsspielräume der Landesregierungen für den Erlass von Abschiebestopppregelungen', *Zeitschrift für Ausländerrecht und Ausländerpolitik*, 19 (1), 23-29.

Goffman, Erving (1974), *Frame Analysis - an Essay on the Organization of Experience*, New York, Harper and Row.

Goodwin-Gil, Guy (1987), 'Refugees, The Functions and Limits of the Existing Protection System', A. E. Nash, (ed.), *Human Rights and the Protection of Refugees under International Law*, Halifax, The Institute for Research on Public Policy, 149-182.

Goodwin-Gill, Guy (1995), 'Asylum, The Law and Politics of Change', *International Journal of Refugee Law*, 7(1), 1-18.

Goodwin-Gill, Guy (1996), *The Refugee in International Law*, 2nd edition, Oxford, Clarendon Press.

Grahl-Madsen, Atle (1972), *The Status of Refugees in International Law*, 2 Vol., Leiden, Sijthoff.

Grewe, Constance and Weber, Albrecht (1993), 'Die Reform des Ausländer- und Asylrechts in Frankreich. Die Entscheidung des Conseil Constitutionnel vom 13. August 1993', *Europäische Grundrechte Zeitschrift*, 20 (20/21), 496-499.

Griffiths, Martin (1992), *Realism, Idealism and International Politics, A Reinterpretation*, London, Routledge.

Guild, Elspeth (1999), 'Discretion, Competence and Migration in the European Union', *European Journal of Migration and Law*, (1) 1, 61-87.

Guild, Elspeth and Niessen, Jan (eds) (1996), *The Developing Immigration and Asylum Policies of the European Union*, The Hague, Kluwer.

Guiraudon, Virginie (1994), 'The reaffirmation of the republican model of integration, Ten years of identity politics in France', *French Politics and Society*, 14 (2).

Guiraudon, Virginie (2000), 'European Integration and Migration Policy, Vertical Policy-Making as Venue Shopping', *Journal of Common Market Studies*, 38 (2), 251-271.

Habermas, Jürgen 1981, *Theorie des kommunikativen Handelns*, 2 vol., Frankfurt a.M., Suhrkamp.

Habermas, Jürgen (1992), 'Handlungen, Sprechakte, sprachlich vermittelte Interaktionen und Lebenswelt', J. Habermas, *Nachmetaphysisches Denken. Philosophische Aufsätze*, Frankfurt a.M., Suhrkamp, 63-104.

Habermas, Jürgen (1994), 'Human Rights and Popular Sovereignty, The Liberal and Republican Versions', *Ratio Juris*, 7 (1), 1-13.

Habermas, Jürgen (1996a), *Die Einbeziehung des Anderen*, Frankfurt a.M., Suhrkamp.

Habermas, Jürgen (1996b), 'The European Nation State. Its Achievements and Its Limitations. On the Past and Future of Sovereignty and Citizenship', *Ratio Juris* 9 (2), 125-137.

Hailbronner, Kay (1989), *Möglichkeiten und Grenzen einer europäischen Koordinierung des Einreise- und Asylrechts, ihre Auswirkungen auf dea Asylrecht der Bundesrepublik Deutschland*, Baden-Baden, Nomos.

Hailbronner, Kay (1993a), *Die Rechtsstellung der De Facto-Flüchtlinge in den EG-Staaten, Rechtsvergleichung und europäische Harmonisierung*, Baden-Baden, Nomos.

Hailbronner, Kay (1993b), 'The Concept of 'Safe Country' and Expeditious Asylum Procedures - A Western European Perspective', *International Journal of Refugee Law*, 5 (1), 31-65.

Hailbronner, Kay (1995), 'Die europäische Asylrechtsharmonisierung nach dem Vertrag von Maastricht', *Zeitschrift für Ausländerrecht und Ausländerpolitik*, 19 (1), 3-13.

Hailbronner, Kay, (ed.) (1992), *Asyl- und Einwanderungsrecht im Europäischen Vergleich*. Köln, Bundesanzeiger.

Hall, Peter (ed.) (1989), *The political power of economic ideas*, Cambridge, Cambridge University Press.

Hall, Peter (1992), 'The movement from Keynesianism to monetarism, Institutional analysis and British economic policy in the 1970s', S. Steinmo and K. Thelen and F. Longstreth, (eds) 90-113.

Hall, Peter and Taylor, Rosemarie (1996), *Political Science and the New Institutionalisms*. Discussion Paper, Max Planck Institut, 96 (6).

Hathaway, James (1984), 'The Evolution of Refugee Status in International Law, 1920-1950', *The International and Comparative Law Quarterly*, 33, 348-380.

Hathaway, James C. (1987), 'International Refugee Law, Humanitarian Standard or Protectionist Ploy?', A. E. Nash, (ed.) *Human Rights and the Protection of Refugees under International Law*, Halifax, The Institute for Research on Public Policy, 183-188.

Hathaway, James C. (1991), *The Law of Refugee Status*, Toronto and Vancouver, Butterworth.

Hathaway, James C. (1993), 'Harmonizing for whom? The Devaluation of Refugee Protection in the Era of European Economic Integration', *Cornell International Law Journal*, 119, 719-735.

Heckmann, Friedrich and Bosswick, Wolfgang, (eds) (1995), *Migration Policies, A Comparative Perspective*, Stuttgart, Emke.

Heine, Regina (1978), 'Ein Grundrecht wird verwaltet', in Amnesty International (ed.), *Bewährungsprobe für ein Grundrecht, Art. 16 Abs. 2 Satz 2 Grundgesetz, Politisch verfolgte genießen Asylrecht*, Baden-Baden, Nomos, 407-504.

Heisler, Martin O. (1992), 'Migration, International Relations and the New Europe, Theoretical Perspectives from Institutional Political Sociology', *International Migration Review* 26 (2), 596-622.

Héritier, Adrienne, Mingers, Susanne, Knill, Christoph and Becka, Martina (1994), *Die Veränderung von Staatlichkeit in Europa. Ein regulativer Wettbewerb, Deutschland, Grossbritannien und Frankreich in der Europäischen Union*, Opladen, Leske und Budrich.

Hesse, Joachim Jens and Ellwein Thomas (1997), *Das Regierungssystem der Bundesrepublik Deutschland*, Opladen, Westdeutscher Verlag.

Hix, Simon and Niessen, Jan (1996), *Reconsidering European Migration Policies. The 1996 Intergovernmental Conference and the Reform of the Maastricht Treaty*, Brussels, Briefing Paper of the Churches' Commission for Migrants in Europe.

Hochet, Agnès (1988), 'L'immigration dans le débat politique français de 1981 à (1988)', *Pouvoirs*, 47 (4), 23-30.

Hoffman, Mark (1994), 'Normative international theory, approaches and issues', A.J.R. Groom and M. Light, (eds) *Contemporary International Relations, A Guide to Theory*. London, Pinter, 27-43.

Hoffmann, Stanley, (1996), *The Ethics and Politics of Humanitarian Intervention*. Indiana, University of Notre Dame Press.

Holborn, Louise W. (1975), *Refugees, A Problem of our Time. The Work of the UNHCR, 1951-1972*, 2 vol., Metuchen, Scarecrow Press.

Hollifield, James F. (1992), *Immigrants, Markets and States, The political economy of postwar Europe*, Cambridge MA, Harvard University Press.

Hollis, Martin and Smith, Steve (1990), *Explaining and Understanding International Relations*. Oxford, Oxford University Press.

Huber, Bertold (1989), 'Artikel 16 Abs. 2 GG und europäischer Binnenmarkt. Zum Spannungsverhältnis von nationalem Verfassungsrecht und europäischer Asylrechtsharmonisierung', in K. Barwig, K. Lörcher and Ch. Schumacher, (eds) 43-64.

Huber, Bertold (1992), 'Asyl- und Ausländerrecht in der Europäischen Gemeinschaft', *Neue Zeitschrift für Verwaltungsrecht*, no. 7, 618-626.

Hullmann, Klaus (1997), 'Germany', J-Y. Carlier and D. Vanheule and K. Hullman and C. Pena Galiano, (eds) *Who is a refugee? A comparative case law study*, The Hague, Kluwer Law International, 225-290.

Hurrell, Andrew (1990), 'Kant and the Kantian paradigm in international relations', *Review of International Studies*, 16 (3), 183-205.

Huysmans, Jef (1995), 'Migrants as a security problem, dangers of 'securitizing' societal issues', in R. Miles and D. Thränhardt, (eds) *Migration and European Integration, the Dynamics of Inclusion and Exclusion*. London, Pinter.

Huysmans, Jef (1998a), 'The Question of the Limit, Desecuritisation and the Aesthetics of Horror in Political Realism', *Millennium*, 27 (3), 569-589.

Huysmans, Jef (1998b), 'Revisiting Copenhagen, or, about the Creative Development of a Security Studies Agenda in Europe', *European Journal of European Relations*, 4 (4).

Ikenberry, John G. (1988), 'Conclusion, An Institutional Approach to American Foreign Economic Policy', *International Organization* 42, 219-243.

Immergut, Ellen (1994), *Historical Approaches to Public Policy*, Entwurf eines Beitrags zum Workshop 'Policy-Forschung und historische Analyse' der DVPW-Sektion Staatslehre und politische Verwaltung, 13 and 14.1.1994, Konstanz.

Immergut, Ellen (1997), 'The Normative Roots of the New Institutionalism, Historical Institutionalism and Comparative Political Studies', in A. Benz and W. Seibel, (eds), 325-355.

Jachtenfuchs, Markus (1993), *Ideen und Interessen, Weltbilder als Kategorien der politischen Analyse*, Arbeitspapier ABIII/Nr. 2, Mannheimer Zentrum für Europäische Sozialforschung, Mannheim.

Jachtenfuchs, Markus (1996), 'Regieren durch Überzeugen, Die Europäische Union und der Treibhauseffekt', in M. Jachtenfuchs and B. Kohler-Koch, (eds) 429-454.

Jachtenfuchs, Markus and Huber, Michael (1993), 'Institutional Learning in the European Community, the response to the greenhouse effect, J.D. Liefferink, P.D. Lowe and A.P.J. Mol (eds) *European Integration and Environmental Policy*, London and New York, John Wiley and Sons, 36-58.

Jachtenfuchs, Markus and Kohler-Koch, Beate, (eds) (1996a), *Europäische Integration*. Opladen, Leske und Budrich.

Jachtenfuchs, Markus and Kohler-Koch, Beate (1996b), 'Einleitung, Regieren im dynamischen Mehrebenensystem', in M. Jachtenfuchs and B. Kohler-Koch, (eds), 15-46.

Jackson, Ivor C. (1984), 'Harmonisierung des Flüchtlingsrechts und der Asylverfahren im europäischen Rahmen', in Otto Benecke Stiftung, (ed.), *Flüchtlinge in Europa*. Dokumentation einer Arbeitstagung 20 and 21.11.1983 in Köln, Baden-Baden, Nomos, 63-70.

Jacobson, David (1996), *Rights across borders, Immigration and the decline of citizenship*, Baltimore, John Hopkins University Press.

Jaeger, Hans-Martin (1996), 'Konstruktionsfehler des Konstruktivismus in den Internationalen Beziehungen', *Zeitschrift für Internationale Beziehungen*, 3(2), 313-340.

Jobert, Bruno and Muller, Pierre (1987), *L'Etat en action, Politiques publiques et corporatismes*, Paris.

Joly, Danièle (1996), *Haven or Hell? Asylum Policies and Refugees in Europe*, London and New York, Macmillan.

Joppke, Christian (1997), 'Asylum and States Sovereignty, A comparison of the United States, Germany, and Britain', *Comparative Political Studies*, 39 (3), 259-298.

Julien-Laferriere, François (1990), 'Le traitement des réfugiés et des demandeurs d'asile au point d'entrée', *Revue Universelle des Droits de l'Homme*, 2, 53-58.

Julien-Laferrière, François (1996), 'L'entrée sur le territoire national', *Migrations Société* 48 (8), 35-44.

Julien-Laferrière, François (1997), 'La 'loi Debré' sur l'immigration', *Regards sur l'Actualité*, 232, 27-39.

Julien-Laferrière, François (1998), 'La 'loi Chevènement' sur l'entrée et le séjour des étrangers et sur le droit d'asile', *Regards sur l'Actualité*, 242, 17-39.

Jun, Uwe (1995), 'Die zweite 'cohabitation' in Frankreich (seit April 1993). Terraingewinne der Parteien und des Parlamentes', *Zeitschrift für Parlamentsfragen*, Sonderband 1/95, 146-161.

Kantemir, Rita 1985, 'Die Vorreiterrolle Lummers in der Ausländerpolitik', *Vorgänge*, 78 (6), 24-27.

Kanther, Manfred (1994), 'Innere Sicherheit in Deutschland', in M. Kanther, B. Seite and H. Eggert (eds) *Innere Sicherheit in Deutschland*, Konrad-Adenauer-Stiftung, Aktuelle Fragen der Politik, Nr. 14, Sankt Augustin, 7-16.

Kapteyn, Paul (1991), ''Civilization under negotiation'. National Civilizations and European Integration, The Treaty of Schengen', *Archives Européennes de Sociologie*, 32, 363-380.

Kastoryano, Riva (1996), 'Immigration and Identities in France, The War of Words', *French Politics and Society*, 14 (2), 58-66.

Katzenstein, Peter (1987), *Policy and Politics in West Germany*, Philadelphia, Temple University Press.

Katzenstein, Peter (1990), *Analyzing Change in International Politics, The New Institutionalism and the Interpretative Approach*, Paper des Max-Planck-Instituts für Gesellschaftsforschung, Köln.

Kauffmann, Heiko (1986), 'Fremdenfeindlichkeit als Regierungspolitik. Von der Demontage eines Grundrechts zum Verlust der politischen Kultur', in H. Kauffmann, (ed.), *Kein Asyl bei den Deutschen. Anschlag auf ein Grundrecht*, Reinbek, 16-34.

Keraudren, Philippe (1994), 'Réticences et obstacles français face à Schengen, la logique de la politique de sécurité', in A. Pauly, (ed.), 123-144.

Kerber, Karoline (1997), 'Temporary protection, an assessment of the harmonisation policies of European Union Member States', *International Journal of Refugee Law*, 9 (3), 453-175.

Kimminich, Otto 1978, 'Die Geschichte des Asylrechts', Amnesty International, (ed.), *Bewährungsprobe für ein Grunrecht. Art. 16 Abs. 2 Satz 2 Grundgesetz, 'Politisch Verfolgte geniessen Asylrecht'*, Baden-Baden, Nomos, 19-66.

Kimminich, Otto (1984), 'Harmonisierung des Flüchtlingsrechts und der Asylverfahren im europäischen Rahmen', in Otto Benecke Stiftung (ed.), *Flüchtlinge in Europa*. Dokumentation einer Arbeitstagung 20/21.11.1983 in Köln, Baden-Baden, Nomos, 53-80.

Kjaergaard, Eva (1994), 'The Concept of Safe Third Country in Contemporary European Refugee Law', *International Journal of Refugee Law*, 6 (4), 649-655.

Kjaerum, Morten (1992), 'The Concept of Country of First Asylum', *International Journal of Refugee Law*, 4 (4), 514-530.

Klein, Josef (1995), 'Asyl-Diskurs. Konflikte und Blockaden in Politik, Medien und Alltagswelt', in R. Reiher (ed.), *Sprache im Konflikt, zur Rolle der Sprache in sozialen, politischen und militärischen Auseinandersetzungen*, Berlin and New York, de Gruyter, 15-71.

Knight, Uwe and Kowalsky, Wolfgang (1991), *Deutschland nur den Deutschen? Die Ausländerfrage in Deutschland, Frankreich und den USA*, Erlangen, Straube.

Knipping, Helge Margaret and Saumweber-Meyer, Uta (1995), 'Basic Principles of Asylum Law and Asylum Procedure in the Federal Republic of Germany', in F. Heckmann and W. Bosswick, (eds) 267-304.

Kohler-Koch, Beate, (ed.) (1998a), *Regieren in entgrenzten Räumen*, PVS Sonderheft 39 (29), Opladen, Westdeutscher Verlag.

Kohler-Koch, Beate (1998b), 'Einleitung, Effizienz und Demokratie, Probleme des Regierens in entgrenzten Räumen', in B. Kohler-Koch, (ed.), 11-28.

Kohler-Koch, Beate and Edler, Jakob (1998), 'Ideendiskurs und Vergemeinschaftung, Erschließung transnationaler Räume durch europäisches Regieren', B. Kohler-Koch, (ed.), 169-206.

Kommers, Donald (1997), 'The Government of Germany', in M. Curtis et al., (eds) *Western European Governments and Politics*, New York, Longman, 153-221.

Koslowski, Rey (1998), *Personal Security, State Sovereignty and the Deepening and Widening of European Cooperation in Justice and Home Affairs*, Conference Paper presented at the Conference 'Dilemmas of Immigration Control in a Globalizing World' of the European Forum on International Migrations, MIG/59, Florence, European University Institute.

Krasner, Stephen D. (1983), 'Structural Causes and Regime Consequences, Regimes as Intervening Variables', in S. D. Krasner, (ed.) *International Regimes*, Ithaca, Cornell University Press, 1-21.

Krasner, Stephen D. (1993a), 'Westphalia and All That', in J. Goldstein and R.O. Keohane (eds) *Ideas and Foreign Policy, Beliefs, Institutions, and Political Change*, Ithaca, Cornell University Press, 235-264.

Krasner, Stephen D. (1993b), 'Sovereignty, Regimes and Human Rights', in V. Rittberger, (ed.), *Regime Theory and International Relations*, Oxford, Clarendon Press, 139-167.

Kratochwil, Friedrich (1986), 'Of Systems, Boundaries, and Territoriality, An Inquiry into the Formation of the State System', *World Politics*, 39, 27-52.

Kratochwil, Friedrich (1989), *Norms, Rules and Decisions*, Cambridge, Cambridge University Press.

Kreuzberg, Hans (ed.) (1984), *Grundrecht auf Asyl, Materialien zur Entstehungsgeschichte*, Köln, Heymann.

Krulic, Joseph (1988), 'L'immigration et l'identité de la France, mythes et réalités', *Pouvoirs*, 47 (4), 31-44.

Kühne, Hans-Heiner (1991), *Kriminalitätsbekämpfung durch innereuropäische Grenzkontrollen? Auswirkungen der Schengener Abkommen auf die innere Sicherheit*, Berlin, Bertelsmann.

Lambert, Hélène (1995), 'Asylum-Seekers, refugees and the European Union, case studies of France and the UK', in R. Miles and D. Thränhardt, (eds) 112-131.

Landgren, Karin (1995), 'Safety Zones and International Protection, A Dark Grey Area', *International Journal of Refugee Law*, 7 (3), 436-458.

Langeron, Pierre (1996), 'Frankreich - eine verfassungsrechtliche Anomalie?', *Juristen Zeitung*, 51 (4), 170-175.

Lavenex, Sandra (1998a), 'Transgressing borders, The emergent European refugee regime and 'safe third countries'', in P. Peters and A. Cafruny (eds) *The Union and the World*, The Hague, Kluwer Law International, 113-132.

Lavenex, Sandra (1998b), 'Asylum, Immigration and Central-Eastern Europe, Challenges to EU Enlargement', *European Foreign Affairs Review*, 3 (2), 275-294.

Lavenex, Sandra (1999), *Safe Third Countries. Extending EU Asylum and Immigration Policies to Central and Eastern Europe*. Budapest and New York, Central European University Press.

Lavenex, Sandra (2000), 'France, International norms, European integration and state discretion', in J. Van Selm (ed.), *Kosovo's 'refugees' in the EU*, London, Pinter.

Lavenex, Sandra (2001a), 'Migration and the EU's new eastern border, between realism and liberalism', in *Journal of European Public Policy* 8 (1), 24-42.

Lavenex, Sandra (2001b), 'The Europeanisation of refugee policies. Institutional legacies and normative challenges', in *Journal of Common Market Studies* 39 (5), forthcoming.

Leggewie, Claus (1993), 'SOS France, Ein Einwanderungsland kommt in die Jahre', in C.Y. Robertson-Wensamer (ed.), *Multikulturalität - Interkulturalität? Probleme und Perspektiven der Multikulturellen Gesellschaft*, Baden-Baden, Nomos, 212-238.

Legoux, Luc (1993), 'La demande d´asile en France, le pic de 1989 et la théorie de la dissuasion', *Revue Européenne des Migrations Internationales*, 9 (2), 31-65.

Legoux, Luc (1995), *La crise de l'asile politique en France*, Paris, Centre Français sur la Population et le Developement.

Leuprecht, Peter (1989), 'Bestrebungen des Europarats zur Harmonisierung des Asylrechts', in K. Barwig and K. Lörcher and C. Schumacher, (eds) 237-250.

Lipschutz, Ronnie D., (ed.) (1995), *On Security*, New York, Columbia University Press.

Lobcovicz, Wenceslas de (1990), 'Quelle libre circulation des personnes en 1993?', *Revue du Marché Commun*, 334, 93-102.

Loescher, Gil (1989a), 'Introduction', in G. Loescher and L. Monahan, (eds) *Refugees and International Relations.* New York, Oxford Universtity Press, 1-33.

Loescher, Gil (1989b), 'The European Community and Refugees', *International Affairs*, 65, 617-636.

Loescher, Gil (ed.) (1992), *Refugees and the Asylum Dilemma in the West*, Pennsylvania, Pennsylvania State University Press.

Loescher, Gil (1993), *Beyond Charity. International Cooperation and the Global Refugee Crisis*, New York and Oxford, Oxford University Press.

Loescher, Gil and Monahan, Leyla (eds) Refugees and International Relations. New York, Oxford Universtity Press, 1-33.

Luchaire, François (1994), 'Le droit d'asile et la révision de la constitution', *Revue du droit public et de la science politique en France et à l'étranger*, 1, 5-44.

Maaßen, Hans-Georg and de Wyl, Marion (1996), 'Folgerungen aus den Asylurteilen des Bundesverfassungsgerichts vom 14. Mai (1996) zur Drittstaatenregelung', *Zeitschrift für Ausländerrecht und Ausländerpolitik*, 20 (4), 158-165.

Maaßen, Hans-Georg and de Wyl, Marion (1997), 'Folgerungen aus den Asylurteilen des Bundesverfassungsgerichts vom 14. Mai (1996) zur Herkunftsstaaten- und zur Flughafenregelung', *Zeitschrift für Ausländerrecht und Ausländerpolitik*, 21 (1), 9-17.

Mahmood, Shiraz (1995), 'The Schengen Information System, An Inequitable Data Protection Regime', *International Journal of Refugee Law*, 7 (2), 179-200.

Maier, Matthias (1998), *Three images of ideas in political science, conceptual and methodological issues*, Paper presented for presentation at the workshop on 'Norms and Interests in International Relations' of the IR Working Group, EUI, Florence, 21-22.11.1998.

Majone, Giandomenico (1991), 'Research programs and action programs, or can policy research learn from the philosophy of science?', in P. Wagner, C. H. Weiss and B. Wittrock and H. Wollmann (eds) *Social Science and Modern State. National experiences and theoretical crossroads*, Cambridge, Cambridge University Press, 290-306.

Manfrass, Klaus (1989), 'Politische Flüchtlinge und Asylbewerber in Frankreich', in K. Barwig (ed.), 149-179.

Manfrass, Klaus (1993), 'Zuwanderer und Asylanten in Frankreich und Deutschland. Vergleichende Überlegungen zu einem dauerhaften Problem', *Dokumente*, 49 (1), 34-42.

Marx, Reinhard (1978), 'Plädoyer für ein liberales Asylrecht', Amnesty International, (ed.), *Bewährungsprobe für ein Grunrecht. Art. 16 Abs. 2 Satz 2 Grundgesetz, 'Politisch Verfolgte geniessen Asylrecht'*, Baden-Baden, Nomos, 111-188.

Marx, Reinhard (1984), *Eine menschenrechtliche Begründung des Asylrechts. Rechtstheoretische und -dogmatische Untersuchungen zum Politikbegriff im Asylrecht*, Baden-Baden, Nomos.

Marx, Reinhard (1992), 'Anforderungen an ein europäisches Asylrecht', *Kritische Justiz* 25, 405-426.

Marx, Reinhard and Lumpp, Katharina (1996), 'The German Constitutional Court's Decision of 14 May 1996 on the Concept of 'Safe Third Countries'' - A Basis for Burden-Sharing in Europe?, *International Journal of Refugee Law*, 8 (3), 419-437.

Meijers, Herman et al., (eds) (1991), *Schengen. Internationalization of central chapers of the law of aliens, refugees, privacy, security and the police.* Deventer, Kluwer.

Melander, Göran 1978, 'Refugees in Orbit', in Amnesty International, (ed.), *Bewährungsprobe für ein Grunrecht. Art. 16 Abs. 2 Satz 2 Grundgesetz, 'Politisch Verfolgte geniessen Asylrecht'*, Baden-Baden, Nomos, 67-96.

Melander, Göran (1987), *The Two Refugee Definitions*, Lund, Raoul Wallenberg Institute of Human Rights and Humanitarian Law, Report no. 4.

Mény, Yves (1996), 'France. The institutionalization of leadership', in J. M. Colomer (ed.), *Political Institutions in Europe*, London and New York, Curtis, 99-137.

Mény, Yves, Muller, Pierre and Quermonne, Jean-Luis, (eds) (1996), *Adjusting to Europe, The Impact of the European Union on National Institutions and Policies*, London, Routledge.

Miles, Robert and Thränhardt, Dietrich (eds) (1995), *Migration and European integration, the dynamics of inclusion and exclusion*, London, Pinter.

Monar, Jörg (1993), 'The European Parliament and Immigration Policy, Its Position and Possibilities of Control', in G. Korella and P. Twomey, (eds) *Towards a European Immigration Policy*, Brussels, European Interuniversity Press, 123-137.

Monar, Joerg (1995), 'Democratic Control of Justice and Home Affairs, The European Parliament and the National Parliaments', in R. Bieber and J. Monar, (eds) 243-258.

Monar, Jörg (2000), *Flexibility and closer cooperation in an emerging European migration policy, opportunities and risks*, Working Paper, No.1, Rome, CeSPI.

Morgenthau, Hans Joachim (1973), Politics among nations. The struggle for power and peace, New York, Knopf.

Moussalli, Michel (1988), 'Reflexions sur l'actualité de la Convention de 1951 rélative au statut des réfugiès', *Chronique de la Ligue Belge des Droits de l'Homme*, June.

Münch, Ursula (1993), *Asylpolitik in der Bundesrepublik Deutschland, Entwicklungen und Alternativen*, Opladen, Leske und Budrich.

Muus, Philip, (ed.) (1997), *Exclusion and Inclusion of Refugees in Contemporary Europe*, Utrecht, Ercomer.

Myers, Philip (1995), 'The Commission's Approach to the Third Pillar, Political and Organizational Elements' in R. Bieber and J. Monar, (eds) 277-300.

Nair, Sami (1994), *Lettres à Charles Pasqua de la part de ceux qui ne sont pas bien nés*, Paris, Editions du Seuil.

Nanz, Klaus-Peter (1994), 'Das Schengener Übereinkommen, Personenfreizügigkeit in integrationspolitischer Perspektive', *Integration*, 17 (2), 92-108.

Niemeier, Michael (1995), 'The K.4 Committee and its position in the decision making process', in R. Bieber and J. Monar, (eds) 321-332.

Niessen, Jan (1996), 'Introduction', in E. Guild and J. Niessen, (eds) 3-66.

Noiriel, Gérard (1991), *La Tyrannie du National. Le Droit d'Asile en Europe 1793-1993*, Paris, Callmann-Levy.

Noll, Gregor (1997), 'The Non-Admission and Return of Protection Seekers in Germany', *International Journal of Refugee Law*, 9 (3), 415-452.

Norek, Claude and Doumic-Doublet, Frédérique (1989), *Le Droit d'Asile en France*, Paris, Presses Universitaires de France.

Nullmeier, Frank (1993), 'Wissen und Policy-Forschung. Wissenspolitologie und rhetorisch-dialektisches Handlungsmodell', in A. Héritier (ed.), *Policy-Analyse. Kritik und Neuorientierung*, PVS Sonderheft, 24, 175-194.

Nullmeier, Frank (1997), 'Interpretative Ansätze in der Politikwissenschaft', in A. Benz and W. Seibel, (eds) 101-143.

Nullmeier, Frank and Rüb, Friedbert W. (1993), *Die Transformation der Sozialpolitik, vom Sozialstaat zum Sicherungsstaat*, Frankfurt a.M. and New York, Suhrkamp.

Nuscheler, Franz (1995), *Internationale Migration. Flucht und Asyl*, Opladen, Leske und Budrich.

O'Keeffe, David (1994), 'Non-Accession to the Schengen Convention, The Cases of the United Kingdom and Ireland', in A. Pauly, (ed.), 145-154.

O'Keeffe, David (1995), 'Recasting the Third Pillar', *European Common Market Law Review*, 32 (4), 893-920.

O'Keeffe, David (1996), 'A Critical View of the Third Pillar', in A. Pauly, (ed.), 1-16.

Oellers-Frahm, Karin (1992), 'Grundlagen des Asylrechts in Frankreich', in K. Hailbronner, (ed.), *Asyl- und Einwanderungsrecht im europäischen Vergleich*, Bonn, Bundesanzeiger, 29-37.

Oellers-Frahm, Karin and Zimmermann, Andreas (1996), 'France's and Germany's Constitutional Changes and their Impact on Migration Law - Policy and Practice', *German Yearbook of International Law*, 38, 249-283.

Ogata, Sadako (1993), 'Refugees and asylum-seekers, A challenge to European immigration policy', The Philip Morris Institute for Public Policy Research (ed.), *Towards a European immigration policy*, London, The Philip Morris Institute for Public Policy Research, 5-17.

Olms, Ellen and Liehmann, Dieter (1989), 'EG-Binnenmarkt, Der 'Europäische Sicherheitsstaat' naht...', *Vorgänge*, 98 (2), 62-74.

Olsen, Johan (1991), 'Political Science and Organization Theory. Parallel Agendas but Mutual Disregard', in R. Czada and A. Windhoff-Héritier (eds) *Political choice, institutions, rules, and the limits of rationality*, Frankfurt a.M., Campus, 87-119.

Olsen, Johan P. (1995a), *European Challenges to the Nation State*. Arena Working Paper no. 14, Oslo.

Olsen, Johan P. (1995b), *Europeanization and Nation-State Dynamics*. Arena Working Paper no. 9, Oslo.

Olsen, Johan P. (2000), *Organising European Institutions of Governance. A Prelude to an Institutional Account of Political Integration.* Arena Working Paper no. 00/2, Oslo.

Opitz, Peter J. (1988), *Das Weltflüchtlingsproblem. Ursachen und Folgen,* München. Beck.

Papademetriou, Demetrios G. (1996), *Coming Together or Pulling Apart? The European Union's Struggle with Immigration and Asylum,* Washington D.C., Carnegie Endowment for International Peace.

Pauly, Alexis (ed.) (1993), *Les accords de Schengen, Abolition des frontières intérieures ou menace pour les libertés publiques?,* Maastricht, European Institute of Public Administration.

Pauly, Alexis (ed.) (1994), *Schengen en Panne.* Maastricht, European Institute of Public Administration.

Pauly, Alexis (ed.) (1996), *De Schengen à Maastricht, voie royale et course d' obstacles,* Maastricht, European Institute of Public Administration.

Peaucelle, Jean-Christophe (1990), 'L'immigration et la libre circulation des personnes en Europe, enjeux et perspectives', *Revue Française du Droit Administratif,* 6 (4), 516-524.

Peers, Steve (1998), *Mind the Gap! Ineffective Member State Implementation of European Union Asylum Measures,* Report prepared for the Immigration Law Practioners' Association and the Refugee Council, London, ILPA and Refugee Council.

Perotti, Antonio (1996), 'L'immigration en France, Fracture de la Droite', *Migrations Société,* 45 (8), 131-140.

Perotti, Antonio (1997), 'Le retour en force du dossier relatif à l'immigration', *Migrations Société,* 50-51 (9), 129-140.

Perotti, Antonio and Thepaut, France (1989), 'Le Président de la République et les Immigrés', *Migrations Societé,* 41-58.

Perrakis, Stelios (ed.), (1995), *Immigration and European Union, Building on a Comprehensive Approach,* Athens, Sakkoulas.

Plender, Richard (1995), 'Asylum Policy, Deficits of Intergovernmental Cooperation', in R. Bieber and J. Monar, (eds) 141-166.

Prantl, Heribert (1993), 'Hysterie und Hilflosigkeit. Chronik der Asyldebatte seit der Deutschen Einheit', in B. Blanke (ed.), (1993), 301-338.

Quermonne, Jean-Louis (1994), 'Chronique d'une révision constitutionnelle bouleversée, La révision constitutionnelle en France, en régime de 'cohabitation'', *French Politics & Society,* 12 (1), 1-15.

Reermann, Olaf (1992), 'Deutschland', in K. Hailbronner, (ed.), 16-28.

Rein, Martin and Schon, Donald (1991), 'Frame-reflective policy discourse', P. Wagner, C.H. Weiss, B. Wittrock and H. Wollmann (eds) *Social Sciences and Modern State National Experiences and Theoretical Crossroads,* Cambridge, Cambridge University Press, 262-289.

Reiss, Hans, (ed.) (1991), *Kant. Political Writings,* Cambridge, Cambridge University Press.

Risse-Kappen, Thomas (1994), 'Ideas do not float freely, transnational coalitions, domestic structures, and the end of the cold war', *International Organization*, 48 (2), 185-214.

Rogers, Rosemarie (1992), 'The future of refugee flows and policies', *International Migration Review*, 26 (4), 1112-1143.

Roos, Alfred (1991a), 'Flüchtlingspolitik und innenpolitische Debatte. Oder 17 Jahre 'Asylmißbrauch'- (noch) kein Jubiläum', *Vorgänge*, 109 (1), 46-60.

Roos, Alfred (1991b), 'Für das Grundrecht auf Asyl. Anmerkungen zur Debatte um eine 'realistische' Flüchtlingspolitik', *Vorgänge*, 111 (3), 84-100.

Roos, Alfred (1992), 'Von Menschen und Wahlen. Neues aus der Asylarena', *Vorgänge*, 115 (1), 77-84.

Roos, Alfred (1994), 'Neue Entwicklungen in der Flüchtlingspolitik', *Vorgänge*, 127 (3), 58-71.

Rothkegel, Ralf (1994), 'Ewigkeitsgarantie für das Asylrecht?', in K. Barwig et al., (eds) 178-196.

Rudge, Philip (1989), 'European initiatives on asylum', in D. Joly and R. Cohen, (eds) *Reluctant Hosts, Europe and its Refugees*, Aldershot, Avebury.

Ruggie, John G. (1986), 'Continuity and Transformation in the World Polity, Toward a Neorealist Synthesis', in R.O. Keohane, (ed.) *Neorealism and its Critics*, New York, Columbia University Press, 131-157.

Ruggie, John G. (1993), 'Territoriality and beyond, problematizing modernity in international relations', *International Organization*, 47 (1), 139-174.

Rupprecht, Reinhard and Hellenthal, Markus (eds) (1992), *Innere Sicherheit im Europäischen Binnenmarkt*, Gütersloh, Bertelsmann.

Sabatier, Paul (1993), 'Advocacy-Koalitionen, Policy-Wandel und Policy-Lernen, Eine Alternative zur Phasenheuristik' in A. Héritier, (ed.), *Policy-Analyse. Kritik und Neuorientierung*, PVS Sonderheft, 26, 116-148.

Sabatier, Paul (1997), *The advocacy coalition framework, revisions and relevance for Europe*. Jean Monnet Chair Lecture, European University Institute and Robert Schuman Centre, 21.10.1997.

Santel, Bernhard (1995), *Migration in und nach Europa. Erfahrungen. Strukturen. Politik*, Opladen, Leske und Budrich.

Sassen, Saskia (1991), *The Global City*, New York, Princeton University Press.

Sassen, Saskia (1996), *Losing Control?*, New York, Columbia University Press.

Schain, Martin A. (1990), 'Immigration and Politics', in P.A. Hall and J. Hayward and H. Machin, (eds) *Developments in French Politics*, London, Macmillan, 253-269.

Schain, Martin A. (1994), 'Ordinary Politics, Immigrants, Direct Action, and the Political Process in France', *French Politics and Society*, 12 (2-3).

Schain, Martin A. (1996), 'The Immigration Debate and the National Front', in J.T.S. Keeler and M.A. Schain, (eds) *Chirac's Challenge. Liberalization, Europeanization and Malaise in France*, New York, St. Martin's Press, 169-198.

Scharpf, Fritz W. (1998), 'Die Problemlösungsfähigkeit der Mehrebenenpolitik in Europa', in B. Kohler-Koch, (ed.), 121-143.

Scharpf, Fritz W. (1999), *Governing in Europe. Effective and Democratic?*, Oxford, Oxford University Press.

Schäuble, Wolfgang (1989), 'Artikel 16 Grundgesetz und europäischer Binnenmarkt aus der Sicht der Bundesregierung', in K. Barwig, K. Lörcher and C. Schumacher (eds) 21-35.

Schäuble, Wolfgang (1991), 'Vorschläge und Bemühungen zur Lösung der Asylproblematik', *Bulletin*, Presse- und Informationsamt der Bundesregierung, 85, 689-691.

Schelter, Kurt (1996), 'Innenpolitische Zusammenarbeit in Europa zwischen Maastricht und Regierungskonferenz 1996', *Aus Politik und Zeitgeschichte*, no. 1-2, 1-18.

Schieffer, Manfred (1997), 'The readmission of third-country nationals within bilateral and multilateral frameworks', in M. de Boer, (ed.), 97-100.

Schmitter, Philippe C. (1996), *Is it really possible to democratize the Euro-polity?*, Arena Working Paper no. 10, Oslo.

Schnapper, Dominique (1991), *La France de l'intégration. Sociologie de la nation en 1990*, Paris, Gallimard.

Schnapper, Dominique (1995), 'The Significance of French Immigration and Integration Policy', in F. Heckmann and W. Bosswick (eds) *Migration Policies, A Comparative Perspective*, Stuttgart, Enke, 99-112.

Schnapper, Dominique (1998), *La relation a l'autre. Au coeur de la pensée sociologique*, Paris, Gallimard.

Scholdan, Bettina (2000), 'Addressing the root causes, Relief and development assistance between peacebuilding and preventing refugee flows', *The Journal of Humanitarian Assistance*, June 2000, *http://www.jha.ac/articles/a058.htm*.

Schor, Ralph (1996), 'L'extreme droite française et les immigrés en temps de crise. Années 1930 - Années 1980', *Revue Européenne des Migrations Internationales*, 12 (2), 241-260.

Schraml, Alexander (1991), 'Das Schengener Übereinkommen und Artikel 16 Absatz 2 Satz 2 des Grundgesetzes der Bundesrepublik Deutschland', *AWR-Bulletin (Vierteljahresschrift für Flüchtlingsfragen)*, 29 (1), 65-71.

Scott, W. Richard and Meyer, John W. et al., (eds) (1994), *Institutional Environments and Organizations, Structural Complexity and Individualism*, Thousand Oaks, Sage.

Seiters, Rudolf (1992), 'Rede anläßlich der ersten Lesung des Gesetzes zum Schengener Übereinkommen vom 19. Juni 1990 im Deutschen Bundestag am 30.4.1992', *Innere Sicherheit*, (2), 1-3.

Selm, Joanne, van (ed.) (2000), *Kosovo's 'refugees' in the EU*, London, Pinter.

Selm-Thorburn, Joanne van (1998), *Refugee Protection in Europe. Lessons from the Yugoslav Crisis*, The Hague, Kluwer.

Silverman, Maxim (1992), *Deconstructing the Nation. Immigration, racism and citizenship in modern France*, London and New York, Routledge.

Skran, Claudena M. (1992), 'The International Refugee Regime, The Historical and Contemporary Context of International Responses to Asylum Problems', in G. Loescher, (ed.), 8-35.

Smith, Steve (1992), 'The Forty Years' Detour, The Resurgence of Normative Theory in International Relations', *Millennium*, 21(3), 489-506.

Smith, Steve (1995), 'The Self-Images of a Discipline. A Genealogy of International Relations Theory', in K. Booth and S. Smith, (eds) *International Relations Theory Today, Pennsylvania*, The Pennsylvania State University Press, 1-37.

Smith, Steve (1997), 'New Approaches to International Theory', J. Baylis and S. Smith, (eds) *The Globalization of World Politics. An Introduction to International Relations*. Oxford, Oxford University Press, 165-190.

Spijkerboer, Thomas (1993), *A bird's eye view of asylum law in eight European countries*, Amsterdam.

Standing Committee of Experts in international immigration, refugee and criminal law (1993), *A new immigration law for Europe? The 1992 London and 1993 Copenhagen rules on immigration.* Utrecht, Nederlands Centrum Buitenlanders.

Steinmo, Sven, Thelen, Kathleen and Longstreth, Frank (eds) (1992), *Structuring Politics, Historical Institutionalism in Comparative Analysis*, Cambridge, Cambridge University Press.

Targuieff, Pierre-André, (ed.) (1991), *Face au racisme*, Paris, Editions la Découverte.

Tarrow, Sydney (1994), *Power in Movement, Social Movements and Contentious Politics*, Cambridge, Cambridge University Press.

Teitelbaum, Michael and Weiner, Myron, (eds) (1995), *Threatened Peoples, Threatened Borders. World Migration and U.S. Policy.* New York and London, W.W. Norton and Company.

Teitgen-Colly, Catherine (1994), 'Le Droit d'Asile, La Fin des Illusions', *L'actualité juridique - Droit administratif*, 20.2.1994, 97-114.

Thelen, Kathleen and Steinmo, Sven (1992), 'Historical institutionalism in comparative analysis', S. Steinmo, K. Thelen and F. Longstreth, (eds) 1-32.

Thorburn, Joanne (1995), 'Transcending Boundaries, Temporary Protection and burden-sharing in Europe', *International Journal of Refugee Law*, 7 (3), 459-480.

Thorburn, Joanne (1996), 'Root Cause Approaches to Forced Migration, Part of a Comprehensive Strategy?', *Journal of Refugee Studies*, 9 (2), 119-135.

Tiberghien, Frédéric (1984), *La Protection des Réfugiés en France*, Paris, Economica.

Tomuschat, Christian (1996), 'Asylrecht in der Schieflage. Anmerkungen zu den drei Asylrechtsurteilen des BVerfG', *Europäische Grundrechte Zeitschrift*, 25 (15-17), 381-386.

Tricot, Bernard, Hadas-Lebel, Raphael and Kessler, David (1995), *Les institutions politiques françaises*, second edition, Paris, Presses de la Fondation Nationale de Sciences Politiques & Dailloz.

Tuppen, John (1991), *Chirac's France, 1986-1988. Contemporary Issues in French Society*, London, Macmillan.

Türk Volker (1992), *Das Flüchtlingshochkommissariat der Vereinten Nationen (UNHCR)*, Berlin, Springer.

Uçarer, Emek M. (1999), *Asylum Harmonization and European Integration, W(h)ither Refugee Protection*, unpublished PhD dissertation, University of South Carolina.

Uibopuu, Henn-Jüri (1983), 'Der Schutz der Flüchtlinge im Rahmen des Europarats', *Archiv des Völkerrechts*, 21, 60-103.

Ulmer, Matthias (1995), *Asylrecht und Menschenwürde. Zur Problematik der 'Sicheren Drittstaaten' nach Art. 16a Abs.2 und 5 GG und die Harmonisierung des Asylrechts in Europa*, Frankfurt a.M. et al., Peter Lang.

UNHCR, (1995), *The State of Refugees in the World*, London, UNHCR.

Vincent, J.Y. (1987), 'Le régime juridique des étrangers en droit français', in J.A. Frowein and T. Stein, (eds) *Die Rechtstellung von Ausländern nach staatlichem Recht und Völkerrecht*, 2 volumes, Berlin et al., Springer, 433-500.

Waever, Ole (1993), 'Societal Security, the Concept', in O. Waever et al., (eds), 17-40.

Waever, Ole (1995), 'Identity, Integration and Security. Solving the Sovereignty Puzzle in E.U. Studies', *Journal of International Affairs*, 42 (2), 389-431.

Waever, Ole (1996a), 'European Security Identities', *Journal of Common Market Studies*, 34 (1), 103-132.

Waever, Ole (1996b), 'The Rise and Fall of the Inter-Paradigm Debate', in S. Smith, K. Booth and M. Zalewski, (eds) *International Theory, Positivism and Beyond*. Cambridge, Cambridge University Press, 149-185.

Waever, Ole et al., (eds) (1993), *Identity, Migration and the New Security Order in Europe*, London, Pinter.

Waldstein, Michael (1993), *Das Asylgrundrecht im europäischen Kontext. Wege einer europäischen Harmonisierung des Asyl- und Flüchtlingsrechts*, Frankfurt a.M., Peter Lang.

Wallace, Helen (2000), 'The Institutional Setting, Five Variations on a Theme', in H. Wallace and W. Wallace (eds), *Policy-Making in the European Union*, Oxford, Oxford University Press, 3-36.

Waltz, Kenneth (1979), *Theory of International Politics*, Reading, MA, Addison-Wesley.

Weil, Patrick (1988), 'La Politique Française de l'Immigration', *Pouvoirs*, 47 (4), 45-60.

Weil, Patrick (1995a), *La France et ses Étrangers*, 2nd edition, Paris, Folio.

Weil, Patrick (1995b), 'Die Französische Politik der Einwanderung, der Integration und der Staatsbürgerschaft', in CiRAC, Cfi, DGAP and IFRi (eds) *Handeln für Europa*, Deutsch-Französische Zusammenarbeit in einer veränderten Welt, Opladen, Leske und Budrich.

Weil, Patrick (1995c), 'Racisme et discrimination dans la politique francaise de l'immigration. 1938-1945 and1974-1995', *Vingtième Sciècle* 4, 77-102.

Weil, Patrick (1995d), *Pour une Nouvelle Politique d' Immigration*, Paris, Notes de la Fondation Saint-Simon.

Weiner, Myron (1992), 'Security, Stability, and International Migration', *International Security* 17 (3), 90-126.

Weiner, Myron (1995), *The Global Migration Crisis, Challenge to States and to Human Rights*, Boulder, Westview Press.

Weiner, Myron (ed.) (1993), *International Migration and Security*, Boulder, Westview Press.

Weir, Margaret (1992), 'Ideas and the politics of bounded innovation', S. Steinmo, and K. Thelen and F. Longstreth, (eds) 188-216.

Weis, Paul (1971), 'Human Rights and Refugees', *Israel Yearbook on Human Rights*, 1, 35-50.

Weis, Paul (ed.) (1995), *The Refugee Convention, 1951*, Cambridge, Cambridge University Press.

Wihtol de Wenden, Catherine (1987), 'France's policy on migration from May 1981 till March 1986, its symbolic dimension, its restrictive aspects and its unintended effects', *International Migration*, 25 (2), 211-220.

Wihtol de Wenden, Catherine (1994), 'Frankreich', in H. Heinelt, (ed.), *Zuwanderungspolitik in Europa. Nationale Politiken. Gemeinsamkeiten und Unterschiede*, Opladen, Leske und Budrich, 255-271.

Williams, Howard and Booth, Ken (1996), 'Kant, Theorist beyond Limits', in I. Clark and I.B. Neuman, (eds) 71-98.

Wolken, Simone (1988), *Das Grundrecht auf Asyl als Gegenstand der Innen- und Rechtspolitik in der Bundesrepublik Deutschland*, Frankfurt a.M. et al., Suhrkamp.

Wölker, Ulrich (1985), 'Das Ausländerrecht Frankreichs', in J.A. Fowein and J. Wolf, (eds) *Ausländerrecht im internationalen Vergleich*, Heidelberg, C.F. Müller, 29-62.

Wollenschläger, Michael and Schraml, Alexander (1994), 'Kriegs- und Bürgerkriegsflüchtlinge im nationalen und internationalen Recht', *Humanitäres Völkerrecht - Informationsschriften*, 3, 128-133.

Yanow, Dvora (1995), 'Editorial. Practices of Policy Interpretation', *Policy Sciences*, 28 (2), 111-126.

Zarjevski, Yéfime (1988), *A Future Preserved. International Assistance to Refugees*, Oxford, Oxford University Press.

Zimmer, Willy (1996), *Die Reformen des Ausländerrechts, des Asyl- und Staatsangehörigkeitsrechts in Frankreich und Deutschland*, Speyerer Forschungsberichte no. 163, Speyer.

Zolberg, Aristide R. (1978), 'International Migration Policies in a Changing World System', in W. McNeill and R. Adams, (eds) *Human Migration*, Bloomington, Indiana University Press, 241-286.

Zolberg, Aristide et al. (1989), *Escaping from Violence, Conflict and Refugee Crisis in the Developing World*, New York, Oxford University Press.

Zolberg, Aristide (1994), 'Commentary on Current Refugee Issues', *Journal of International Affairs*, 47 (2), 341-350.

Index

For Product Safety Concerns and Information please contact our EU
representative GPSR@taylorandfrancis.com
Taylor & Francis Verlag GmbH, Kaufingerstraße 24, 80331 München, Germany